Fundamentals
of Research Management

Fundamentals
of Research Management

William G. McLoughlin

American Management Association, Inc.

International standard book number: 0-8144-5208-6
Library of Congress catalog card number: 70-114204

FIRST PRINTING

To the one person
who makes it all worthwhile—
my favorite proofreader and critic

Preface

I f this book had been written in the form of a modern novel, the plot's misunderstood heroes and victims would have been the industrial life cycles of various commodities and services. Villains would have been supplied by the forces of the social, economic, geopolitical, and technological world as aided and abetted by indifferent managers.

This is no "how to" handbook for the individual suddenly thrust into the role of a direct manager of research efforts. Quite the contrary, every effort has been made to show that management of research extends outside the research organization to reach every corner of the company. As will be seen, if management of the research function begins in any one place within the company, it must begin in the office of the chief executive.

The viability of any industrial concern is inseparably tied to the life cycles of all its products and services. Each such cycle has its beginnings in research; each progresses through the various stages of development to market introduction; each provides a financial offset for the total investment of money, facilities, people, and—most important—time, which cannot be regained.

From its inception to its last market sale, the life cycle is a thing of management risk, uncertainty, and decision. As a baby's later life will be shaped by the way in which he is protected, fed, and cared for in infancy, so a product's life cycle is shaped by the way in which it is managed in research. Hence a very real effort is made in this book to bring research and research management into proper perspective.

The ways to fail in the initiation and early nurturing of a life cycle are legion, and no real effort is made here to describe them. The major effort is directed toward positive management guidelines. Of paramount concern are the concepts required to pace the movement through a life cycle so that the resultant product or service arrives in the right market at the right time at the right price. Similarly, evaluation methods for the investment are presented with the admonition that management efforts should be directed toward termination of development when it is obvious that the investment cannot be recovered and a profit realized.

If there is one underlying idea or precept in this book, it is that research represents an investment which is controllable if managed properly. With this precept as a basis for writing, it is reasonable that this book is addressed to *all* managers within a company.

William G. McLoughlin

Contents

1

Introduction

Effective planning and control of research and development programs determine the success of these efforts. Without control, there can be no purposeful adherence to planning or meaningful achievement of established goals. In and of itself, the organizational chart with its lines of authority and statements of responsibility is not control, either real or imagined. This book treats of the problems of control for research and development; far more important, it treats of the basic reasons for control: investment and return on investment.

The Researcher

As a beginning, consider the individual who gives himself to the role of a research or development scientist or engineer. A true scientist in today's definition of the term freely gives or shares his knowledge and findings while also carefully seeking the experience and derived knowledge of his peers. (Sometimes his giving and his seeking transcend the rules of military security, and the scientist finds himself in difficulties beyond his comprehension—as witness

Klaus Fuchs and others.) The scientist reaches for the unknown with the type of reasoning and meaningful analysis characteristic of scientific inquiry. It is a reasoning alien, even incomprehensible, to the uninitiated.

Too often, those outside the realm of science look upon those within as akin to the gods—as people set apart or possibly as just freaks. The researcher is none of these. At best, he may be highly creative; at worst, he may be a charlatan. Thus those within the realm tend to run the same gamut as other mortals. However, it is impossible to keep telling a select group of people that they are a group apart without having some members of the group adopt some of the expected characteristics. It is interesting to consider what characteristics are attributed to researchers by management.

Twenty-three graduate business majors (many of whom had had extensive work experience) were asked to characterize the research scientist on a word-association basis. The characterizations were poor company man, individualistic, absentminded, unsocial, snobbish with pride, not time-oriented, nonconformist, professional, dedicated to science, inquisitive, creative, analytical, objective, disciplined, methodical, logical, introspective, narrow viewpoint, poor organizer, opinionated, need for achievement, need to excel, need for recognition among peers, different view of ethics, introverted extrovert, poor manager of others, perseverance, high I.Q., egotistical, highly motivated, and highly communicative with own kind. These are the characteristics any nonscientific group can be expected to list, and they echo words repeatedly used about members of the scientific community. As with all generalities, they contain a modicum of truth; but, if they were all truthful, management of research and development would be impossible.

The objectives of the professional manager in directing the efforts of the scientist and engineer should be to obtain the maximum creative output from each. Thus enter the twin problems of motivation and control of the individual scientist or engineer.

Industrial Research

This book is addressed primarily to the problems of industrial research. Because industrial research is a phenomenon of the modern era, its definition becomes exceedingly complex. Nor is the definition made easier by any reference to the activities customarily conducted within industrial research laboratories. So-called industrial research laboratories have performed and sponsored basic research, applied the fundamental knowledge derived in basic research to discover the practical approaches to new technologies, developed those approaches to the point of commercial product practicability, seen them through the pilot-production stages, acted as troubleshooters for market and production difficulties, been responsible for quality control of production, and even, in a few cases, engaged in routine testing and production control. Obviously, the term "industrial research" can loosely cover a wide spectrum of "scientific" activities.

In the broadest sense, industrial research involves the following four elements:

1. It is nearly always organized research and, as such, excludes the individual inventor and the lone, cut-and-try experimenter.
2. It employs scientific methods and scientifically trained personnel.
3. It is concerned with the natural sciences and their related technologies to the exclusion of such areas as the social sciences.
4. In the long run, it is utilitarian, since the investigations, whether fundamental or applied, are connected in one way or another with industry, being directed primarily toward improving technology and maximizing economic satisfactions.

Contained within the foregoing elements is the fundamental principle that industrial research is conducted for a monetary purpose which is normally expressed in terms of profit or return on investment. In the chapters that follow, industrial research is not considered in any other light, although it is recognized that what is called industrial research in some companies does not fit these objectives.

Science Versus Technology

Historically, science and technology have occupied two separate and largely independent spheres of human activity. Science devoted itself to the development of a fuller and more satisfactory philosophical understanding of the world of natural phenomena. Interest in science was largely confined to members of the educated upper classes who pursued its rewards out of curiosity and boredom. The characterizing of science as either natural philosophy or natural history, even into the nineteenth century, was symptomatic of the separation or demarcation between science and practical technology. During this period, technology was concerned with the manipulation of things and the production of economic goods. Technology was essentially traditional knowledge, handed down with only minor refinements from one generation of eminently practical craftsmen to the next. Innovation was the result of crude empiricism of the cut-and-try character. This was partly because of the differing social status of the scientist and the craftsman, but in larger measure it was due to the fact that science had little or nothing to offer for the improvement of technology.

It would be inaccurate to say that there has been no contact between the scientific and technological traditions in Western civilization, for there have been a number of notable exceptions. Archimedes mixed the two as he formulated the law of specific gravity. Christiaan Huygens and Robert Hooke utilized the scientific theories of mechanics in the development of clocks and watches; astronomical discoveries were applied to the problems of navigation: and James Watt found that the theoretical work being performed in the field of heat helped him to improve the steam engine. Yet it is fair to state that even in the seventeenth and eighteenth centuries science was relatively helpless in the face of technological problems requiring advanced solutions.

The development of science to a point where its principles had application in economic activity occurred at various times, depending on the branch of science and the type of economic activity involved. The importance of science in agriculture was revealed relatively early in the nineteenth century. The work of the German chemist Justus von Liebig in the 1830s was the crucial development in this field, and it eventually led to the modern agricultural revolution. In the broad field of engineering, the convergence of science and technology came in the middle of the nineteenth century after it became apparent that close attention to basic scientific principles could result in significant savings in the cost of production and fabrication.

Marriage of Science and Technology

The most spectacular early marriage of science and technology occurred in the dye industry. Although the English chemist William Henry Perkin synthesized the first dye in 1856, it remained for German chemists to seize the development leadership and to open the synthetic dye industry. By World War I, the German dye industry had completely ruined the once flourishing business of producing indigo and had established Germany as a technological pioneer. The scientific feats performed by the German dye manufacturers and the profits that resulted from their application of scientific knowledge to technological needs are often cited as evidence of the profitability of the marriage of science and technology.

By the end of the nineteenth century, the burgeoning petroleum industry, which was destined to become one of the true leaders in industrial research, had begun to realize that scientifically trained geologists were more effective than divining rods in locating pools of oil beneath the earth's surface. More recently, Carl Zeiss's success in improving optical instruments through the application of scientific principles of analysis strengthened the marriage. However, it was the development of the electric and electronics industry that consummated the affair, for here was created an entirely new technology independent of any preexisting traditional craft techniques.

Science in Industry

The still growing realization of the importance of science to industry is evidenced by the increasing use of scientifically trained persons in the advancement of industrial technology. Today, few companies of any significance lack a scientific staff to perform research or supporting development. Physicists and chemists now work in close cooperation with engineers to establish the best technological designs on the basis of the fundamentals of science and the handbook principles that characterize so much of engineering.

Industrial research began to assume its modern form in the late nineteenth and early twentieth centuries, primarily in Germany and the United States. In Germany the electrical, chemical, and optical industries made systematic use of scientific personnel in large-scale laboratories before World War I, while German industry as a whole supported the establishment in 1911 of the Kaiser Wilhelm Gesellschaft, a group of scientific institutes conducting both fundamental and applied research. In the United States, industrial research began to attract an increasing amount of attention in the technical press during the decade preceding World War I, and these years saw the establishment of some of the most important industrial research laboratories, notably at General Electric, Du Pont, Bell Telephone, Westinghouse, Eastman Kodak, and Standard Oil (Indiana). Rapid technological advancement in chemicals and electricity made the need for systematic research apparent, while the growth of large corporations provided these economic organizations with sufficient capital to support and exploit research.

It remained for World War I to convince Western Europe and the United States of the necessity for systematic industrial research. Both England and the United States were cut off from German dyes, chemicals, medicines, and glass. A vigorous effort to bring science to the aid of industry immediately resulted. In the United States, existing industrial research laboratories turned toward support of the war effort, while the government set up the National Research Council to coordinate the activities of scientists in industry and the academic communities. The results were astounding. Applied research gave a tremendous boost to the U.S. chemical industry in addition to solving innumerable special war-related problems. In the United Kingdom the problems were similar, but the approach was different. There the government formed the Department of Scientific and Industrial Research (DSIR), an agency which has since played a leading role in encouraging cooperative British industrial research.

Following World War I, research became an established part of the industrial scene. The rate of expansion and the patterns of organization have shown significant national variations. Similarly, research activity has depended on technological and economic conditions which have varied widely from industry to industry and from country to country.

The Impact of World War II

World War II brought important changes in industrial research, the principal one being a sharp increase in the total amount of research. The war also emphasized the importance of the cooperative approach and brought new experience in the techniques of organization for scientific endeavor. Above all, the success of Allied arms and the awesome results of atomic research brought new prestige to science and a renewed confidence in its utilitarian potentialities. The net result has been a marked increase in applied and basic research in the United States since that war.

Industrial research has tended to be dominated by big business and large laboratories. The major research leader has been the electrical/electronics industry, with Bell Laboratories, Westinghouse, General Electric, and RCA heading the list. The chemicals and allied products industry is an almost entirely new industry that is based on the discoveries of the nineteenth century. Du Pont, the leader of the U.S. chemical industry, has consistently used research as a method of expanding company interests. Next in line within this industry are Union Carbide, American Cyanamid, Dow Chemical, and Allied Chemical and Dye, all of which have developed substantial research programs. Other industries closely related to basic chemicals have also engaged in extensive research. Eastman Kodak is a prime example, having used professionally trained scientists almost from the company's beginning. Also noteworthy is the pharmaceutical industry, which spends more for research in relation to its sales than does any other U.S. industry.

Although the prime responsibility for U.S. research has remained in the hands of private agencies, the government has expanded its role to a point where it is probably the most important single force shaping the direction, character, and destiny of research. The government has become involved in research for several reasons, of which the most important is national defense. World War II, the subsequent Cold War, and the development of atomic energy have all contributed to the growing importance of the government in the research picture. Now it is to be anticipated that the socioeconomic problems besetting this country will be an added stimulus. Some of the research has been and will continue to be done in government facilities, but a significant portion will be contracted, as before, to industrial organizations, private laboratories, and universities.

Industrial Research Today

Between 1962 and 1965, there was a slowdown in the expenditures on research and development in U.S. industry. Expenditures in this period increased by only 4 percent per year. However, the 1966 increase was 9 percent greater than the 1965 increase, and the 1967 increase was a gain of 7 percent over 1966. If past patterns continue, expenditure in the 1970s for research and development in industry will be 25 percent greater than the 1967 commitment. Expressed in real dollars, these percentages become $14.2 billion industrywide in 1965, $15.4 billion in 1966, $16.6 billion in 1967, and an estimated $20.8 billion in 1970.

As previously noted, industrial research is the result of the marriage of science and technology in industry. It has not been an isolated phenomenon. Nearly all the industrially and scientifically advanced countries of the Western world have participated with "backward" nations demonstrating an ever increasing interest. There has been an immense variation in the amount and type of research performed in different industries. This has resulted in part from the variation in the level of technical advancement within an industry and in part from the organization of the industry as well as its ability to support large-scale research programs. But, whatever its character, industrial research has clearly become a major factor in industry as well as in society.

With its current and expanding position in industry, research has assumed a major role in the continued growth, if not the survival, of many corporations. Corporate managers can no longer ignore the research efforts of their firms, and they must exercise control over such efforts on the basis of both profit and investment.

Concept of This Book

The chapters that follow are designed as a guide to the manager directly concerned with administration of research efforts and to the managers who have a responsibility to insure that research is properly managed. Much of what is written here is also applicable to development efforts, and consequently the terms "research" and "development" are used together where joint applicability is particularly strong or evident.

This book offers a number of management concepts to be applied to research (and in some cases to development). Some of these concepts are not entirely new, but most of them are ignored by industry today. Where the concepts are ignored, this is noted and the reasons are given. The fact that the concepts are not used does not make them wrong, nor does it make the industries any less sound. The real name of the industrial game is "maximize the return on investment." A company may be showing a significant profit and its investors may be delighted, but the company may be less than optimally successful because there is still room for an increased return on investment. When this condition prevails, it is usually because the managers fail to analyze the situation adequately, shirk a part of their control responsibility, or willingly settle for less.

Twelve concepts are detailed in the pages of this book.

1. Basic research is the proper province of the not-for-profit laboratories and universities. It should not be performed by an industrial research laboratory and presented to stockholders and would-be stockholders as evidence of investment in the future of the company.

2. Applied research is the proper province of the industrial research organization. All research and development should be conducted with a firm objective to produce a proprietary position for the company.

3. Research represents an investment of capital funds, and it should produce a proprietary position which is a capital asset. This is then consumed in the production of profit or is salable as an asset to a second firm.

4. As a capital asset, the results of successful research deserve the same careful investment analysis as any other capital asset investment.

5. Patents and trade secrets are the evidence of a proprietary position, and the objective of research should be patents and trade secrets. The failure to obtain these from industrial research efforts is indicative of improper control and motivation of research.

6. Research organizations deserve to be treated as separable profit centers, even negative ones. The accounting procedures for research should be adapted to the problems of research, and control should be exercised through accounting methods.

7. Research and development efforts should be controlled by professional managers utilizing the most advanced management control techniques. Scientists and engineers should be encouraged to pursue careers in their fields and not attempt to convert to management per se.

8. Proper motivation is the key to successful research, but motivation without control or purpose is meaningless. Procedures and organization can provide both motivation and control to a significant but not a total degree.

9. Network analysis through a modified PERT (program evaluation and review technique) is applicable to control of both research and development. Each program in these two segments of the corporation should be afforded such evaluation and control to properly reflect the investment being made in the program.

10. Investment goals and limitations on research efforts should be established before the initiation of such efforts, and the efforts should be terminated promptly when it becomes clear that the limitations are being exceeded.

11. Research and development sold outside the industrial research laboratory or firm require the same marketing attention as any material product or service of the company.

12. Planning for research and development is as critical as for any other segment of the firm. Such planning requires the application of the most advanced prediction techniques, including those of technological and economic forecasting.

These concepts raise many problems in their implementation and application. Many managers will find them difficult to accept, and some will reject them outright as alien to their own concepts of what research and development should be. Yet no apologies are made for them. Experience, observation, and study have proved their efficacy, and any manager would do well to consider each of these concepts within his own corporation's frame of reference.

2

Process of
Technological Innovation

Few words suffer from more misuse than "research," "development," "invention," "innovation," "scientist," "technologist," and "technician." Even "engineer," in recent years, has become a badly abused term, with janitors and custodians being called sanitary engineers! Yet every manager who directly or indirectly exercises control over industrial or government research and development functions should have a firm and meaningful definition established for each of these terms. An initial effort is made in this chapter to provide a working frame of reference within which these terms should be used and understood. All these terms are applicable to the process of technological innovation.

Research: Fundamental Meaning

Of itself, *research* has two rather distinct meanings and uses in everyday conversation. The first and most general usage covers all inductive and experimental processes from an initial theoretical concept to a proven, useful principle, reducible to a practical product. It is this very broad usage which is called to mind when we speak of industrial research and research laboratories. The second use of the word "research" is sometimes applied to a much narrower segment of the total research process and may be applied to specific tasks in experiment or theory through which a scientific or technological precept or concept is brought to a new level of understanding.

Depending upon its use, "research" can be either a noun or a verb. As a noun, it implies a systematic investigation relative to a specific subject. The investigation is generally characterized as diligent and all-inclusive, dealing primarily with applications, facts, and theory. When used as a verb, the word implies the actions required to accomplish the purposes of research. These are the broad definitions. The real danger exists, however, in carrying such extremely broad definitions over into the industrial research environment.

In the industrial environment, research is the prelude to development. Taken together, research and development carry a scientific or technological concept from its initial inception in the minds of the originators to a product or service in the marketplace. There are a series of distinct steps in this process, and the manager should consider each as providing a means for evaluation and possible termination of effort at a minimal investment loss when infeasibility becomes obvious. How the steps are divided becomes something of personal choice. For example, the eight stages of Professor James R. Bright of Harvard are fully compatible with the four steps of David Novick of RAND Corporation. For planning purposes, Bright's eight stages seem more adaptable, while Novick's four steps provide an excellent base for definitions. Since it is always best to begin with definitions, first consider Novick's four steps. These steps, together with appropriate definitions, were presented during his testimony before the U.S. Senate's hearings on the subject of administered prices in April 1960.

Step I: Basic Research

The terms "basic research," "fundamental research," and "pure research" are sometimes used interchangeably. Mr. Novick characterizes step I as basic research, experimental research, and basic development. The promise in all these terms is great but not identified as to specific purposes. But still more important, the possibility or even the probability of ultimate product or service fulfillment is highly uncertain. At best, the output of this first step is merely an understanding of the universe and an organization of knowledge about it to (1) permit major changes in ways of looking at phenomena and activities; (2) create new devices and methods of accomplishing scientific objectives; and (3) identify phenomena and activities which permit revolutionary changes in existing products, methods, and approaches.

Even a cursory consideration of this first step reveals that the scientific and technological effort it fosters is not performed with a specific product or service objective. This naturally raises the question as to whether it should be a function of an industrial research organization. In fact, it is the province of universities and pure research centers. On the other hand, an industrial research organization should have at least a future profit motivation. If basic research provides the concepts from which product concepts can be originated, can profit motivation begin before the conclusion of basic research efforts? It cannot. For this reason, industrial research organizations should not engage directly in basic research. However, basic research must be performed, since it is the foundation for all that follows. Industrial organizations and the federal government should provide the support needed for basic research in the universities and pure research centers.

Whenever a company permits basic research within its own organization, there is a very real danger that such research may be presented to the investing public as an actual investment in the future of the company. Few people realize that only an insignificant fragment of basic research ever produces a patentable concept, and it is highly doubtful that true basic research has ever produced a trade secret of real value.

Step II: Applied Research

The output of basic research is a concept in either expressible or understandable form. Moving from this concept to a product which has large-scale acceptance and potential commercial success is both costly and time-consuming. Various studies of major technology conversion from an initial expression of concept to the commercial success of the ultimate product reveal a historically unchanged 14 years. Today, the time span is therefore assumed to be 14 years for efficient technological transfer. The fact that not every technological concept is reducible to a product or that not every start toward a product from an established concept will produce a successful product is frequently overlooked. In considering undertaking the transfer, those responsible for research and development must recognize that the period of 14 years is nearly three times as long as the period normally selected for corporate long-range planning.

Assuming that an evaluation of the output of step I apparently justifies further effort, then applied research, advanced development, basic evaluation, and basic testing constitute step II. Within this step, there is a singling out or identification of specific potentials or applications with a view toward developing devices or methods for utilizing the general knowledge obtained in step I. The promise is for great new things, but the question remains—How soon? The economy, efficiency, and acceptability of the promise remain uncertain. This step is the true beginning of the industrial research process. The profit motive is now identifiable, and some measure of anticipated return on investment can or should be made for evaluation of progress through this and subsequent steps.

Do not be misled. The output of step II is not a product, although it may be substantiation of the original precept or concept in real terms, as in a quantitative experiment or a conceptual breadboard. Step III is the first effort at actual product development.

Step III: Product Development

Step III has as its objective product development, product testing, product evaluation, and even pilot production. Within this step specific devices or methods which appear as likely solutions must be brought reasonably close to final application with a view to determining effectiveness, economy, and acceptability. At the successful conclusion of the third step, "do-ability" has been established and major advances are promised. Step III is the most expensive step and the one that requires the maximum application of good managerial judgment. Throughout this step, managers responsible for the program direction should rigorously apply an ongoing program evaluation process or system such as PERT. In the evaluation process, continuing evaluation should be conducted not only to determine the probability of technological success in reaching a practical product, but also to establish the potential financial return on the total research and development investment up to the point of product acceptance within the market.

Step IV: Product Introduction

Product application, application research, applied testing, and applied evaluation constitute the final step in Novick's research and development process. Step IV, emerging as it does from step III, provides some reasonable assurance of product success, since what happens next is evolutionary rather than revolutionary. But success is not absolutely assured. Within this last step, new uses or applications for existing uses or applications should be sought for the methods, products, or components, with the specific objective of substantial benefits to both users and producers. This is the beginning of the payoff for the technological innovation process which has preceded this step. It is the beginning of the reduction in the investment of money, people, and facilities, but it is not the beginning of the realization of profits.

The investment in money, people, facilities, and time from the initiation of step I to the product or service introduction at the successful conclusion of step III can be enormous and will seldom be insignificant. But the investment procedure is not completed. Step IV will require still more investment, with the first profits (in the sense of sales revenues exceeding costs) not materializing until the end of the product introduction period of the life cycle (see Exhibit 1). This life cycle is divided into four distinct phases following initial marketing of the product: product introduction, market growth, market maturity, and sales decline.

During the product introduction phase, additional funds must be invested to insure product acceptance and possibly to make any

Exhibit 1

PRODUCT LIFE CYCLE

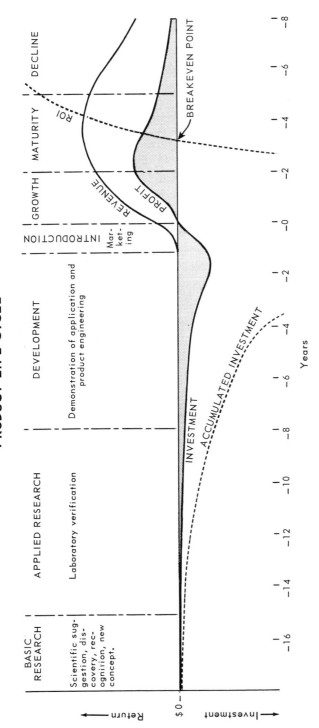

The product life cycle represents the history of a commodity or service from the time of its initial conception to its ultimate withdrawal from the market because of inadequate profit margin. There are four distinct phases of the life cycle after the initial introduction to the market: introduction, growth, maturity, and decline. Profit during these phases may be defined as the margin realized after both fixed and variable costs have been covered. The return on investment (ROI) does not begin until breakeven on the total accumulated investment is realized. The position of the breakeven point is determined by the effectiveness of management in controlling the investment prior to market introduction and in providing a correct pricing policy thereafter.

product refinements dictated by the marketplace. With the passage of time, these funds are increasingly offset by the income derived from product sales. Initially, the rate of offset equals the rising revenue from sales; but, if the product begins to win consumer acceptance, the rate of offset moves into an exponential rise.

The product introduction phase ends when the revenue from sales exactly matches the cost of sales. In a very real sense, this is the end of step IV and the beginning of the return on investment (ROI), an investment which extends back over a period of years. This investment could have been made entirely by one organization, or it could have been made by several organizations, with some actually realizing none of the return or, at best, only a small part of it.

In today's fast-developing technological society, new products can anticipate a good profit period (represented by the growth and maturity phases of the life cycle) of only five to ten years. This compares rather unfavorably with the estimated 14 years of gestation in research and development. However, it clearly demonstrates the necessity for careful evaluation of the accumulated investment as well as the anticipated return on investment at the beginning of each new step and at appropriate turning points within each step.

It is frequently suggested that a company trade upon the completed research and development of another company. The implication is that a sure thing can be grasped and large profits for a small investment can be exacted. General experience shows that this cannot be done. The market growth phase is obviously the most profitable. It is also the phase in which the competitors can first recognize the potential of the profits. With recognition, there still must be reaction. The competitors need time to copy and market the competing product. At best, the competitive product can reach the market near the beginning of the maturity phase, when profits are beginning to peak out before their decline. The market growth period is the most profitable, but the real profits are to be realized in the growth phase as combined with the first half of the maturity phase. Thus, with few exceptions, new technologies prove to be more profitable than a marginal improvement of an existing technology in a highly competitive market.

If these life cycle relationships are accepted, they provide the basis—even the need—for both technological forecasting and long-range planning (subjects which will be discussed in later chapters).

That these relationships should be accepted as fact is demonstrated by the number of companies, both large and small, which now engage in long-range planning with some degree of technological forecasting to facilitate product selection as well as selectivity in research and development efforts.

Stages of Technological Innovation

In the preceding paragraphs, the four steps in product research and development as defined by David Novick were analyzed. At this point, it is worthwhile to retrace the process of technological innovation on the basis of Professor James R. Bright's eight stages.* They are

Stage 1: Scientific suggestion, discovery, recognition of need.
Stage 2: Proposal of theory or design concept.
Stage 3: Laboratory verification of theory or design concept.
Stage 4: Laboratory demonstration of application.
Stage 5: Full-scale or field trial.
Stage 6: Commercial introduction or first operational use.
Stage 7: Widespread adoption (profits, significant usage, significant impact).
Stage 8: Proliferation.

Viewed in terms of the product life cycle, these eight stages may be divided as follows: Stage 1 represents the process of basic research or other input. Stages 2 and 3 are the applied research phase, which precedes the development phase represented by stages 4 and 5. The product introduction phase and stage 6 correspond, as do the growth phase and stage 7. Stage 8 is represented by both the maturity and decline phases of the life cycle.

Bright's stages of innovation include the possibility of invention by other than the orderly process of basic research, applied research, and the rest. A scientist may be an innovator and an originator of inventions, but the business manager should always look upon the

* "Some Management Lessons from Research in Technological Innovation Research." Lecture at the Bradford University and Ministry of Technology Seminar, England, March 1969.

"inventor" in an area apart from the scientist. Even though inventive scientists may originate inventions, most of them prefer not to be classified as inventors. The difference is one of degree, and it is a significant difference.

Inventor Versus Scientist

A true scientist in today's definition of the term freely gives or shares his scientific and technological knowledge and findings while carefully seeking the related experience and derived knowledge of his peers. In his research and development efforts, the scientist establishes each new plateau of personal knowledge through a careful pyramiding of derived knowledge (his own and that of others) upon a base of established scientific and technological facts. He seldom, if ever, reaches new plateaus of knowledge by sudden, intuitive guesses or rationalizations.

Within the scientific community, as each new technological fact or phenomenon is understood, knowledge relating thereto is made available in many formal and informal ways. Most scientists resent any effort to impose a barrier to the exchange of such information— a barrier such as company restrictions or the military classification and espionage code. That is why so many prominent scientists have run afoul of the military and why there is opposition to the military on many university campuses.

The true scientist knows that technology feeds upon technology and that technological events are usually bred within related technology. The scientist who gives of himself receives as he gives, and his own level of knowledge advances to the extent he is willing to share.

The conventional inventor is everything that the true scientist is not. He is generally motivated by a desire for esteem that is based upon his astuteness in recognizing the things others have missed and by a desire for sudden wealth. The rationale by which inventors reach a plateau of knowledge is sometimes beyond the comprehension of others. Many inventors state categorically that they will not read anything beyond fundamental scientific and technical works so as not to be unduly influenced by the "mistakes of others." The "pure" inventor concerns himself with immediate ends and as a rule only with limited problems relating to materials and methods. As a general practice, if he experiments at all, he uses cut-and-try methods on a random basis; and his experiments are usually designed to support his own, often intuitive, beliefs relative to the subject of the invention. Invention in this case is not a continuous activity of developing a concept by an orderly process to a practical level of usefulness; rather, it is a sudden discovery of an idea which the inventor hopes is exploitable, preferably for his personal gain. Rarely does he try to see his invention within the context of the totality of science and technology.

Although there are significantly fewer inventors than scientists, engineers, and technicians in research and development programs, some inventors do make meaningful discoveries. Many unsuccessful but persuasive inventors, however, live quite comfortably, supported by gullible people who hope to share in the eventual wealth expected from "the invention" or who are merely satisfied to be "close to greatness."

The real tragedies of business are those companies that have irresponsible managers who rely in the main upon the anticipation that an Edisonian invention will arrive from out of the blue. They pay lip service to research and development, maintaining a research organization but providing no managerial guidance or control over its activities. When they receive nothing in return for the investment in research and development, they consider themselves fully justified in seeking inventors and inventions.

Invention and Innovation

Invention is the province of both the inventor and those engaged in planned research and development. True invention is the exposition of a new concept or idea in an objective form which is open to examination and test for validity. It will withstand all legitimate examination and test and will prove its worth as another logical step in technological advancement. The United States and most other governments recognize any invention properly presented for examination and test by awarding a patent to the originator.

Innovation is the first cousin of invention. Innovation is the introduction of something new and novel relative to something already understood and in existence. Possibly, the innovative feature may be nothing more than a new combination of common items which results in a synergistic effect not otherwise possible. Some innovation is considered to be creative enough to justify the award of a patent, but not all innovation is that fortunate.

The Innovation Cycle

Exhibit 2 presents the process of technological innovation as a closed system. Within this system, basic research is seen to produce increased human understanding, new or extended theory, and prediction. The performance of basic research is most directly stimulated by the new techniques, new knowledge, and new materials which result from efforts in applied research. The usual concept of applied research is an effort which naturally emerges from basic research efforts. Yet this cycle indicates that applied research efforts may also be suggested by the prior output of applied research or may result from human knowledge of needs and possibilities, intelligent inquiry into natural or other phenomena, the application of imaginative thinking, or serendipitous observation. The output of applied research provides the basis for development, which takes the new techniques, new knowledge, and new materials to a point where new or improved commodities and services can enter the market to expand the technological state of the art. But the state of the art encompasses far more than the commodities and services in the marketplace. It actually includes all of man's technological knowledge and his efforts in basic research, applied research, and development.

The state of the art in technology should be viewed as a sphere of activity within the world of man. However, it is not an independent sphere. This fact is illustrated by Exhibit 3, as well as by the influence arrow pressing the state-of-the-art box in Exhibit 2. In a very real sense, the technological sphere is surrounded by the economic, social, and geopolitical spheres. Each of these spheres can include activity which will either repress technology or provide the motivation for its expansion. At the same time, technology is interacting with the other spheres to influence them, even challenge them, as a result of technology's basic pressure to expand and grow.

Exhibit 2
TECHNOLOGICAL STATE OF THE ART

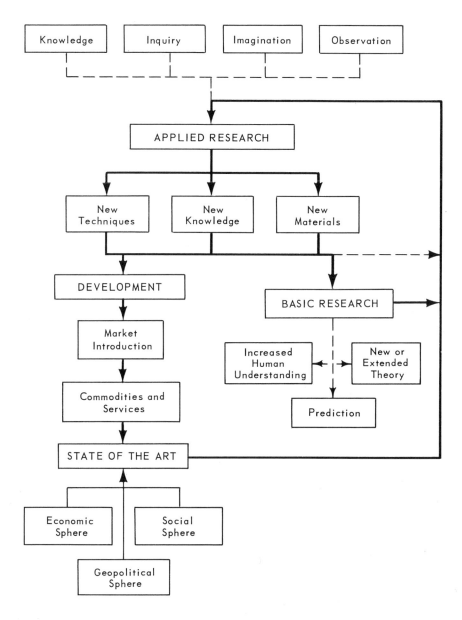

The state of the art in technology comprises all man's knowledge of the natural world, his technical abilities to perform tasks in that world, and his tools and facilities for the performance of the tasks undertaken. In some sense, state of the art also includes innate capabilities either unused or unrealized. However, purists will disagree with the latter viewpoint.

Exhibit 3
SPHERES OF ACTION AND REACTION

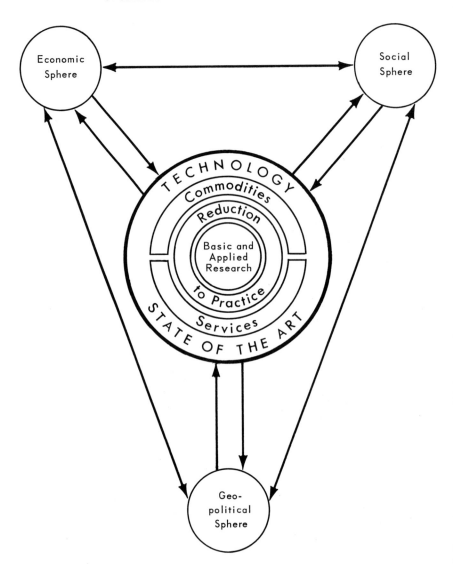

The world in which we live consists of four basic spheres of action and reaction. Each sphere influences events in the other spheres and in turn is influenced by them. While each sphere is an orderly complexity, only the complexity of the technology sphere is suggested here. In Exhibit 2 this sphere is presented in more detail, and the relationships of the other three spheres is suggested as an interaction with the box labeled "state of the art." Although the term geopolitical is disliked in some quarters, it must be recognized that the environmental and political aspects of any community are closely interlaced and can be treated as a single sphere of action in these interrelationships.

As pressure is applied unevenly to the technological sphere, it expands unevenly along the paths of least resistance, but generally not for very long. While technology is not independent, neither are the other spheres of influence independent from each other. As a result, there is a total world of interrelationships and interaction which results in counterbalancing forces through the weak reactive spheres from the more dominant. With the passage of time, today's weak reactive spheres become tomorrow's dominant force.

Consider again the Exhibit 3 representation of the state of the art. At the core of the technology sphere is research encased by the layers of reduction to practice and of commodities and services. If the external pressure on the sphere is repressive, the pressure inward will ultimately be felt by research. When the converse is true, a real stimulus to increased research will exist. A part of any company's long-range planning must be directed toward prediction of the periods when there will be repression or encouragement of expansion in technology so as to program and properly commit resources to research efforts.

Engineer, Technologist, and Technician

In concluding this chapter, it would be wise not to forget the contributing personnel in research and development programs. They are the research and development engineer, the technologist, and the technician. Akin to the scientist, they apply scientific and technical principles to the orderly solution of problems. Like the scientist, these contributors may be the originators of both inventions and innovation. Few among them show much respect, however, for the inventor or the inventor's approach to problem solving.

3

Proprietary Position

THE proper role for industrial research and development in support of a competitive market situation is to (1) provide the new product which will create a new competitive demand in that market; (2) establish an old product on a new demand plane; or (3) introduce a new method of producing an old product in a more economical and therefore more profitable form. Accomplishing any or all of these three objectives is meaningless if the firm does not have a proprietary position in the marketplace as a result of the investment made in the research and development effort. Proprietary position comes primarily from one of two possible sources: trade secrets and patents.

Trade Secrets

Though not generally acknowledged, trade secrets still play a major role in modern industrial practices. Interestingly enough, such secrets are preserved in many different and effective ways. For example, a formula for a chemical combination, such as a flavor syrup from which a soft drink is manufactured, may be known to only one or two key management people. The mixing of the combination is conducted by several key employees who measure and add a single ingredient to the batch mix in the absence of the others. Thus no one individual is able to derive the formula for the mix without the collusion of all the others involved in the measuring and mixing process. However, as no military secret ever remains a complete secret, industrial secrets also have a habit of "leaking." In some cases the leak is accidental; but in other cases the leak may be the result of industrial espionage. Unlike the military, which has no recourse against the recipient foreign nation (and probably not against the spy who committed the espionage) to protect the secret, an industrial source which has lost a trade secret by unethical acts of an employee or nonemployee can appeal to the courts to prevent unfair exploitation of the lost information.

An employee made privy to an industrial secret, in the view of many courts in the United States, assumes the role of an agent to his employer, whether an express agreement to protect the company's industrial secrets has been entered into or not. It is a well-established principle of law that the chief duties of the agent to his principal (or employer) are to be loyal, to give notice of all material facts, to obey instructions of the principal, and to account for all things of value entrusted to him by his principal. Further, the agent is required to act for only one principal at a time, never for himself, and to safeguard all secret or privileged information of his principal however such information may come into his possession. In interpretation the last point is frequently enlarged to restrain the agent from using such information for his personal benefit or his principal's detriment, even after the agent–principal relationship has been terminated unilaterally or by common consent. There are many cases on record where an agent and his new employer have been legally restrained from the benefits which they might have received from exploitation of a trade secret gained in the agent's former agent–principal relationship.

In a typical agent–principal case involving trade secrets, as heard in the courts of New Jersey (*A. Hollander & Son* v. *Imperial Fur Blending Corp.*, 66 A 2nd 319), an employee contract was accepted by Phillip A. Singer from the firm of A. Hollander & Son, a fur dyeing and blending company. By this contract, Singer covenanted with Hollander to perform his duties as a dresser and dyer of furs faithfully, not to divulge any of the trade secrets or processes of A. Hollander & Son, not to use those secrets for profit to himself or others, and to make the Hollander firm sole owner of all discoveries he might make relative to any shades of color, new formulas, and processes used in the dressing and dyeing of fur skins during his employment there. While still employed by Hollander, Singer assisted Imperial Fur Blending Corp. in establishing itself in the industry, giving it trade secrets of the Hollander firm and new processes which he had developed while working for Hollander but had withheld.

The Hollander company discovered the duplicity and sought relief by requesting that the court enjoin both Singer and the Imperial company from using Hollander's trade secrets *and* Singer's new discoveries. The purpose of the action was clearly to limit Imperial's ability to compete. The law of the case, as expressed in the final decision, was, "a stranger and its employees may be enjoined where, with knowledge of the employee's covenant [with another] and in violation thereof, the stranger applies to his own use the property of the complainant [that is, the rightful owner as a result of the covenant]."

At this writing, another trade secrets case is before the courts, a case which cannot but have a significant effect upon all future cases of a similar nature. The magnitude of this case is such that it will probably be settled ultimately by the Supreme Court of the United States. This case involves two electronic manufacturing giants. The second firm succeeded in luring away the general manager of the first firm's semiconductor division to become the president and chief executive officer of the second. The lure was composed of a substantially larger salary and a stock bonus plus stock options supported by an interest-free loan to assist in their purchase. The exiting general manager was followed by seven senior managers of the semiconductor division, who also joined the second firm's management team. It was well known in the industry that, at that time, this firm was in desperate need of the management and technical skills represented by these eight men. Since its earliest beginnings, such competitor personnel raids have been a natural hazard within the electronics industry, with even the first firm acknowledging that it once hired 18 engineers from another competitor's semiconductor division at a critical point in the corporate development. However, in this case, the first firm reacted to its loss of key personnel with righteous indignation. It entered a suit against the second firm, charging "unfair competition, interference with advantageous personnel relations, antitrust violations, and unjust enrichment." Furthermore, it sought to exact penalties under the legal action of the constructive trust, an obscure precedent usually buried in the back pages of the law books. On this basis, the first firm asked to receive any profits which its ex-employees might make as a result of stock options *and* increased salaries. In the first decision of the lower court, the second firm did emerge victorious, but the first firm has vowed to fight on for ultimate vindication. It can be assumed that if its position in the semiconductor industry is weakened in the future while the second firm emerges anew as a significant factor in the industry, the first firm's case will be strengthened in the courts.

Patents to Provide a Proprietary Position

A patent has been characterized as a piece of paper which confers upon its owner the right to sue anyone who violates the protection afforded by it. In a very real sense, a patent is such a right; but it is a right far more meaningful and protective than a trade secret. The principal difference between a patent and a trade secret lies in the exposure of the concept, idea, process, application, and so on of the patent to public inspection and knowledge. The awarded patent is published for all to see and analyze (except for certain patents bearing a military classification as secret or confidential documents), and each patent is printed and for sale at a nominal fee to anyone who wishes a copy. Given the details of a patent and the knowledge that the ideas contained in it could result in a new and profitable product, any individual or company is at liberty to attempt to circumvent the patent's afforded protection and compete for a portion of the resultant market. If the patent is in fact circumvented, the patent holder has no recourse at law or elsewhere to prevent the competition; and then the patent holder must compete in the marketplace on the basis of quality and price. On the other hand, if the patent holder can prove in a court of law that the patent has not been circumvented successfully, he can obtain an enjoiner to prevent further exploitation of his patent and then sue for damages in recompense for his prior losses. In many cases, the patent holder will discover that the costs of proving his prior claim and the actual degree of infringement, plus the costs of suing to receive damages, may be substantially in excess of any money he might hope to recover through the complex trial processes.

Through research and development, each company should be seeking new proprietary positions which are insured by either patents or trade secrets. As the research and development programs progress through their several stages, it becomes the responsibility of the company's managers to decide whether to seek a patent or attempt to hold the derived knowledge as a trade secret. There will be less opposition from auditors in declaring the value of a patent to be a capital asset than there will be in so classifying a trade secret.

Patent Law Development

Patent law in the United States predates the establishment of the federal government. In those early times, individual colonies awarded patents as special acts of their legislatures. The earliest known special act was passed in 1641. When the Constitution of the United States was ultimately adopted, Section 8 of Article I gave Congress the power "to promote the Progress of Science and useful Arts, by securing for limited times to Authors and Inventors the exclusive Right to their respective Writings and Discoveries."

The first act passed by Congress under this constitutional authority is dated April 10, 1790—the date normally recorded as the beginning of the patent system in this country. However, the actual beginnings of modern patent procedure date from July 4, 1836, when by an act of Congress an examination system was established to approve the award of every patent issued by the government. This system provided that each concept submitted to the government for award of a patent would be treated as an application until it had been examined by officials with the power to reject the application on the basis of conflict, lack of novelty, or established prior art. In the case of patent refusal, the inventor was given recourse in an appeal from the examiners' decision. Accordingly, the Patent Office was created to control and perform the examinations. Since 1836, the patent laws have been revised regularly on a minor scale and twice on a major scale. The basic law was rewritten and extensively revised last in 1952. Present patent law is to be found in Title 35, "Patents," of the United States Code.

The present code provides for the award of patents for the invention of "any new and useful process, machine, manufacture, or composition of matter, or any new and useful improvement thereof." Each of these words is carefully defined within the code, and research and development managers should become acquainted with their defined meanings as expressed in the code and as modified from time to time by changes of the code. The important aspect here is that the invention must be new and useful. To be new, the invention cannot have been known or used previously in the United States or patented or described in a publication anywhere in the world. Mere knowledge without publication in a foreign country will not exclude the possibility of a patent in the United States. Another important exclusion of the code provides that a patent cannot be awarded if the inventor provides public printed awareness or public use of his invention for a period in excess of one year prior to making application for a patent. Publication or use within the one-year period, however, has no effect upon the validity of a patent award.

Many people applying for a patent make the mistake of believing that the concept of new and useful is really all that is required or important. On the other hand, in their role as public protectors the examiners of the Patent Office have historically taken a different view. They have tended to require that an inventor prove differences between the new subject matter and prior art, showing that these differences are not generally obvious to anyone skilled in the art. This interpretation of the code by the examiners has been one of the major sources of conflict in the award of patents.

The Patent Process

Application for a patent must be made by the actual inventor if he is alive. In the event of his death before an application can be filed, all other things being acceptable, the administrator or executor of the inventor's estate may make the required application. Incompetence of an inventor by reason of insanity opens the possibility for the legal representatives of the inventor to file a patent application in the name of the inventor during his lifetime. The resultant patent, if awarded, will have the full rights of any patent, but the ability of the inventor's legal representatives to exercise those rights will be in accordance with the laws governing the capacity of a party to contract.

Many patents are the result of the formal and informal efforts of more than a single inventor. The code provides that the patent application must include the names of *all* parties to the invention. A coinventor who discovers that a patent has been awarded to another coinventor without his knowledge and his name as a coinventor may bring legal action to have his name included on the patent. Similarly, a person whose name has been appended to a patent application as a coinventor may take legal action to have his name removed if he can show that in fact he made no contribution to the invention.

The patent application must set out all the claims of the inventor relative to his patent. These claims must cover the full scope of the invention and must be free of all ties with inventions for which patents have previously been awarded when such ties are required to insure the new invention's validity. Most patent attorneys recommend that a patent be submitted with a graduation of claims from extremely broad to very specific, hoping thereby to obtain the maximum possible coverage with the claims that win the acceptance of the examiners. The total patent is submitted in the legalistic jargon which has become traditional and must be supported by drawings which become a part of the issued patent. (An example of a typical patent as awarded is included in Appendix C of this book.)

Every patent application must be accompanied by a filing fee, which covers the costs of examination only. If the examiners decide favorably for the award of a patent, the inventor is sent a notice of acceptance. The inventor then has six months in which to pay the final fee. On receipt of this final fee, the patent is formally awarded by the government and made a matter of public record, being synopsized in the official *Patent Office Gazette* and made available for purchase through the Government Patent Office as an exact copy of the original patent document.

The examination process can be a lengthy one, covering in some instances several years of review, analysis, and appeal to achieve a final decision. Beyond existing patents, the examiners consider prior art in the public domain and technological principles which are fundamental or general knowledge. Technical literature of the United States and foreign countries is surveyed to assess applicability and worth. At the conclusion of their examination, the examiners, acting for the U.S. Patent Office, may decide to accept some of the claims made by the inventor and disallow others. Or they may disallow all the claims and reject the application in toto. If the application or any of its claims is rejected, the inventor can appeal the decision of the examiners to a board of appeals in the Patent Office. An unfavorable decision by that board may be appealed, in turn, to the United States District Court for the District of Columbia. In rejecting a patent or disallowing claims, the examiners cite previously awarded patents (furnishing the appropriate patent award numbers for reference) or historical references or technical treatises to establish conflicting prior art.

As finally issued and printed, the patent contains only the allowed claims plus the supporting information and drawings of the original application. From the date of issuance, the inventor or his assignee is granted the exclusive right to use, practice, or license to others the rights of the invention for a maximum period of 17 years. As stated previously, the U.S. Patent Office grants a patent only to an individual and never to a business enterprise or an organization. However, since a patent is recognized as a species of real property and has all the attributes of personal property, the inventor may assign the patent (even prior to application) to any company, organization, or person either with or without receipt of money. If the patent has been assigned prior to issuance, the application must reflect this fact and the patent is issued with a statement as to the assignment which has been made.

Pending Patents

The content of a patent application is not made public prior to its issuance. From the time of submission to the Patent Office until award of the final patent, one or more years may pass. In the interim, the company owning the patent assignment may want to reap the benefits which are to be derived from the final patent. To do this, the company may decide to proceed with the production of the resultant product pending the final decision relative to a patent award. This action to produce and market the product will not jeopardize the patent award. In fact, it may encourage a favorable decision, since a product being sold in the market proves "reduction to practice" or technical feasibility.

As a protection in the preaward period, the company should place all other companies on notice of potential protection from a patent by clearly marking the product in some conspicuous place with the words "Patent Pending" or the abbreviation "Pat. Pending." This marking has no validity in law if the patent is never awarded, and any company is free to risk the possibility of patent infringement by copying the product directly or indirectly for competitive sale. If a patent is never awarded, the originator has no legal recourse against these competitors; if a patent *is* awarded, the originator must prove deliberate infringement.

Although it is illegal to do so, it is not an uncommon practice for a company to mark a new product with a "Patent Pending" stamp, even when there is no intention of filing a patent application or when it is already recognized that the application for a patent will be rejected. The hope is to stay competition by this ruse.

Disputed Patents

It is not unusual for two inventors to file on the same idea within a short period of time. It is also not unusual to have an awarded patent challenged by another inventor on the basis of prior discovery. The rights of the true inventor can then be established by an "interference proceeding." The first person to apply for a patent is not necessarily the rightful owner of the patent rights. At the interference proceedings, each contender is required to prove his prior authorship.

Any research or development manager is well advised to document fully and carefully all ideas that might lead to patents. Research and development personnel should be encouraged to keep diaries or notebooks in bound volumes. New or advanced concepts written in these notebooks should be dated and signed by the originators with witnesses' signatures added to attest to the date of entry and the authenticity of the originators' signatures. Anything less than this can be self-defeating.

Worldwide Coverage

Many people have the mistaken belief that a U.S. patent confers patent protection around the world. Nothing could be further from the truth. Efforts are now under way to establish a worldwide patent system. In the meantime, however, it is still necessary to file separate patent applications in most other countries.

In regard to foreign coverage, it is noteworthy that the Union of Soviet Socialist Republics will provide patent coverage for inventions made outside that country. Such patent coverage is expensive to obtain, and the fate of the patent in any litigation in Russian courts is an undetermined factor. The patent holder would be forced to sue the Russian government in the courts of that country. While, in essence providing the basis for patent coverage in the USSR, the Russian government, through a specialized front company, attempts to sell licenses for patentable ideas developed within that country and other Eastern bloc countries.

It is also noteworthy that the Russian government, through its Washington embassy, has a standing purchase order for copies of all patents issued by the United States. It can only be assumed that this is done for exploitation within the Soviet Union.

The international patent situation is but one of the many reasons that a company (and especially its research and development managers) should turn to a qualified patent attorney in any matter pertaining to coverage of new ideas, concepts, and the like. A company with a well-planned and well-executed research and development program will find it more profitable in most cases to engage a full-time patent attorney as a member of the management staff.

Patents Under Government Contracts

Since expenditures made under government-funded research and development contracts with industry account for more than half the total research and development expenditures in our economy, it is worthwhile to consider the rules and regulations which govern patents or patentable concepts derived under or in conjunction with such programs.

Inventions arising from federally underwritten research and development contracts are subject to the same standards of patentability as those arising from private inventive activity. The specific rules and regulations differ among the many government agencies, and the rights and limitations should be the subject of precontract negotiation and inclusion in the formal terms of any written contract. In the case of military contracts written with the Department of Defense, the contract clauses pertaining to patents must be in accordance with the Armed Services Procurement Regulations (which are generally referred to as ASPeRs). In contracts signed with the National Aeronautics and Space Administration, the patent clauses must fall within the printed regulations of that agency.

It is extremely important for any industrial research and development organization contemplating a contract with any government agency to become fully aware of its rights and limitations relative to patents under such contracts. Occasionally, a government agency may attempt to include terms within the contract "boiler plate" (that is, the preprinted, basic clauses added as addenda to the negotiated clauses—the part of the contract sometimes called the fine print) which would give the agency rights to the company's related prior art as expressed in patents of the company, regardless of how those patents may have been obtained or financed. Without question, this is something to be guarded against. If such clauses are accepted, it should be on the basis of full knowledge of what is being sacrificed to obtain the contract.

The reasons most often advanced for the federal government's financing of research and development through contracts with industry are to discharge specific missions by specific agencies and to promote technological change, productivity improvement, and economic welfare on an economywide or industrywide basis. Most of the government research and development contracts are granted by the Department of Defense, the Atomic Energy Commission, and the National Aeronautics and Space Administration, with the other agencies accounting for only a small percentage of such contracts.

The Department of Defense, in precontract negotiations, determines whether the government shall receive title (with a free license to the contractor) or a license to inventions conceived or first reduced to practice in the contract work. This is determined by the status of the contractor in the corresponding commercial area. Traditionally, the Department of Defense's departments have granted free licenses under any patents it holds to anyone requesting such licensing. A violation of any Department of Defense patent (for example, production of a device covered by a DOD patent without an appropriate license) is a serious matter, one to be avoided as all other patent violations are to be avoided.

The Atomic Energy Commission, by statute, generally acquires title to all inventions made under its contracts and also acquires rights relating to some noncontract inventions pertaining to nuclear energy applications, devices, and the like. In some cases, the Atomic Energy Commission will grant licenses under its patents.

The National Aeronautics and Space Administration, by statute, acquires title to inventions covered under its research and development contracts. However, through its regulations, this agency has relaxed that title position by granting waivers (with certain restrictions) of the government's title and by an aggressive licensing campaign.

Other government agencies follow inconsistent policies on inventions covered under contract work, with many agencies providing that the contracting officers determine what rights shall accrue to the government and the contractor after the invention is reported. It is advisable that all government research and development contracts be entered into with full awareness and knowledge of what is being sacrificed to gain the contract and that precontract negotiations be conducted to gain the best position granted to any other contractor by that agency.

The existence of these differing policies controlling patents under government contracts has resulted in difficulties when industrial research and development efforts are conducted by one company for different agencies. For example, NASA and DOD sponsor research and development in identical technological areas and with the same industrial firms. Because differing patent rights clauses have resulted in controversies in which one government agency is opposed to another and the industrial contractor is placed squarely in the middle, there are increasing demands for a new uniformity of government patent policy in contracts from all government agencies.

Morality of the Government Patent Policy

If the government patent issue is worth arguing at all, the patents being granted to private contractors under the present policies must have some significant value. If there were no value, there certainly would be no objection to the government's holding them. Arguments are being offered pro and con regarding the licensing policies, and the research and development manager should be fully aware of both sides in order to make intelligent contracting decisions.

On one side the argument says in part that, under the government contract, something of commercial value is created at public expense and then turned over to individuals or individual companies with neither an explicit rationale for the transfer nor an explicit evaluation of the worth. Further, given the existing concentration of companies engaged in large-scale, government-financed research and development efforts, the granting of patent monopolies to these contractors tends to increase this concentration and to reduce the probability that new sources of research and development capability will appear.

On the other side of the argument, research and development as financed by the government is seldom financially rewarding for industrial contractors. Such contracts normally bring a fixed fee of 7 or 8 percent of the contract's actual cost up to a set ceiling. If the contract suffers a cost overrun, the company's fee is not increased; but, if the cost of the contract is less than estimated and set by the contract terms, the fee is reduced accordingly. It must be recognized that the fee is not profit. In the final audit, the contractor can fully expect the government auditors to disallow various expenses of the contract as a matter of practice. When the costs of borrowing money to support the contract effort while awaiting government payment are added to the unrecoverable costs disallowed in the final audit, the contract may yield a true profit of only 2 or 3 percent.

The acquisition of a patent license with commercial potential as a result of the contract may completely offset this poor return and provide the incentive for performing the work required by the government. Also, among a new breed of government employees, many of whom are moving into positions of responsibility, there is an expressed belief that American industry must serve the government and, through the government, the people. This attitude is making research and development for the government ever less attractive and defeating the purpose of the government contract with industry.

It is clear that there is a great need for a new study of government patent policies and practices. Such a policy study should be conducted with representation from all segments of society with a view to adoption of better policies to meet the dynamic demands of the current situation. Only Congress can bring about such an event.

A Patent as a Monopoly

The patent concept is an anomaly within our economic system and is generally considered alien to our moral precepts of business conduct, inasmuch as the patent is a grant of an exclusive monopoly by the government to an individual or (by assignment) to a company. This is of course true only in an abstract sense; but, disregarding that fact, the purpose of the patent program is to

1. Stimulate inventive activity, as well as a flow of inventions and technological changes for the benefit of the economy and the public as a whole.
2. Promote investment in research and development facilities required to bring the results of inventive activity into a commercially operable state.
3. Encourage the disclosure and dissemination of the results of inventive activity among potential users and producers of subsequent inventions.

While a patent does award a monopoly relative to a product and is issued by the U.S. government through its Patent Office under the strict laws established by Congress, other agencies of government may turn around and declare that the owner of a patent may not use the conferred monopoly for his sole benefit. In a classical example of this duplicity of action, the Securities and Exchange Commission took note of the fact that automobile wheel production in this country was confined to three firms on the basis of interlocking patent agreements. Ruling that this type of action is in violation of the principles of the Sherman antitrust statutes, the commission issued an order that enjoined these firms to grant a manufacturing license to any other firm desiring to enter the business in competition with the patent holders. The companies lost their case and agreed to the stipulated terms. In spite of this effort of the commission, no other company has attempted to challenge the three principals—not because of the royalty payments which might be exacted, but because of the capital investment which would be required to establish a production line.

Assignment of Patents

Patents and patent assignments have played a significant role in the function of concept and invention control within industry. As previously mentioned, many companies require that their employees, as a condition for employment, sign a patent and invention waiver agreement written in contract or covenant form. An example of such an agreement taken from the files of a major company is as follows:

Assignment of Inventions

A. I agree to disclose promptly, completely, and in writing to ABC, Inc. and I hereby assign and agree to assign and bind my heirs, executors, or administrators to assign to ABC, Inc. or its designee, its assigns, successors, or legal representatives any and all inventions, processes, diagrams, methods, apparatus, or any improvements (all hereinafter collectively called inventions) whatsoever, discovered and/or developed, either individually or jointly with others, during the course of my employment with ABC, Inc., or using ABC, Inc.'s time, data, facilities and/or materials, provided the subject matter is one within the fields of interest of ABC, Inc. My obligations under this paragraph apply without regard to whether an idea for an invention or a solution to a problem occurs to me on the job, at home, or elsewhere. I further agree that all such inventions are ABC, Inc.'s exclusive property, whether or not applications are filed thereon.

B. Subject matter within a field of interest of ABC, Inc. includes any field of interest that has been worked on by ABC, Inc. in the past or in which there is work in progress at ABC, Inc. at the date of or during my employment with ABC, Inc., and projects or other operations at ABC, Inc. planned for the future. It is expressly understood that this agreement does not apply to any of my patents or patent applications filed or based on inventions made prior to my employment with ABC, Inc. or to matters (other than those within a field of interest of ABC, Inc.) which are exclusively of personal interest.

C. I shall assist ABC, Inc. at any time during or after my employment is terminated, at ABC, Inc.'s expense, in the preparation, execution, and delivery of any disclosures, patent applications, or papers within the scope and intent of this agreement required to obtain patents in this or in other countries and in connection with such other proceedings as may be necessary to vest title thereto in ABC, Inc., its assigns, successors, or legal representatives. If such assistance takes place after my employment is terminated, I shall be paid by ABC, Inc. at a reasonable rate for any time that I actually spend in such work at ABC, Inc.'s request.

Exhibit 4 is still another typical agreement taken from the files of a major company.

In these agreements, which are common forms of contracts between a new employee and a company willing to hire him, an obvious conflict appears between a patent as a management control function and a patent as an employee motivational means. From the studies made regarding a motivating environment (known as the Pittsburgh Studies), it is clear that "motivation only begins with the traditional rewards of employment, reaching its full flower in the removal of restrictions, regulations, and controls." * Of course, if the employee is what David C. McClelland calls achievement-motivated, there may be no motivational conflict, since an individual so motivated finds accomplishment to be an end in itself. However, if an individual is motivated by money or other rewards, there is a need for a change in the present concepts of industrial patent programs. This is a matter which will be explored more fully in the chapter dealing with motivation. In the interim consider that many companies now lose their most productive, inventive employees as

---

* Frederick Herzberg, Bernard Mausner, and B. Snyderman, *The Motivation to Work* (New York: John Wiley & Sons, 1959).

Exhibit 4

ASSIGNMENT OF INVENTIONS AND
COMPANY INFORMATION AGREEMENT

In consideration of one dollar ($1.00), the receipt of which I hereby acknowledge and in consideration of my continued employment by ABC, Inc. during such time as may be mutually agreeable to ABC, Inc. and myself, I hereby agree as follows:

I. I agree to assign to ABC, Inc., its successors and assigns, all my rights to inventions which, during the period of my employment by ABC, Inc. or its successors in business, I have made or conceived, or may hereafter make or conceive, either solely or jointly with others:

    (a) In the course of such employment,

    (b) Or with the use of the employer's time,

    (c) Or with the use of the employer's materials or date or facilities,

    (d) Or relating to any problems arising in the employer's business, the question of relation to be determined by ABC, Inc.

II. I agree to promptly and fully disclose to ABC, Inc. in writing all of said inventions and/or discoveries.

III. I agree, without charge to ABC, Inc., but at the expense of ABC Company, to execute, acknowledge, and deliver all such further papers, including applications for patents, as may be necessary to obtain patents for said inventions in any and all countries and to vest title thereto in ABC, Inc., its successors and assigns.

IV. Further, I agree to keep secret and not to disclose any secret process, trade secret or confidential information concerning the business of ABC, Inc. disclosed to me or knowledge of which was gained by me in the course of my employment.

V. Still further, I agree that, during the period of my employment by ABC, Inc., I will not perform any service for any other company or person in competition with ABC, Inc. without written approval of ABC, Inc.

Date _____

STATE OF

COUNTY OF

The above-named_____

personally appeared before me and acknowledged the foregoing instrument to be his free act and deed.

_____

Notary Public

My commission expires:

SEAL

This patent agreement is an altered copy of an agreement taken from the files of a major company. Typed and mimeographed on cheap paper rather than printed, the form's appearance completely belies its importance. It is normally presented to a new employee with a group of other forms which the employee is asked to sign on the first day of employment. The employee is not given a copy of the form, which disappears in his file, and one dollar is added to his first paycheck as a special employment "benefit."

a result of poor patent programs. A responsible manager might find that the cost of suitable rewards for patent disclosure is actually less than the cost of hiring new employees, who will probably be as reluctant to disclose their patentable ideas. This matter of control, however, still remains.

Protecting Your Rights

The managers of a company must recognize that they have nothing to protect if the information they consider to be proprietary is in fact known outside the company. Similarly, no company can appropriate as proprietary information facts or knowledge which is in the public domain or is known generally in the trade or industry. If the company fails to warn its employees that certain data, information, equipment, and so on are in fact considered to be proprietary and confidential, the courts cannot be expected to accept such things as proprietary and confidential. Further, if a company permits the publication in open literature of papers or articles which reveal too much information about proprietary matters, the company cannot continue to claim these matters as proprietary. Finally, the company which exposes proprietary information on a label or in directions, specification sheets, or even catalogs forfeits its right to continue claiming such information as truly proprietary.

Protecting proprietary information requires that managers exercise due restraint and reasonable control. Besides cautioning employees that certain matters are proprietary and confidential, the managers must take appropriate action to restrict such matters to a limited number of employees. It is highly desirable to enclose an area and restrict admission to specially qualified personnel who work with or use the proprietary items. Such an area is prima facie evidence that the company is attempting to guard its proprietary information from all competitors.

Beyond a restricted working area, all documents, drawings, formulas, and other easily removed proprietary items should be registered as to content and kept in an adequate safe or in combination-lock containers. All such items should be marked with a warning or restrictive notice that is obvious as well as clearly inclusive.

Restrictive Clauses on Information

There are a number of possible restrictive clauses that can be used to mark proprietary property. Each manager should consult the company's legal staff before selecting and using any such clause. An improperly drawn or invalid clause could actually be self-defeating.

One major company uses the following restrictive clause on all proprietary items:

> This document discloses subject matter in which ABC, Inc. has proprietary rights. Neither receipt nor possession thereof confers or transfers any right to reproduce or disclose the document, any part thereof, any information contained therein, or any physical article or device, or to practice any method or process, except by written permission from or written agreement with ABC, Inc.

Still another firm uses a less restrictive clause which reads:

> ABC, Inc. proprietary rights are included in the information disclosed herein. Neither this document nor information disclosed herein shall be reproduced or transferred to other documents or used or disclosed to others for any purpose except as specified herein, without authority in writing from ABC, Inc.

Whenever a company prepares a proposal in response to a government agency's request for proposal leading to a contract, or when a company submits an unsolicited proposal to a government agency seeking a contract response, the proposal document and all the proposal addenda should bear a limiting clause. One major company uses the following clause for this purpose:

> The contents of this document are the exclusive property of ABC, Inc. and are provided to the government for its evaluation only. These contents are not to be disclosed to other parties outside the U.S. government or to be duplicated, used, or discussed in whole or in part, except as provided by a contract with ABC,

Inc. This restriction does not limit the government's use of identical, similar, or related data and information obtained from other sources.

This clause normally appears on the title page of the documents and also appears on each page which definitely presents proprietary information.

Employee Control

In matters relating to proprietary secrets, employees present the major source of difficulty. A good deal of later difficulty can be avoided by a carefully organized program of personnel management. Each prospective employee or job applicant should be thoroughly screened if he is to become privy to any proprietary matters. A check with former employers should be carried out to establish whether the applicant has previously had access to a competitor's proprietary matters. It is also wise to establish whether the applicant is under any contractual or convenant obligation to former employers.

When a new employee is hired, he should not be given immediate access to proprietary matters beyond those necessary to the performance of his assigned tasks. To avoid lawsuits from a former employer and competitor, assign the new employee to a project removed from the type of project to which he was formerly assigned. In spite of the new man's best intentions and highest ethical standards, he may be sorely tempted to use a former employer's secrets to improve his own position.

When the employee leaves (and he must be expected to leave if he is one of today's creative but highly mobile scientists or technicians), precautions must be taken to protect the company's future. A departure agreement is one legal way of accomplishing that purpose, and a warning to his next employer is another. The departure agreement should be designed to have the employee acknowledge that he has been privy to proprietary matters and that he is aware of his limitations with regard to these matters. He should also be asked to affirm that he possesses no company property of any type or character obtained directly or indirectly as a consequence of his employment.

If the employee is hostile at the time of his leaving and refuses to sign a departure agreement, a departure interview should be conducted with appropriate witnesses present. In this interview, the employee should be made aware of his rights and his limitations relative to proprietary matters of the terminated employment. The interview should be recorded and transcribed, with the witnesses and the principal interviewer signing the transcription. A certified copy of the transcription should be sent to the employee by registered mail, and a return receipt should be secured. The courts will view such an action as correct and prudent provided the company recognizes that the departing employee is entitled to all special and general skills he may have acquired previously and any skills he acquired during his employment just terminated.

With both amicable and hostile departures, it is wise to write a letter to a competitor making a flat and unembroidered statement that the ex-employee was privy to proprietary information, data, and the like and that he is under an obligation, both implicit and explicit, to withhold such matters from his new employer while the employer is restrained from using any such information which might be given by the employee. If there is any embroidery in the statements, the ex-employee can bring suit on the grounds that his job opportunities have been damaged. This is a legal tightrope, and it should be walked only under the guidance of a lawyer.

Copyright as Protection

One means of protection for proprietary information is the copyright. All specification sheets, catalogs, instruction booklets, and other printed material which cover a firm's products should be copyrighted. Considering the small fee required to accomplish this, it is difficult to understand why the protection of a copyright is not obtained more often.

To obtain a copyright on any information, first produce the work in copies by printing or other means of reproduction (even dry copy processes). Each copy must have the copyright notice on the title page or first page. In the case of any work with a title page, the copyright notice may appear on the reverse side of the page. This notice must have each of three elements. The first element is the word "Copyright," the abbreviation "Copr.," or the symbol ©. The second element is the name of the copyright owner. Finally, the notice is completed by the date of publication. Examples of such notice are

Copyright by ABC, Inc., 1970.
Copr. John Doe 1970.
© ABC, Inc., 1970.

Use of the symbol, as in the last example, insures the securing of a copyright in countries which are members of the Universal Copyright Convention.

The date of publication is the earliest date when copies of the first authorized edition were placed on sale, sold, or publicly distributed by the proprietor of the copyright or under his authority. If for any reason copies of the work are published without the required notice, the right to secure copyright is lost and cannot be restored. The act of publication with the required notice actually secures the copyright protection. Confirmation of the copyright is obtained by filing Form A, which is both application and certificate. This form should be completed as soon as practical after publication. Two copies of the material, the form, and the fee should then be sent to the Register of Copyrights, Library of Congress, Washington, D.C.

Statutory copyright lasts for 28 years from the date of first publication. In the event that this period is not long enough, the copyright may be renewed for an additional 28 years. The law does not provide for registration of material in an unpublished form. Material which has not yet been published is protected from unauthorized use by common law.

4

Financing Applied Research

ALTHOUGH a firm may not be consciously oriented to the profit center concept, in a very real sense the portion of corporate management represented by the president and his executive staff must assume the role of corporation banker to the several distinct company profit centers. Like any good banker, these corporate managers are expected to invest the firm's available assets and funds wisely, choosing from among the many available alternatives to obtain the maximum promise of return on investment. As with a commercial bank, each profit center of the corporation must come to top management within each fiscal year, seeking the "loan" of corporate funds and assets for the year to follow. As the corporation approaches a commercial bank to attain its financing, the individual profit centers must approach the corporation's financial control center; that is, the need for funds and assets, as well as a cash flow schedule and return to the bank, must be documented to the full satisfaction of the loan reviewers.

Within the corporation, the documentation must provide full disclosure of such data as the assets that will be used, how these assets will be applied, the funds flow planning schedule, and the rate of return to be anticipated from direct support of the profit

48

center's request. Such documentation is best supplied by a profit plan as incorporated within a conventional planning report. The planning function will be dealt with separately in a later chapter.

Research as a Separable Profit Center

The principle was advanced earlier that the province of research for any firm attempting to realize a profit from its operations is properly that of applied research. An applied research effort begins with a specific and well-defined objective—a new product, an improvement of an old product, a new or improved production process—and it perseveres toward that objective in a scientific and businesslike manner, avoiding the inviting tangents that are revealed as progress is made toward the objective.

The path from initiation of a research effort to tangible, useful results is an investment that involves both risk and uncertainty. It is an investment that must be studiously considered and evaluated in the same light as any other corporate investment. In a very real sense, it is the commitment of current dollars to obtain tomorrow's discounted dollars. When the commitment has been made, the investment must be managed and guarded with the same care and diligence as any other investment made by the company.

Whether as part of a corporate structure or as a separate entity, a research (and, for that matter, development) organization has all the attributes of a separable profit center. Although it may not be treated in that manner, there are very sound reasons for accepting the research organization as a separate profit center—even an acknowledged negative profit center—since, in this way, the top managers of the corporation can affect control over the company's very real investment in the research and development efforts.

Adjusting Accounting Procedures for Research

It is entirely true that the accounting procedures which apply effectively to production processes become cumbersome and even unmanageable when applied to research and development programs. But can this fact ever be accepted as justification for excluding these organizations from detailed accounting and proper audit control? The answer to that question must be an obvious *no!* Management at the highest levels must place upon the corporate accounting function a requirement to adapt or adopt methods which serve the needs of research and development accounting as well as the principles of good program management. The justification for performing a particular accounting procedure may be a historical one rather than a matter of accommodation to the need of the business segment. But this should not deter those in positions of management responsibility from requiring new or modified accounting precepts and principles to accommodate the control and specialized audit problems inherent in research and development programs. However, the problem arises because, within today's conventional accounting and planning procedures, there are only subjective means of evaluating the contributions of a company's research efforts.

To exercise control over a defined profit center, research and development managers should be able to plan and apply both cash flows and assets in a predictable manner, either with or without anticipated income from external contracts. Then these managers, following procedures paralleling those of other company profit centers, can also apply to the corporate banker for the loan of assets required to operate the research and development activity over the projected planning period, fully documenting and justifying the proposed asset applications. In seeking such a loan, the R&D managers' statement of anticipated returns on the loan can be made in two different forms. The return can be expressed either as a potential patent or other proprietary advantage to the firm, which can be assigned an estimated value in terms of sale by the company when the appropriate research and development effort is completed, or as production savings or a potential corporate profit increase.

The Need for Accountability

From both accounting clues and analysis of the individual programs, the managers directly responsible for research and development and those managers above the R&D organization are able to assess the ongoing probability of ultimate success for a program and to determine the possibility of altered completion value. Unprofitable research and development efforts, like unprofitable production programs, should not be continued to the detriment in cost and scheduling of other efforts or to the detriment of the company's planned investment program. Effective management will result in informed corporate managers who recognize the unprofitability of any effort or program long before that effort fully expends the investment judged to be adequate.

The scientist as a general class is not immune to the desire for empire building, and for all his scientific astuteness he may still tend to equate bigger with better. If the corporate management staff is to keep the company's assets productively employed—an essential activity in the growth and success of any enterprise—conscious control of the return on investment must be extended to all areas of the company, including the research and development area. A motivation incentive plan for research and development personnel, if coupled with detailed accounting for each effort or program, will do much toward establishing economically rational decisions relative to the acquisition of assets and relative to their use in research and development. The manager of research must be in a position to stress maximum productivity relative to the available resources. He must be able to discourage pressures toward indulgent or wasteful use of assets by citing the effect upon organization and individual incentive plans, or he must be able to enforce a limitation on the application of assets in a specific program.

Research as a Capital Asset

The asset derived from an investment in research and development fits all the requirements normally established in the definition of a corporate capital asset. Capital assets are economic goods or resources used in or consumed by production and as such include real property, materials, cash, and intangibles. The cost of the research and development derived asset is determinable; and, like a fixed asset which is expected to be consumed and is therefore depreciated or amortized according to some acceptable time schedule, the R&D derived asset is consumed in the business by production utilization or is squandered by inactivity with the passage of time.

If the asset is wasted by idleness, the upper echelon of the corporate managers is not performing its delegated responsibility to insure the proper and efficient application of all available assets for profit maximization. By the same token, no productive profit center should be allowed to squander any asset or utilize it uneconomically in the production of profit. Consideration must be given to the proposition that any profit center in the firm must be required to bid for any asset created by research and development investment, paying an appropriate charge to the corporate bank for its use and consumption.

If this concept of valuing research and development generated assets is accepted and applied, how will the R&D organization realize the profit which justifies its continued existence? Can a profit be applied to the organization to remove its performance evaluation from the subjective methods now generally used by industry? These objectives of profit assignment and subjective evaluation can be accomplished by assigning to the product of each research and development effort an asset value which is the *lower* of either (1) the costs of the effort plus some fixed profit percentage or (2) the estimated market value of the resultant patent or proprietary right when sold outside the company. Then, when the corporate managers consign or lend a research and development generated asset to a production profit center or sell the asset for a direct financial return, the books of the R&D organization can be credited with the inventory reduction and debited with the value of the return on the original investment. The responsibility for economically sound use of the generated asset at that time passes from the research and development organization to the production organization accepting the asset. Thus the production managers must accept full responsibility for achieving a profit from the consumption of the asset.

Control of Research Through Accounting

As a means of management control over a defined and separated profit center, the managers having direct responsibility for research and development programs must be able to plan and apply both cash flow and asset application in a predictable manner, either with or without anticipated income from external contracts. They must be able to justify their expense and asset application in terms of anticipated return on investment. This return might be expressed as a potential patent or other proprietary advantage to the company, or it might be expressed in terms of production savings or potential corporate profit increase. The method of expression, however, should be understood by and be agreeable to all affected managers.

The demand for full accountability for specific efforts in progress is far more important in and to a research (and even a development) organization than to a production organization. The accounting centers of the research and development organizations should be diligent in accumulating and apportioning all the costs attributable to each individual effort. In these efforts, the costs associated with travel as well as with telephone and telegraph communications take on a larger significance than in other profit centers. The same is true of the printing function and space charges. Whereas such charges would become normal burden costs in a production organization, they should become direct charges to a specific research and development effort whenever they can be identified in terms of specific efforts. These less than obvious direct charges, when combined with the obvious direct charges of labor and materials, assist managers in ascertaining that the several efforts or programs are progressing in accordance with preprogram planning and costing.

The accounting clues added to the analysis of the research and development programs' technical advancement permit the upper echelon managers to assess the probability for ultimate success of various programs on an ongoing basis. It is also possible for them to determine the likelihood of altered completion value. Unprofitable efforts should not be continued to the detriment in cost and scheduling of other efforts or to the detriment of the corporation's planned investment program. Effective management will result in informed corporate managers regarding the unprofitability of any effort long before that effort fully expends the investment loan made by the corporate management staff.

It is not unreasonable to assume that there will be research-generated assets which none of the company's other profit centers will seek or accept on assignment. This does not mean that these generated assets have no intrinsic value. But it does impose an obligation upon the corporate managers either to establish a new profit center that will exploit the asset or to market the asset as quickly as possible—that is, sell it (preferably at a profit) to some other firm for exploitation.

This method of handling accounting for research, including asset transfer, is not without its inherent dangers. The principal danger lies in the area of establishing right and reasonable value for the asset. This danger is magnified by the possible analysis and derivation of the firm's true worth by financial experts and potential investors. The effectiveness of corporate managers in planning for the future will then become far more evident, and the false façades which characterize so many research organizations will be torn down for brutal inspection of the worth of the corporation's supported research efforts—the firm's true investment for future profits.

Government Research and Development Contracting

Some companies attempt to rationalize their façade research on the basis of necessity in the solicitation of government production contracts. It is true that, when bidding for these production contracts, a company without a research capability may be disqualified for system and subsystem production programs. The government's estimate of the need for a research organization to solve the complex problems that could arise in the manufacture of the system may be highly debatable; but, since the procurement policies of the government are relatively inflexible, this will be of no consequence in the award of the contract. In some cases, a company without a research organization can convince government personnel that the required research backup is available, but this is generally difficult to do. The need for government contracts seems a poor justification for maintaining a façade research organization when the same financial investment applied through proper management can accomplish this purpose while also providing a direct financial return reflected in improved future profitability.

Beyond the need for a research organization to support government production contracts, such an organization should be considered in terms of deriving a part—and possibly a significant part—of its operational financing from direct government research and development contract awards. In the science-based industries, the most profitable government business involves the mass production of major military or social systems (for example, mass urban transit). Such system programs generally begin with the award of a number of small research projects to a variety of companies. Although the research efforts are defined as to objectives and requirements, they generally leave significant room for original thinking and creativity.

After the results of the research efforts have been received and analyzed by government scientists and technologists, these results may be combined for a system study under appropriate "definition contracts" generally negotiated with one or more companies chosen from the participating research organizations. Within most companies, a definition contract study effort can be most effectively conducted by the research division or organization that performed the initial research studies, since the system study must combine proven concepts with the most advanced technology, while utilizing the work originally performed in the research studies.

Contrary to what may be supposed, it is not unusual to find that more than one company will compete with definition contracts in the system study phase. The company that will win the development of the system and ultimately receive the prized initial production contract is the company that performs the most comprehensive analysis of all facets of the system problem. Inasmuch as the government generally awards the initial production contract—the contract with the most direct and indirect profit potential—to the successful development contract firm, it is worth a company's investment of management talent, scientific/technical talent, and facilities to perform the system study with attention to the most meticulous details and the highest quality workmanship.

The management that does not realize that a prerequisite for military system development contract consideration is participation in the research studies and analyses leading to the definition contract phase may well have excluded itself from the highest potential profits. At the same time, the companies that perform the initial research studies have the right to anticipate the possibility of progressing toward production of the ultimate system. To achieve that end, quality performance must begin in the research phase and persist through all subsequent phases. Each phase must be viewed as an independent investment in the future, requiring careful management action.

Making the Most of Government Contracts

Tangents and subtangents which are revealed en route to the objective of a system production contract should not be explored to the detriment of the principal objective. However, at any point at which the company loses to its competition, the research and development managers should be ready to exploit these tangents and subtangents as a hedge to the investment now lost.

Also in regard to government contracts which result in system production programs, corporate managers must recognize that the company which develops the system is in most cases able to establish a proprietary interest in the system by including the company's own manufactured components and subsystems as integral parts of the design. Even with the introduction of second-source procurements, the company is in a position to establish a high order of profitability that would not be possible if it waited to compete in the government's solicitation of second sources for production.

Since it is never possible fully to recover the cost of research and applied development in government contracts, each contract for research and development efforts requires some company investment. However, the fact that a contract is accepted from the government for research and development efforts leading to a military system reduces and at the same time increases the risk to the company's investment in government sponsored research.

The government is becoming more and more insistent that significant contracts become fully competitive in each phase. Corporate management should note, therefore, that it is not entirely necessary for a company to engage in contractual research with the government in order to arrive at the production of an important system. There are companies in the United States which have successfully performed—in house and at their own expense—the preliminary research, system definition studies, and first-phase engineering development of a major system. These companies have then been able to sell the resultant program as a sole-source, proprietary, final development and production contract.

For the large company with an aggressive management staff and financial resources which permit the assumption of larger risks, the in-house approach to a system seems one of the more desirable means of reaching production profits. On the other hand, smaller companies that are less financially secure and larger companies with conservative management will choose to obtain contracts from the government covering the major portion of research and development in the system preproduction phases. Corporate management must decide the form of investment it wishes to make, and this decision will vary with each company's varying circumstances.

The corporate group seeking government research and development contracts to support or reduce costs of operation must approach the problem of contract solicitation in a manner somewhat different from that of pure production to government specifications and drawings. Literally, the reputation of the company is at stake with each government research and development contract accepted. The government expects—and has a right to expect—that the work performed under a research contract will be accomplished within defined time schedules, defined objectives, and a defined price. The contracting company cannot view the money paid by the government for corporate-performed research and development as a gift which does not require sound company control over every facet of the effort.

The product of a research effort is in a sense paper, and the company must recognize that the paper product should be of the highest quality the company can supply. A well-written and properly published report covering a worthwhile research effort will come to the attention of a greater number of important government personnel than the company's highest-quality manufactured component. A poorly written and improperly prepared report will also come to the attention of a vast segment of government personnel, and it will have a more adverse impact upon the company's image than any unsatisfactorily manufactured component. In a very real sense, the quality of the research report reflects upon the overall competence of the company.

It is not inappropriate to print and hardbind all research reports submitted to the government under government contracts. While most of these contracts will specify publication procedures for final reports, the government agencies will willingly amend these contract terms to permit company printing and hardbinding of final research reports when the contractor certifies that the cost to the government will not be increased by this technique. In many cases, a truly objective analysis of the comparative costs will reveal that there is no increase in cost when the work is performed by professional publication and bindery personnel.

The Profit Decline in Military Contracts

In 1956, the government's Renegotiation Board began to publish defense contractors' profits on renegotiable sales. The revealed percentages cover average profit regardless of quality of performance, contractors' assumption of financial risk, or other factors affecting profitability. Expressed as pretax and pre-renegotiation, the 1956 figure was 6.3 percent, and this was cut in half in 1962. The 1968 figure has been estimated at something less than 3 percent. On this basis, why do companies even consider the acceptance of government contracts? Obviously, the reasons have to be more than purely financial and, as such, are beyond the scope of this particular chapter.

The significant fact to note here is that the government is aware of the problems it is creating not only for the defense industry as a whole but also for itself through the production of less than optimum equipment. In an attempt to provide industry with an opportunity to earn a reasonable profit, Congress at the urging of the Defense Department has amended the Armed Services Procurement Regulations to encourage fixed-price and incentive contracts as opposed to the more common cost contracts.

In theory the government is willing to reward superior performance with increased profits, while penalizing substandard performance with reduced fees. Like so much that is theoretical in the realm of complex economics, when put to practice this theory has been less than successful. The fixed-price contract is an open invitation to the marginal company to undercut the more qualified (and reputable) firm on any procurement. The most qualified firm, to stay in competitive contention, must cut its profit to a subsistence level, and the whole theory is sunk by the same regulation which says that fixed-price contract awards must be given to the "lowest bidder among the qualified firms." Since qualification of a firm is all too frequently a subjective matter, government contractor-evaluation personnel are fooled into qualifying the marginal firm, awarding it the contract, and then literally having to move into the manufacturer's plant to manage the program and insure delivery of needed equipment. The contracting agency may also find itself in the position of having to award the contractor financial relief in the form of larger payments. When such relief is granted, it usually raises the cost to a figure substantially above the offered price of the more qualified but rejected bidders.

In conjunction with the government's recognition of the profit decline and of the defense industry's need to conduct research and development as well as incur substantial bidding expenses on major systems and subsystems, the Defense Department willingly enters into triservice shared expenses with established and qualified contractors covering both internal research and development and bidding costs. These annual agreements are discussed in somewhat more detail in the chapter on marketing of research.

Research as an Investment

The principal point of the foregoing is that research and development, regardless of how or why they are conducted, require an investment by corporate management. In the acquisition of such significant items as fixed assets, management will usually evaluate a proposed purchase by an appropriate and in-depth investment study. To cover the acquisition, the purchase funds must be taken from the owner's equity, subtracted from profits, or covered by increased corporate debt. The proposed expenditure is analyzed in terms of future cash flow both to and from the proposed investment; and, to give this future cash flow financial meaning, it is converted to current money value through the process of discounting. Generally, the number of years required to achieve full recovery of the investment is also computed.

Why should the firm's investment in research and development not be afforded this same financial planning? One rather weak excuse for not so doing—an excuse which is sometimes offered by an indifferent management staff—goes like this: Science and scientific research are not understandable in the same terms as conventional capital investment in fixed assets; the scientific research processes establish, in the average mind, an aura of black magic and thus become too intangible for proper comprehension and planning.

Any manager who accepts such a statement has abdicated his managerial responsibilities and prerogatives. Competent, professional managers willingly accept research as management-controllable factors in business. There is absolutely no reason why research and preproduct development cannot be controlled effectively. In seeking control over research, however, all managers must immediately accept the fact that in research there are higher risks as well as higher potential long-range profits. This means that managers must realize and be willing to accept another fact—that the potential profits will be obtainable at a more deferred time than might be expected with many other potential capital investments.

In the company in which managers accept their full responsibilities, research and preproduct development will not be financed on the basis of a general allocation of corporate funds, with the allocation charged as a general and administrative expense or divided among the other direct profit centers as a burden charge. Instead, the research and development function will be treated as a separate profit center engaged in the delivery of a salable service to the corporation as a unit or to the corporation's customers. Within the profit center there will be costed services offered to and purchased by the corporation.

As with any other corporate profit center, the research and development center will accumulate its actual burden costs. By management design, a significant part of that burden cost should be devoted to the center's own self-preservation. A competent research and preproduct development organization will invest not less than 10 percent—and more nearly 20 percent—of its scientific and technical talent resources in the acquisition of data and information from which new research and development recommendations are drawn. This burden expense is comparable to the lost productivity charges to overhead which come from time spent—at all corporate levels—for both current and future planning.

Selecting the Research Investment

Upper echelon managers should receive periodic recommendations of potential research investments from the research organization. Each such recommendation should be described as to objective and should reveal an estimated potential worth or return in a specific time frame. Further, the research organization should give corporate managers an estimate of the risk or uncertainty of success as well as an estimate of the probability of achieving a proprietary advantage with a corresponding improvement in the oligopolistic competitive structure characterizing today's markets. When corporate managers evaluate all such data, consider the subjective factors involved in having such capability within the firm, and arrive at an investment decision relative to research, they are fulfilling the role expected by the corporate owners—a role the managers must perform without abdication of responsibility.

To assist in the selection of the appropriate research efforts for investment, the company should establish some form of ongoing evaluation sheet to be completed within the research organization. Preferably, this sheet should become a regular form on which the research director or project initiator enters appropriate information in the indicated blocks. Each company should undertake to develop a form most suited to its specific requirements. Whatever the layout and whatever the general considerations, the form might be considered as divisible into product identification, marketing data, research and development requirements, production engineering and production considerations, and financial analysis.

The objective of the research and development effort, as has already been stated, should be to establish a proprietary position. Most probably, this position will be embodied in a product, although some other type of position (for example, a new manufacturing process) might be the objective. Whatever the objective, it should be identified and defined as a basis for accomplishing the proposed task. In the case of a product and of most other objectives, the extent of both domestic and foreign competition should be stated. Further, the estimated useful market life of the product, process, or whatever should be stated in terms of the most likely situation rather than the most optimistic.

In any evaluation of a research and development investment, it is an absolute necessity to consider all relative marketing data. Among the questions to be answered are those affecting the salability of the product and the requirements to achieve the sales objectives. Particularly important in any evaluation is the answer to this question: How will the new product fit within present product lines? The answer must consider whether present marketing procedures and sales forces are adequate or whether new marketing methods are required and the sales force will have to be retrained.

Next in importance, some estimate should be made of the market stability. Specifically, the question must be answered as to whether the introduction of this specific new product or process will result in extensive price cutting in both competitive and correlative products. Also, in terms of markets and marketing, there should be some indication of any specialized postsales service support requirements. If these requirements exist, the question becomes one of meeting them with current support service groups and facilities or establishing new groups and facilities. Finally, in terms of marketing, some measure is needed of the advertising and promotion necessary to bring the resultant product to market.

The research and development requirements must provide the data necessary to predict the final return on investment. These data include estimates of research and development costs at each stage or phase (including historic and projected costs) and the schedule for completion. Next, the technological posture of the company to accomplish the research and development effort should be clearly delineated in terms of what is available and what will be required in the way of personnel and facilities. Finally, some measure must be made of the proprietary position that will result. This might be expressed in terms of a patent, an exclusive license granted on the basis of the extension of some other firm's patent, or a trade secret.

Production and production engineering considerations provide the essential data relative to bringing the product from the research and development phases into full production for marketing. There are considerations of materials, materials handling, equipment requirements, and facility requirements. In essence, it is necessary to establish whether new production facilities will be required, whether the old facilities can be adapted without production interruption, or whether there will be a fundamental interruption in the flow of the company's products when the switchover to the new product takes place.

The financial analysis wraps all the other data into a single tabulation which provides an estimate of the return on investment and of the time when the return will be achieved. An example of a typical form is given in Exhibit 5.

Exhibit 5

PROGRAM CONTROL FORM

PROGRAM DESCRIPTION (attach specification):

Phase:	Date:	Previous Review:	Program No.:
Originator:		Director:	

APPROVALS:

Office Chief Executive	Controller	Division Manager

MARKETING INFORMATION:

Markets: _____

_____

Competition: _____

Uniqueness: _____

Product Follow-on: _____

Duration: _____ Entry Date: _____

Expected Penetration: _____

Position Estimate: _____

Patentability: _____

Support Requirements: _____

INVESTMENT DATA:

	This Phase	To Date	Total Estimate
Personnel	$	$	$
Materials			
Equipment			
Facility Allocation			
Tooling			
Engineering Prototype			
Production Setup			
Other (define)			
TOTALS:	$	$	$

SCHEDULE:

Phase	Estimate Completion	Estimate Completion

Date of First Approval:	On Cost-Target?

PRICING TARGET: Percent

List Price	$ _____
Factory Price	_____ 100
Less:	
Standard Organization Cost	
Direct Cost	
Gross Income	
Return-on-Investment	
Standard Net Profit	

SALES TARGET:

Year	Sales Volume	Sales Revenue	Gross Income	Standard Profit	ROI	Percent ROI	Probability	
1		$	$	$	$			
2								
3								
4								
5								

PROBLEMS TO BE RESOLVED THIS PHASE:

Probability of Resolution:	%	Prepared by:

The program control form provides a means for ongoing evaluation of research and development efforts. Completed quarterly or before the start of each phase of effort, the form provides managers at all levels with the information necessary to assess the accumulated investment and the predicted return on investment.

Controlling the Research Investment

The program form in Exhibit 5 provides the means for ongoing control of the investment in each research and development program. Although the form should be completed anew with the conclusion of each phase of the program, it would not be unreasonable to require that the form be completed quarterly whenever any phase of the program requires more than three months to complete. If the form is filled in conscientiously, the division manager, the company's controller, and other upper echelon managers will be in a position to evaluate whether it is reasonable to expect that the investment being made in the program can be recovered and a profit can be obtained.

This form has one other distinct value in terms of control. It is unreasonable to expect research and development personnel concerned with the program to complete the marketing, pricing, or even preproduction costing data. Whoever prepares the form must therefore bring representatives of marketing, accounting, and production into the preparation activity. These representatives will be interested in insuring that the data are as nearly accurate as possible and that the picture presents their goals within a reasonable frame. In the future, these same representatives may be expected to achieve the indicated sales targets and profit targets on the basis of prior commitment. The corporate managers should be free to consider what is put on these forms to be firm goals, against which the performance of the appropriate divisions can be measured.

5

Planning for Diversification

GIVEN the thrust or incentive to diversify, a company must consider
the means at hand and the potential courses of action which may
be followed utilizing the available resources. Means at hand are
represented by the company's financial position, its personnel resources, and its facility resources. The potential course of action may
be selected from one or a combination of three distinct possibilities.
These are research and development in new product areas, completion of development of innovative concepts that originated outside
the company, and acquisition of companies with diverse technology.
However, ill-conceived action in any one area can be the ruination
of the company.

When a company's managers commit it to any potential course
of action, there must be a *full* commitment, with a realization of the
limitations of the means at hand. In a very real sense, the means at
hand represent the equity of the stockholders. Few stockholders
even attempt to understand the problems of resource allocation or
reallocation designed to insure company growth and future prosper-
ity. To many stockholders, long-range planning is a business nicety
that is completely overshadowed by immediate price-earnings ratios
and current profit and loss statements. Thus the managers must

shape the course of action to protect the equity position of both present and future stockholders.

With this simplified background, it is possible to consider the effects upon a company when adopting each of the three suggested courses of action.

Research and Development

The process of technological innovation, as has already been discussed in Chapter 2, is bound within the product life cycle and includes eight distinct stages of progression, beginning with scientific suggestion, discovery, and recognition of need. Stages 2 through 6 carry the proposal of theory or design concept through laboratory verification, laboratory demonstration of application, and full-scale or field trials to commercial introduction or first operational use. These six stages represent a filtering process and the commitment of an investment in money, personnel, facilities, and *time* which can be enormous and is seldom insignificant. The first profits to offset this prior investment are not realized until the conclusion of stage 6, which is the product introduction phase of the life cycle, and the investment to bring the product to market is not finished until this time.

Studies have been conducted by many prestigious individuals and organizations to determine the character and commitment of a company entering the market with a new product derived from its own research and development efforts. As Edwin Mansfield * and others have shown, the first six stages of technological innovation have historically taken more than fourteen years. This time span has been independent of the nature of the product and of the scientific disciplines embodied in it. The time span through the first six stages has shown no propensity toward decreasing. But stage 7 (widespread adoption with attendant profits, significant usage, and significant market impact) and stage 8 (proliferation of competition with declining profit margins and increased product support demands) are shortening, thus limiting the possibilities of a return on the investment. In advanced technologies such as electronics, stages 7 and 8 have been reduced to fewer than five years, while less

* "The Speed of Response of Firms to New Techniques," *The Quarterly Journal of Economics* 77 (May 1963).

advanced technological products have market lives reduced to fewer than eight years. Thus, at best, a company must anticipate recovering and realizing a return on its investment in less than half the time span over which the investment was made.

Probabilities with Research and Development

One of the major problems associated with technological diversification through performance of research and development is the filter process as represented by the decay curve (Exhibit 6). Booz, Allen & Hamilton Inc. performed a study of the filter process by which potential products are eliminated during the research and development as well as product introduction stages of the life cycle and discovered some interesting relationships. For example, if a company starts with sixty new product concepts which are suggested by basic research, human knowledge, human inquiry, human imagination, or observation, the natural filter processes of stage 1 will reduce the possibilities to approximately fourteen. Using the information generated in stages 1 and 2, hard-headed business analysis will reduce the potential product ideas to approximately six. Actual development efforts represented by stages 3 and 4 will reduce the potential products to three, and one of these may be expected to fail in the precommercialization efforts of stage 5. Of the two product concepts which actually reach commercialization in stage 6, only one product will survive to reach stage 7, where profits and a return on the investment can be realized.

In reinforcement of these probabilities, a recent National Industrial Conference Board report which analyzed the marketing experiences of 87 consumer and industrial goods manufacturers pointed out that three out of ten *major* new products failed in some important respect to reach expectations. Further, one of these three proved so disappointing that it was withdrawn from the market. Thus of the one idea in sixty that reaches the market there is only a 70 percent chance of full return and a 90 percent chance of partial investment return. Yet it must be acknowledged that 75 percent of the sales increase in all markets in the next three years will come from brand-new products not offered today. In this same time span, approximately 18 percent of all sales of manufactured items will come from products not offered today. Thus it must be concluded

Exhibit 6

DECAY CURVE OF PRODUCT IDEAS (MORTALITY CURVE)

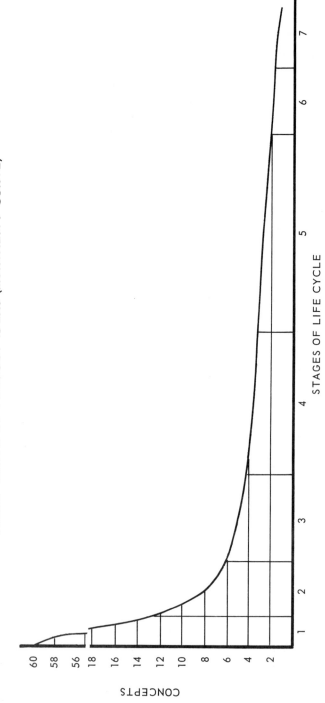

CONCEPTS

STAGES OF LIFE CYCLE

Booz, Allen & Hamilton Inc. has made extensive studies of the success of products from initial concept to market acceptance. The results of these studies have been equated in this figure to the developing stages of the life cycle (see Exhibit 1). The selection process decay curve of product ideas is here called a mortality curve. While many of the concepts are dead as the life cycle process proceeds through the stages, others are fully capable of resurrection in a different environment or in different circumstances.

that research and development proceeds in spite of the low probabilities that any one idea or concept will be a full marketing success.

Possibly the most significant aspect of these probabilities is the commitment to future spending. At the outset, the level of spending to support a concept through stage 1 is merely one hundredth of the support required in stage 5 and one thousandth of the support required in stage 6. Thus a company with a level of available equity for diversification today can commit that full level to internal research and development of new product concepts only if the company can *wait* some 14 years for the outcome and can raise its level of commitment manyfold before the full 14 years have passed.

Acquiring Someone Else's Product Development

The second route to diversification is the purchase of an innovative concept at some stage beyond stage 3. Less frequently than most people believe, a remarkably innovative product concept enters the technological arena from the work of an independent innovator who recognizes his development and entrepreneurial limitations. Companies often seek such innovators, and the innovators seek companies with compatible interests. Bringing the two together is difficult. The innovators, having little acquaintance with business, are extremely suspicious of business managers, and the managers recognize the costs of screening a concept and establishing the marketability of the ultimate product. In the end, the company managers recognize that the cost of the concept is significantly greater than equal internal development to the same stage. However, the company is buying lead time in the life cycle, a factor which may prove of major significance if the thrust toward diversification is moderately strong. If the company does its homework correctly, the more developed product concept increases the probability of product profitability to a level of 16 to 30 percent (as compared with the 1.7 percent at stage 1). These are still long odds in any gambling game.

Assuming that a firm had several possible innovation product opportunities from several outside sources, it would still be foolish to commit all the immediately available resources to these opportunities. First off, the investment return is still several years in the future; second, the level of support for the efforts must rise in each subsequent year.

Diversification Through Acquisition or Merger

The final possibility for diversification is to acquire new and broader technologies through the acquisition of respected companies that utilize these technologies. When a company makes such an acquisition, it has two new courses of action open relative to the acquired firm. In the first course of action, the acquiring company can exploit the technological advances of the acquired company, conducting only the continuing research and development that are required to support prior management commitments to new product concepts. This course leads to an inevitable emasculation of the acquired firm for the purpose of deriving the maximum in quick profits. The second course is to recognize the technological base of the acquired company, including its research and development programs, and then to strengthen and expand this base through committed support for internal research and development in the newly acquired technologies.

It is clear that any company faced with a thrust toward or a desire for diversification can apply all its available resources to acquisition and can thus achieve the maximum immediate benefits. It is less clear that this is wasteful. Consider the technological base of the acquiring company. What is its future to be? These research and development efforts and their base could be abandoned and new gains made either through emasculation of new acquisitions or the expansion of the acquired firm's technologies. This approach weakens the acquiring company's corporate base. Such a course of action is most advantageous for the stockholders on the short term, but it smacks of questionable business ethics. In acquisition, the ethically minded firm continues to build both its own technological base and that of the acquired company. This requires that the commitment to the future be preserved and that the level of application of available resources be distributed proportionately.

Establishing a Research Capability

Assume now that a firm does not have an internal research capability and wants to establish an applied research organization to permit diversification in both products and technologies. It is perfectly clear that the pattern which the company should follow must reflect its needs and resources as well as its desire to establish the organization.

For the purposes of general guidance in planning for a new research organization, a financial analysis of a hypothetical group has been prepared. This particular group has established that it will conduct research leading to products in the electronic instrumentation field. The nature of the products is such that outside contracts for both product research and supporting research can be obtained from the government. A key nucleus of six scientists and technologists is available to establish the group, and these individuals are considered highly creative—an essential factor in initiating the research organization. The resultant financial plan is drawn for a three-year period on the premise that the company has limited resources to commit and that the research organization will minimize the corporate investment in research.

The Capital Investment

The initial capital investment assumes that no capital equipment currently exists to establish an applied research and, in this case, advanced development division. Only items having a unit cost in excess of $50 will be capitalized, and write-off will be on the basis of three years for laboratory and five years for office investments. With the exception of the library, the estimated costs that follow are for new items. It is assumed that a suitable used technical library can be purchased.

Laboratory instrumentation (electronics, etc.)	$100,000
Laboratory equipment (tools, tables, etc.)	15,000
Office furniture (desks, chairs, files, etc.)	15,000
Office equipment (typewriters, calculators, etc.)	5,000
Library	2,000
Total	$137,000

The initial capital investment provides the base on which to build an organization. With the development of a broader technological base and greater in-depth penetration of that technology, a need will arise for personnel and program expansion. In terms of capital investment in the second and third years, the following is considered a planning minimum:

Second year	
Laboratory instrumentation	$50,000
Laboratory equipment	10,000
Office furniture	2,000
Office equipment	1,500
Total	$63,500

Third year	
Laboratory instrumentation	$15,000
Office equipment	5,000
Total	$20,000

The initial noncapital investment assumes that facilities and general items do not currently exist or are not available to the new organization without cost. The facilities preparation costs are predicated upon in-plant construction within the firm's current plant facilities. In certain accounting systems, it is recognized that these costs can be capitalized. There is also a distinct possibility of including these costs in the lease costs if the organization leases its facilities outside the firm's present plant.

Laboratory supplies (chemicals, small tools, etc.)	$ 5,000
Office supplies (stationery, etc.)	1,500
Facilities preparation ($2.50 per square foot)	10,000
Total	$16,500

All noncapital investments or costs in subsequent years can be considered an integral part of the overhead or burden costs of operating the research organization.

Direct and Indirect Costs of Operation

In a research organization such as the one considered here, the major direct and indirect costs of operation are the results of labor.

Inasmuch as in-house efforts will be controlled in the same manner as contracts, the application of scientific and technical talent to either in-house or contract efforts should be considered a direct labor charge. Thus the research organization might typically have the following direct labor charges in the first year of operation:

Scientist	$17,000
Scientist	17,000
Associate scientist	15,000
Assistant scientist	12,500
Research associate	11,500
Research assistant	10,000
Total direct labor	$83,000

The salaries of scientific and technical personnel are rising more rapidly than those of any other group, and adjustments in salaries must be adequate to hold these people. At best, the salaries indicated here are merely examples of what might have been accomplished in 1968. A later chapter includes an incentive plan to enlarge and expand the salaries of scientific and technical employees. It must be assumed that an incentive payment plan of this type cannot be established within the three-year span of the organizing example used here, since there would not be sufficient historical performance data on which to develop the plan. Therefore, the direct labor charges for the second year might be as follows:

Scientist	$18,500
Scientist	18,500
Associate scientist	16,000
Assistant scientist	13,250
Assistant scientist	12,500
Research associate	11,000
Research assistant	8,500
Total direct labor	$98,250

In the second year, it is assumed that the research associate of the preceding year completes such additional education as is required to advance to the status of assistant scientist, at a salary of $12,500. The research assistant is promoted, and a new one is added to the staff. It is only in the third year that real signs of growth within the organization begin to appear. Thus:

Scientist	$ 20,000
Scientist	19,000
Scientist	17,500
Associate scientist	15,000
Assistant scientist	13,500
Research associate	12,000
Research associate	10,000
Research assistant	8,000
Total direct labor	$115,000

As in the previous year, it is assumed that the junior scientist, the associate scientist, and the junior research associate complete such additional education as is required to attain a higher position, while the research assistant is an addition to the staff. In a later chapter, these position titles and the accompanying requirements—expressed in terms of experience and education—are explored in some depth.

Indirect Costs

Indirect costs of operation are compounded of the indirect labor costs; the personnel supporting costs such as social security (FICA), unemployment insurance, and benefits; facilities charges for the space actually occupied on the parent company's premises or lease cost if the facilities are rented apart from the parent company; utilities not included in the facilities costs; printing, binding, and related publications costs; maintenance costs for the facilities and equipment; business liability and other insurance; and educational assistance costs. As is shown in a later chapter, educational assistance to the personnel of the organization has a twofold effect and is a worthwhile investment in the organization's future profitability.

In the example here, it is assumed that four indirect-labor employees will be required throughout the three formative years to provide administrative control and support the scientific and technical staff.

The indirect costs for the first year of operation are estimated as follows:

Indirect labor

General manager	$ 24,000
Administrative manager	16,000
Secretary, security and personnel	6,600
Secretary and accounting clerk	6,000
Labor costs (FICA, unemployment insurance, etc.)	29,832
Facilities (4,000 square feet at 36 cents per square foot per month) (lease)	17,280
Utilities (phone, power, gas, water)	9,600
Publications (printing, binding, etc.)	5,000
Maintenance (facilities, equipment, etc.)	2,000
Insurance and miscellaneous	2,000
Educational assistance	2,500
Total indirect costs	$120,812

It is assumed that starting supplies will be sufficient to sustain the operation of the organization and its laboratory for the first year. During the second year, it will be necessary to provide in-process supplies on an ongoing basis. Also, allowances will have to be made for recruiting costs associated with finding and relocating needed personnel. Both in-process supplies and recruiting costs will be continuing expenses of operation so long as the organization continues to function.

One assumption has been made for simplification: that the general manager and the administrative manager have a personal stake in the future development of the research organization and will accept a fixed salary for the full period of the first three years. This is based on the expectation of larger rewards when they have proved their capabilities in establishing the organization on a sound footing and controlling it to achieve the company's profit objectives.

Thus, in the second year of operation, the cost schedule for the indirect costs might be as follows:

Indirect labor

General manager	$ 24,000
Administrative manager	16,000
Secretary, security and personnel	6,800
Secretary and accounting clerk	6,200
Labor costs	33,275
Facilities rental	17,280
Utilities	9,600
Publications	5,000
Maintenance	2,500
Insurance and miscellaneous	2,500
Educational assistance	3,000
In-process supplies	4,200
Recruiting	3,500
Total indirect costs	$133,855

No new factors should be added to the indirect costs within the third year, but most costs will have risen significantly over equivalent costs of the first year. The third year's estimate follows:

Indirect labor

General manager	$ 24,000
Administrative manager	16,000
Secretary, security and personnel	7,000
Secretary and accounting clerk	6,500
Labor costs	36,850
Facilities rental	17,280
Utilities	9,600
Publications	5,000
Maintenance	2,750
Insurance and miscellaneous	2,500
Educational assistance	3,300
In-process supplies	5,800
Recruiting	5,000
Total indirect costs	$141,580

Labor Charges

In the real world of research and development contracting, contracts are won competitively on the basis of the quality and qualifications of the scientific and technical staff *and* on the basis of cost. The actual hourly labor costs for each of the first three years are as follows:

First year labor cost per hour
Direct labor	$ 6.917	(100 percent)
Burden	9.891	(143 percent)
General and administrative	2.760	(39.9 percent)
Total	$19.568	

Second year labor cost per hour
Direct labor	$ 7.018	(100 percent)
Burden	9.561	(136.2 percent)
General and administrative	3.410	(48.6 percent)
Total	$19.989	

Third year labor cost per hour
Direct labor	$ 7.188	(100 percent)
Burden	8.849	(123.1 percent)
General and administrative	3.720	(51.8 percent)
Total	$19.757	

The direct labor cost is computed on the basis of the total annual direct salaries divided by the number of direct labor employees times 2,000 hours of labor per year. Burden is computed on the basis of the annual indirect costs divided by the number of direct employees times 2,000. General and administrative expenses (G&A) are taken to be the interest charged on corporate investment in the capital assets plus estimated marketing and selling expenses. As would be anticipated, the burden cost decreases with an increase in scientific and technical staff and no increase in the indirect labor personnel. As the capital investment increases and the need for greater selling efforts increases with added staff, the G&A expense rises.

To be competitive and obtain external contract business, the research organization must be prepared to make cost adjustments in its labor charges. Such adjustments can be made by performing external contracts on a total fixed-price or fixed-labor-price basis. Whatever method is used, the company must be prepared to absorb the loss generated by these cost adjustments.

Profit and Loss Estimate

As has already been stated for this example, it has been assumed that the company will permit its research organization to seek and perform external research contracts to support its level of technological competence and to achieve secondary fallout from the advancements made on such contracts. The principal assumption is that these contracts will be performed for the government. In the first year of operation, it is assumed that the organization will obtain and perform $30,000 worth of fixed-price contracts at an absorbed labor cost of $14.30 per hour. In the second year, it is assumed that external contract performance will equal $175,000. With the development of position and status, the absorbed labor cost can rise to $17.50 per hour. By the third year, it is assumed that external contracting will amount to $350,000 to provide a profit on contracts of $61,401.80 before unabsorbed operations costs. The actual profit and loss statements for each year, using these assumptions, would be:

First year profit and loss

Contracts:

Contract income, external	$ 30,000.00	
Contract cost (2,100 hours)	41,092.80	
Profit or (loss) on contracts		($ 11,092.80)
Unabsorbed operations costs:		
Direct costs	$ 68,478.30	
Indirect costs	97,920.90	
General and administrative	27,324.00	
Total unabsorbed costs		(193,723.20)
Total first year profit or (loss)		($204,816.00)

Second year profit and loss

Contracts:

Contract income, external	$175,000.00	
Contract cost (10,000 hours)	199,440.00	
Profit or (loss) on contracts		($ 24,440.00)
Unabsorbed operations costs:		
Direct costs	$ 28,072.00	
Indirect costs	38,244.00	
General and administrative	13,640.00	
Total unabsorbed costs		(79,956.00)
Total second year profit or (loss)		($104,396.00)

Third year profit and loss

Contracts:

Contract income, external	$350,000.00	
Contract cost (14,600 hours)	288,598.20	
Profit or (loss) on contracts		$ 61,401.80
Unabsorbed operations costs:		
Direct costs	$ 10,063.20	
Indirect costs	12,388.60	
General and administrative	5,208.00	
Total unabsorbed costs		(27,659.80)
Total third year profit or (loss)		$ 33,742.00

By the end of the third year, the research organization should be established. The assumptions that have been made here lead to a most optimistic picture of what can happen during those three years. The realities of the situation may be much harsher.

In a recapitulation, consider the following totals:

Three-year capital assets investment	$220,500
Three-year noncapital investment	16,500
Three-year operational loss	275,470

Thus the total cost to establish the research organization during this initial three-year period is $512,470. If the depreciation allowance is applied to offset this amount, the cost is $321,190. In all these calculations, the initial personnel relocation costs have been ignored. Without the contributions of external contracts, the cost would have risen an additional $555,000 to a total establishment cost of $1,067,470.

Cash Flow Analysis

The actual commitment of cash to accomplish the establishment of the research organization is not a uniform one. The initial capital outlays might easily be spread over the first ten months. By the same token, income derived from external contracts will not be received until the contracts have been successfully completed. Before entering upon the program to establish the research organization, it is wise to provide a cash flow analysis. Exhibit 7 provides a month-to-month analysis of the expenditures which might be anticipated, using the assumptions of the previous example. These expenditures run from a low of $17,320.27 in the eleventh and twelfth months to a high of $37,320.27 in the second through sixth months. Exhibit 8 considers the effects of offsetting income from external contracts. In the twentieth month, income begins to have a pronounced effect upon the cash flow, and by the end of the twenty-first month the accumulated investment will have peaked at $442,252.07 if the accumulated investment has been offset by income. Exhibit 9 presents a graphic picture of the accumulated investment and accumulated depreciation over the three-year establishment period.

Exhibit 7
CASH FLOW ANALYSIS

Month	Capital	Salaries	Other	Total
1		$ 5,650	$ 16,500.00	$ 22,150.00
2	$ 20,000	11,301	6,019.27	37,320.27
3	20,000	11,301	6,019.27	37,320.27
4	20,000	11,301	6,019.27	37,320.27
5	20,000	11,301	6,019.27	37,320.27
6	20,000	11,301	6,019.27	37,320.27
7	10,000	11,301	6,019.27	27,320.27
8	10,000	11,301	6,019.27	27,320.27
9	10,000	11,301	6,019.27	27,320.27
10	7,500	11,301	6,019.27	24,820.27
11		11,301	6,019.27	17,320.27
12		11,301	6,019.27	17,320.27
13	15,000	12,382	6,737.91	34,119.91
14		12,382	6,737.91	19,119.91
15	15,000	12,382	6,737.91	34,119.91
16		12,382	6,737.91	19,119.91
17	15,000	12,382	6,737.91	34,119.91
18		12,382	6,737.91	19,119.91
19	7,500	12,382	6,737.91	26,619.91
20		12,382	6,737.91	19,119.91
21	5,500	12,382	6,737.91	24,619.91
22		12,382	6,737.91	19,119.91
23	5,500	12,382	6,737.91	24,619.91
24		12,382	6,737.91	19,119.91
25	5,500	14,042	7,340.00	26,882.00
26		14,042	7,340.00	21,382.00
27	5,000	14,042	7,340.00	26,382.00
28		14,042	7,340.00	21,382.00
29	5,000	14,042	7,340.00	26,382.00
30		14,042	7,340.00	21,382.00
31	5,000	14,042	7,340.00	26,382.00
32		14,042	7,340.00	21,382.00
33		14,042	7,340.00	21,382.00
34		14,042	7,340.00	21,382.00
35		14,042	7,340.00	21,382.00
36		14,042	7,340.00	21,382.00

Investment Analysis

Ideally, the new research group will have launched into one or more programs designed to attain a proprietary position for the company. More realistically, during the first three years the group will be occupied fully with the task of becoming established. Possibly in the latter half of the period the group may be engaged in practical, planned programs of research directed toward company future interests. From a true investment basis, with the resultant

Exhibit 8

CASH FLOW ANALYSIS WITH CONTRACT INCOME

Month	Expenditures	Income	Cash Flow	Accumulated Investment
1	$ 22,150.00		$ 22,150.00	$ 22,150.00
2	37,320.27		37,320.27	59,470.27
3	37,320.27		37,320.27	96,790.54
4	37,320.27		37,320.27	134.110.81
5	37,320.27		37,320.27	171,431.08
6	37,320.27		37,320.27	208,751.35
7	27,320.27		27,320.27	236,071.62
8	27,320.27		27,320.27	263,391.89
9	27,320.27		27,320.27	290,712.16
10	24,820.27		24,820.27	315,532.43
11	17,320.27		17,320.27	332,852.70
12	17,320.27	$ 10,000	7,320.27	340,172.97
13	34,119,90	20,000	14,119,90	354,292.87
14	19,119.90		19,119.00	373,412.77
15	34,119.90	7,000	27,119.90	400,532.67
16	19,119.90	15,000	4,119.90	404,652.57
17	34,119.90	15,000	19,119.90	423,772.47
18	19,119.90	15,000	4,119.90	427,892.37
19	26,119.90	15,000	11,119.90	439,012.27
20	19,119.90	20,000	(880.10)	438,132.17
21	24,119.90	20,000	4,119.90	442,252.07
22	19,119.90	22,000	(2,880.10)	439,371.97
23	24,119.90	22,000	2,119.90	441,491.87
24	19,119.90	25,000	(5,880.10)	435,611.77
25	24,119.90	25,000	(880.10)	434,731.67
26	19,119.90	25,000	(5,880.10)	428,851.57
27	24,119.91	25,000	(880.09)	427,971.48
28	19,119.91	25,000	(5,880.09)	422,091.39
29	24,119.91	25,000	(880.09)	421,211.30
30	19,119.91	25,000	(5,880.09)	415,331.21
31	24,119.91	25,000	(880.09)	414,451.12
32	19,119.91	30,000	(10,880.09)	403,571.03
33	19,119.91	30,000	(10,880.09)	392,690.94
34	19,119.91	35,000	(15,880.09)	376,810.85
35	19,119.91	35,000	(15,880.09)	360,930.76
36	19,119.91	45,000	(25,880.09)	335,050.67

Exhibit 9
ACCUMULATED INVESTMENT AND DEPRECIATION

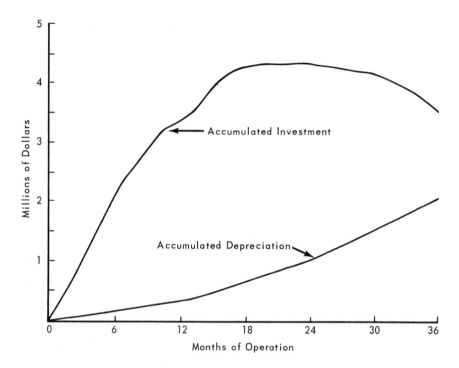

Months of Operation

In the formation of a new research organization, even with the successful acquisition of outside contracts by that organization, there is a substantial investment
with time. If the growth of the organization is held to a moderate level as presented in the text, the investment recovery will occur at some point substantially
downstream. The more usual investment in a research organization provides for
relatively rapid development and a high rate of investment. In the latter case the
probability of investment recovery without the development of improved proprietary positions as a result of the research efforts is extremely slim.

---

program value carried or transferred to the balance sheet as an asset
of the firm, the program must provide a proprietary position. All
other costs of the group must be written off as costs of doing
business. From a purely control point of view, it would be advisable
to separate the nonproprietary directed programs and measure their
individual costs, recognizing that these costs cannot be entered as
assets.

6

Principles of Organization and Operation

A corporate manager who would have a research organization as an integral part of the corporation must be willing to accept and put into practice concepts of management which offer the customer (inside or outside the company) the highest quality of scientific and technical endeavor for the lowest cost. In this chapter, a number of concepts are advanced for consideration in the application of management to research and preproduct development. The concepts advocated here are predicated on the premise that such efforts can be managed and controlled so as to be performed in accordance with time scheduling and price planning, as exemplified in network analysis and other proven planning and control techniques.

Concept of Dual Operational Components

It is a fundamental premise here that a research organization will achieve its maximum effectiveness when its internal organization is divided into two interrelated components. One of these should

84818

provide the direct application of scientific and technical disciplines through its theoretical and experimental personnel. The other should provide essentially all the management support functions required by the organization. This second component thus relieves the individual scientific and technical personnel from most management and administrative responsibilities while also providing all such support services as instrumentation and equipment procurement (or fabrication), laboratory installation, servicing, calibration, and operational support. Thus the scientific and technical personnel are permitted to be career scientists and engineers, and their scientific and technical specialties are contributed with minimum dilution for the betterment of the firm as a whole.

The management and administrative component within this dual organizational concept has the usual form of organizational structure essential to a support group; that is, the structure is well ordered and relatively rigid. In contrast, the scientific and technical component should avoid rigid structural organization. A manager should acknowledge that scientific and technical personnel with the desired research and development flair are fundamentally specialists and, since they are creative, abhor rigid organizational confinement. They function most effectively as individuals or as part of a technical team of individual specialists, each making his own contribution in his own area of specialization. Following this approach, all tasks that a scientist or engineer in research is requested to perform can be put on a specialist or consulting basis, with each individual recognized for his personal contributions.

Technical Management

In establishing such a dual organization, care must be exercised to insure that technical management of the research and development tasks is provided. Technical management must come from within the scientific and technical component. To that end, it is recommended that each scientific and technical task be formally assigned to an individual investigator or to an investigative team with a team leader responsible for the task, including the technical contributions of the assigned support specialists.

The objective here is to approach the type of environment in

Exhibit 10

ORGANIZATION CHART

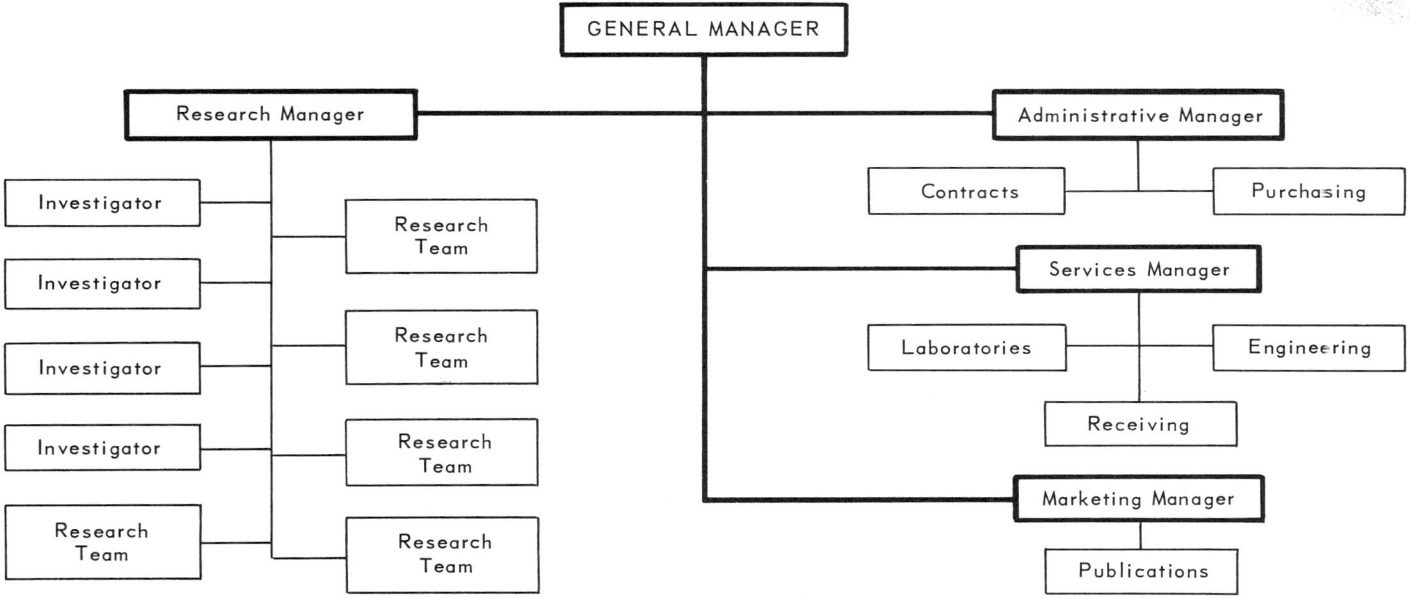

The dual concept of organization provides for all scientific and technical inquiry to be conducted in a loosely structured research organization in which all the scientists and research specialists are assigned. All administrative and management functions are in a rigidly structured organization. The general manager is a "professional manager" and his span of control is relatively limited. By contrast, the research manager, who is also essentially a professional manager with depth of technical understanding, has a span of control which conceivably includes each individual scientist.

which the scientist feels most at home—an environment which approaches the academic. It is possible within an industrial concern to approach the academic environment on both a tangible and an intangible plane without sacrificing management control.

Consider the skeleton organization chart in Exhibit 10. The scientific and technical disciplines required to conduct both applied research and preproduct development are put to use through the theoretical and experimental scientific personnel in the principal component. These people are hired and promoted in strict accordance with academic and performance qualifications that should be made a matter of record for everyone in the organization. If the structure is flexible and titles are controlled according to individual academic attainment and acceptance by peers, each person in the scientific and technical component will realize that he can follow a career as a scientist or technologist without having to convert to a management position so as to achieve a higher salary.

Selecting the Director

One of the most common practices of industry when organizing a research division is to find a scientist of national repute and, regardless of his demonstrated managerial experience or qualifications, to place him in charge of the division. Many, but not a majority, of the scientists placed in such a position of control encourage and foster the widely held upper management belief that the established rules of business management cannot be applied profitably to industrial research and preproduct development programs. The managers who accept this fallacy must be prepared to excuse or overlook managerial inefficiency as well as gross miscalculation in the research division. Knowingly or not, they are also accepting the research division as a façade operation which is not expected to produce anything of proprietary value.

In direct contrast to this point of view is the view that the direct management of research is in itself an administrative art—an art which requires as much painstaking study and development as any other form of business management. If this view is accepted, the broad indifference of upper managers to the control of hours and schedules in the performance of research or development will disappear, and an entirely different philosophy governing the management of these efforts will be adopted: that the concept of dual components within the research organization is consistent with the requirements of management and control.

In a very large research organization, all the direct scientific and technical activities might effectively be placed under the cognizance of a research manager who reports to the general manager. The research manager's functions are purely administrative; and, though he may have a limited technical background, his specialized training and experience must be in research planning and planning implementation. Ideally, he will have at least an M.B.A. degree with additional training in the psychology of personnel management. As a matter of motivation, scientists should be made to understand that the position of research manager is not one for which the top salary has been established and that it is not a position to which they should aspire. In keeping with this limitation, the man who occupies the position must know it is necessary and must be willing to recompense the group's scientific personnel at rates above his own salary when their individual contributions so warrant.

Within the corporation as a whole, managers must recognize that the research manager and division general manager should receive salaries which may be slightly higher than those of managers who fill seemingly comparable administrative positions (that is to say, in terms of the number of people supervised and the dollar volume of the organization). The corporation is making a calculated investment in its future, and the return on this investment will be controlled almost exclusively by the division's general manager and the research manager. Those in upper management must be able to rely upon these individuals for interpretation and control; for unlike production procedures, it is difficult at best to assess scientific productivity directly. However, the fact that the contact of upper managers with the division will be through professional managers will ease the problems of communication and of assessing the division's contribution to the corporation.

Assigning Research Tasks

For psychological reasons, scientific and technical personnel engaged in creative efforts do not respond as effectively in a rigidly structured organization as in a loose yet well-defined organization characteristic of most university research groups. Scientific and technical personnel with the creativity essential to perform research are fundamentally specialists, and all too frequently they possess many of the attributes of prima donnas. Such people perform more effectively when they are permitted to function as individuals or as contributing members of research teams comprised of specialists. Each team should be assembled so that the specialists are able to make their contributions to the required effort through their particular areas of specialization.

The typical scientist, like his associate in the university group, is acutely aware of titles and academic ranking. The avoidance of a rigid organizational structure in the scientific and technical component offers a practical way around this problem. If all scientists in the organization are made aware of the specializations and capabilities of the other members, and if each is made to feel that he is able to contribute something to someone of a lesser rank without demeaning himself, the total effort will proceed more smoothly and more effectively. The most aloof scientist will readily work for or with someone who has a lesser title or rank if the task he is asked to perform is put on a specialist or consulting basis.

Exhibit 11 suggests minimum qualifications for the scientific and technical positions in a research organization. The positions are arranged in financial grades but controlled in title according to academic attainment and scientific recognition. In such a system, each individual may continue his career in a title at the maximum of his academic attainment, and the best qualified and most productive can expect to earn the maximum corporate salary without converting to a managerial position. The qualifications for each position directly parallel the qualifications of an academic position of related title (for example, the rank of scientist is generally equivalent to the rank of professor, associate scientist to associate professor, assistant scientist to assistant professor, and so on).

Individual scientific and technical tasks may be categorized as scientifically or technically complex, semicomplex, or routine. In the case of a complex task, a senior scientist, scientist, or senior development engineer should be considered for assignment as an individual investigator or a team leader. A semicomplex task should be limited to a scientist, an associate scientist, or a development engineer as individual investigator or team leader. A routine task can be handled

Exhibit 11

MINIMUM QUALIFICATIONS FOR PERSONNEL

Research Assistant, Advanced Development Assistant

Grade III: A.A. or A.S. degree, or two years' related equivalent technical experience.

Grade IV: A.A. or A.S. degree plus three years' related equivalent technical experience, or six years' related equivalent technical experience.

Research Associate, Advanced Development Associate

Grade III: B.S., A.B., or engineering degree. A.A. degree plus three years' equivalent technical experience, or six years' related equivalent technical experience.

Grade IV: B.S., A.B., or engineering degree plus two years' related equivalent technical experience; A.A. or A.S. degree plus five years' related equivalent technical experience, or seven years' related technical experience.

Grade V: B.S., A.B., or engineering degree plus three years' related equivalent technical experience; A.A. or A.S. degree plus six years' related equivalent technical experience; or eight years' related equivalent technical experience.

Assistant Scientist, Junior Development Engineer

Grade V: Master's degree; or baccalaureate degree with three years' related equivalent technical experience.

Grade VI: Master's degree plus two years' related equivalent technical experience; or baccalaureate degree with graduate training plus four years' related equivalent technical experience.

Associate Scientist, Development Engineer

Grade VII: Doctoral degree; master's degree plus three years' related experience; or baccalaureate degree with graduate training plus five years' related experience.

Scientist, Senior Development Engineer

Grade VII: Doctoral degree plus two years' related experience; or master's degree with doctoral work plus five years' related experience.

Grade VIII: Doctoral degree plus five years' related experience; or master's degree with doctoral work plus seven years' related experience.

Senior Scientist

Grade VIII or Grade IX: Doctoral degree plus eight years' experience; or master's degree with doctoral training plus eleven years' experience. Individual must also have acceptance by the scientific community as a whole as an acknowledged scientist in his area of specialization.

Research Coordinator

Grade V or Grade VI: Baccalaureate degree with technical or marketing specialization, plus five years' experience in direct sales or contract coordination.

Services Manager

Grade VI or Grade VII: Baccalaureate degree with engineering specialization and ten years' experience in engineering support administration functions; or fifteen years' such experience.

Administrative Manager

Grade VII or Grade VIII: Baccalaureate degree with engineering or business administration specialization and ten years' experience in administrative functions; or fifteen years of such experience.

by an assistant scientist or a junior development engineer acting as an individual investigator. A team performing a routine task, on the other hand, would be properly headed by a scientist, an associate scientist, or a senior development engineer, depending upon the total level of effort required for its completion. The research or advanced development associates and the research or advanced development assistants should serve as either direct members of investigative teams or part of the service group supporting division efforts. In the latter functional area they become responsible for setup, calibration, and required laboratory support for a team or an individual investigator. The research associates and research assistants and their engineering counterparts may be appropriately switched back and forth between the two components as requirements and services vary.

Providing Program Continuity

Within the total corporate structure, the research division and its efforts should be separated as much as possible from the day to day production-related programs. General production engineering and production personnel should not be associated in any way with or intimately aware of the research efforts. It is recognized that such production-oriented personnel could easily become too interested in what is coming out of research for possible future production, to the detriment of their current problems and programs. However, as a regular practice, engineering development personnel from the product development groups—especially those who have shown a high technical competence—should be rotated into and out of the research division to provide an understanding of the problems associated with research and preproduct development. This approach will serve to add a new dimension to these engineers' often apparent routine efforts.

Certainly, one objective of this rotation plan is to prime these individuals as potential project leaders for the product development and production phases that will follow. Thus a customer will be assured of complete program continuity from "birth to death." Along this line of reasoning, research division managers should at regular intervals conduct a program of top and outside or other division management indoctrination relative to the research and preproduct development programs, including predictions of potential impact upon the firm. This must be done in full recognition that the output of research and preproduct development is perishable and frequently must be realized immediately to prevent its value from being lost. The transition from research to development to production must be a smooth, uniform flow and must not require relearning and interpolation with each transitional stage, as is the usual situation when research is performed by one company and then transferred to a different company for ultimate refinement and production.

Cooperative Research

To fulfill its role properly, a research division should stand ready to assist development and production divisions with complex problems that arise through the efforts of these other divisions. For example, assume that a company is producing a storage container in which a customer has attempted to store a new chemical. Fumes from the chemical are penetrating the normal paint and plating of the metal and corroding the base metal. The customer is a significant purchaser of the company's products and particularly interested in obtaining a more suitable storage facility. The company's materials engineers normally handle the selection of the metal, the plating and plating technique, and the finish paint, but lack the experience and information to perform this particular design chore properly. Both the facilities and talent to reach a quick and satisfactory solution to the materials problem exist within the research division. The usual course of action is to assign the problem to the research division and then leave it alone until a solution is forthcoming. Such an approach has several disadvantages.

When the research division undertakes to solve a problem in production or development—a problem which is in fact applied research—the researchers must do considerable homework regarding the applications affected and the methods employed. They assume a job which those most directly responsible for the project have been unable to perform. There may have been major reluctance to release the job to research. These conditions could result in strained relations, with the production personnel taking an uncooperative attitude: "If the research men are so smart, let them figure out the answer!" Similarly, the researchers may feel that they are demeaning themselves by asking the mundane questions whose answers are essential to doing the job effectively. Not infrequently an impasse develops and the output of the research division is inadequate. Or it may be adequate but not accepted by the production personnel, who are surreptitiously seeking an empirical solution so as to reassert their capability to exist without the research division. In such a situation, everyone suffers—the research division, the production division, the company, and the customer—and the resultant strained relationships may create breaches which never heal.

A far better approach is cooperative research and the co-op researcher. In this approach, the production division recognizes the problem that has to be solved and appeals to the research division for assistance. The research division then establishes a planned effort using qualified research personnel and division facilities. The production division assigns its materials engineer to the research division as a co-op researcher. Working as a participating member of the research division's investigative team, the co-op researcher provides the production and related information needed to assure a solution within the abilities and interests of the production division. His participation in the name of the production division increases the likelihood that the ultimate solution will be accepted and at the same time establishes great rapport between the two divisions for future cooperation.

What is more, the members of the research division gain a greater insight into the problems of production—an insight which may be of fundamental assistance in choosing between alternative courses of action in the applied research and preproduct development stages. It is impossible to assess how many unsuccessful products or product ideas are the result of selecting the wrong alternative in the early stages when the rationale of production methods and the limitations of production facilities are frequently ignored or simply not understood.

The Working Environment

It is highly improbable that applied research and preproduct development could be conducted effectively or economically if a purely academic atmosphere and mode of operation were established within an industrial structure. Yet there is no valid reason for failing to adopt as much of the academic atmosphere as is practical from a managerial–administrative point of view. Although the titles of professor, associate professor, and the rest have no meaning in a corporate organization, there is no reason why a corporate organization should not adopt titles paralleling those of the academic world (as suggested previously). However, as a simple matter of prestige, these titles should be reserved for the scientific and technical personnel of the research organization.

Carrying this concept to its next logical phase, the working environment should be separated as much as possible, either by placing the research division in an entirely different physical location or by placing it in a restricted area with limited access. This would be in accordance with the recommendations made earlier relative to guarding company proprietary information.

Separating the research division and its efforts provides a means, in a corporate marketing sense, for obtaining extra mileage from an advanced technology organization which is actually productive. This is accomplished by making the organization a moderate showpiece with facilities that reflect a scientific atmosphere. This atmosphere can be created by an air of studious quietness; a readily available technical library; source files of information; and a neat, clean, yet obviously functioning laboratory which is well equipped with modern instrumentation and support equipment. Ostentatious display is not necessary and in some cases will actually cause a negative reaction. But the research management staff should be prepared to arrange a little "pony and dog show" within the facilities to demonstrate for visitors the potential of the research organization. Such shows should be designed so as to prevent interference with normal operations and should be staged in a manner that will not detract from the general impression of studious dedication to advancing technology to meet the needs of the company.

Structuring the Research Efforts

With the advent of the mid-twentieth century, technology reached a point in its development where all mankind could be served by technology rather than the reverse. With this rather recent change in the technological balance, the Edisonian approach to further technological advancement was doomed, becoming impractical in terms of both economics and time. Mankind can no longer afford the luxury of reinvention or the squandering of resources which occurs in experiments isolated from reality and from established scientific knowledge. In today's real world of science, any imbalance between theoretical and experimental personnel or effort within a research organization must favor the theoretical side as opposed to the experimental side. This premise is based on the belief that theory, not intuition, must form the foundation for experimentation.

Unlimited expansion of research is irreconcilable with proper management of ordered progress toward corporate goals or objectives. The research efforts must serve the corporation and should never become the tail that wags the dog. At some point a balance between these efforts and total corporate effort has to be reached. Further or more rapid expansion of research and preproduct development after that point is not economically justified or practical.

If one of the operational objectives of the research organization is to obtain external contracts, solicitation of these contracts should be conducted to initiate and establish "proprietary positions" in product programs. The research managers must recognize that the scientific and technical personnel of the research organization—as opposed to outside contracting agencies acting as investigators—must be scientifically noncontroversial. At the same time, they cannot be bland nonentities. They must be acknowledged or acknowledgeable on the basis of their education and prior experience expressed in terms of projects, publications, and presentations before their peers.

Countering Knowledge Perishability

Managers at all levels must be acutely aware of the perishability of technological knowledge, as well as the exponential rise in human knowledge in technological areas. As a measure of this fact, consider the example given by the instructors of the Industrial College of the Armed Forces. They point out that between 1750 and 1900 the increase in human knowledge was equal to all the knowledge gained by man before 1750. Between 1900 and 1950, man's knowledge doubled again; and between 1950 and 1960 it doubled again. Finally, between 1960 and 1968 it doubled yet again. Thus the level of knowledge in 1968 was 16 times the level of knowledge in 1750. This is a dramatic example of the rate of change. It is also indicative that the new graduate has less than one-sixth the knowledge he will need in the course of his professional career.

In technological research, an individual's inability or unwillingness to compensate for the perishability of his knowledge can be disastrous to him and detrimental to his company. Consequently, the firm, through its research and development divisions, should establish a policy of selecting its creative personnel on the basis of their willingness to renew and expand their knowledge in order to meet the demands of an ever changing and expanding technology. Accordingly, all personnel should be encouraged either to continue their education toward higher or broader academic degrees or to assist the local universities and colleges by teaching specialized, advanced science or engineering courses. As part of this encouragement to go on learning, the company should pay the full cost of schooling and provide ample opportunity for the employees to attend courses even at times which conflict with normal operating hours.

7

Motivation of Personnel

T HE effective corporate management staff recognizes that research must be motivated and that motivation of research begins with motivation of the scientific and technical personnel within the research organization. But what constitutes motivation for this class of specialized personnel?

Two interesting and obvious signposts indicate that the majority of corporate managers responsible for research and development efforts in the United States are failing in their motivational efforts. For one thing, we are told that, in a very real sense, the United States is advancing so rapidly it is creating a technological gap between itself and the other countries of the world. This gap is reported to be widening at an exponential rate. Yet at the same time the fact remains that, in a span of only 50 years, the United States has dropped from first to seventh place in new product and advanced technology patents.

How should the managers of industrial research and development interpret this apparent contradiction? It seems likely that the average U.S. scientist or engineer is withholding his patentable ideas from his employer whenever he perceives the possibility of using those ideas at some future date for his personal gain rather than that of his employer.

The second indicator which should disturb many corporate managers—especially those affected by it already—is the increasing number of instances where a small company is formed by a group of scientists or technical personnel who have left a much larger firm in order to exploit a specific technology or product which was quite obviously generated in or from the larger firm's research and development programs. In many cases, these groups establish firms which quickly grow and prosper by direct competition with former employers.

Where is the failure? Paternalism should have ended with Uncle Tom's log cabin. Certainly, there is no room in modern industry for the paternalistic approach by company managers to any of the company's employees. Yet, strange as it may seem, astute companies which would not consider attempting the paternalistic approach with their relatively unsophisticated general production personnel will turn right around and adopt such an approach toward their scientific and technical personnel in research and development efforts.

The usual side benefits such as pension plans, group insurance, aids to education, and plush working conditions are not motivating forces to scientific and technical people. They view these factors as norms to be expected in research and development positions. The company manager is sadly mistaken if he believes that the scientific and technical employees, because of their deep concern for and involvement in the sciences, are unconcerned with or pay little attention to compensation or promotions. Universities and university professors are promoting the idea that their science and technology students have a right to expect, each year, higher and higher starting salaries with guarantees of rapid financial promotion on the job to "compensate for the flagrant exploitation of their creative powers." The average new scientist of today expects and demands such salary treatment on the basis that he will be exploited by his industrial employer and will not receive the recognition he deserves, much less share in the gross financial rewards his ideas will bring to the company.

Characteristics of the Creative Individual

It is very revealing to ask a group of managers responsible for the overall control of research and development, but not skilled in the direct management of creative personnel, to characterize such personnel. The first comments will generally be directed to the relationship of the creative individual and the company. Typically, the manager views the scientist as a "poor company man" who is too individualistic to conform to the social patterns of the company or the industry as a whole. Most managers will go further and say that the scientist is basically unsocial and excessively snobbish or vain. Nearly all managers recognize that the general scientist is a poor organizer and poor manager of others. Even when the scientist is given the responsibility for managing programs or efforts of direct scientific interest to him, he does not perform well.

In all fairness, the scientist does not fall into a stereotyped mold. Each of us feels most comfortable when we are confronting and solving the problems we understand best. Similarly, we are able to converse most informally and un-self-consciously when we are talking with our peers in the vernacular of our specific interests. Scientists are no different in this respect.

Now consider the specialized training a scientist receives. While he is naturally inquisitive, he has learned the rules of deductive reasoning and readily applies them beyond the limits of his particular research effort. These rules require that he be objective in the extreme, methodical and analytical in approach, and persevering to a point where an opinion can be expressed and adequately defended against all counterarguments. If he is egotistical, his is an egotism born of a knowledge of the solidity of the position or viewpoint assumed. He naturally tends to see things as primarily black or white, with few shades of gray in between.

Almost without exception, the creative scientist displays a need for recognition and a need for achievement, as well as a need for communication which grows out of the other two needs. Recognition from his peers can be attained through publications and presentations before various scientific societies. Gaining recognition from the rest of the world is somewhat more difficult. Certainly this seeking for

recognition outside the peer group results in the individualistic appearance characterized by beards, sandals, and those clothing eccen-
tricities essentially satirized by the hippie generation. Yet the scientist who has achieved recognition outside his peer group will
generally be clean-shaven and conservatively dressed, though not
the usual picture of the "man in the gray flannel suit."

The one danger which all managers must guard against is the
generalization about scientific and technical personnel. Far too many
managers are ready to retreat behind such generalizations and
rationalize research and development failures with the standard
clichés. If the manager avoids the rationalization and clearly defines
what he expects of scientific and technical employees before they are
hired and then actively insures that these objectives are pursued,
the performance level of all personnel, management and technical,
will be unusually productive.

Needs of the Creative Individual

We cannot know, except in general terms, what the professional
scientist or development engineer engaged in industrial research
and development actually expects of his company employer. In
general, the individual in research has a higher order of demands
than the individual in development. Presumably, the professional in
research not only expects but is prepared to require

1. The opportunity to advance his scientific or technical training and education at company expense.
2. The encouragement and assistance required in preparing
   technical papers and presentations wherever given.
3. The encouragement to join and financial assistance to participate in appropriate professional societies.
4. Adequate financial rewards for direct and indirect contributions to the company, including patent royalties and other
   contribution awards.
5. Financial and status advancement on the basis of merit as
   measured by tangible and intangible technological contributions.

6. Competent managerial supervision.
7. Relief from the tedium and intrusion of routine managerial and administrative problems.
8. The opportunity to engage in scientifically challenging work.

These are not inordinate expectations even for creative development personnel, and many of these extras are currently offered by industrial firms. But the question remains as to how they are offered. All too frequently, they are given grudgingly and without grace by the managers most directly associated with the scientific and technical personnel. If the scientist and engineer are made to feel that the only reason these extras are given is to buy their continued favorable response to the orders or control of management, it is far better that the extras not be offered at all.

Interaction Between Scientist and Manager

Within the research group, the research manager, in the terms set forth in earlier chapters, is always a colleague to the scientific and technical personnel; he rarely or never exercises the prerogatives of a boss. At times he may appropriately assume the role of consultant, while at other times he may serve as a teacher to clarify the mysteries of management policy. The manager must give the scientific and technical personnel as much freedom in planning their activities as is consistent with the demands of both technological research and management of that activity. Finally, the manager must be prepared to tailor the rewards for achievement in terms of each individual's effectiveness and creative contributions to the group as a whole.

In giving the researcher freedom in planning his activities, the manager may require the researcher to set work accomplishment goals for any reasonable period of time, even as little as two or three days. A popular buzz word currently is SIS, which is an acronym for short interval scheduling. Essentially, SIS is the division of any significant long-range effort into short-term efforts with goals and timetables for the individual to meet. Improvements of up to 30 percent in performance have been claimed for the method.

In applying SIS, the manager asks the researcher to break his proposed effort into a series of minor efforts whose objectives can be fulfilled (in his estimation) in a sequence of equal time periods. Then at the conclusion of each period the manager requests an informal or a formal estimate of the attainment of the objectives as set by the researcher. The theory is that everyone, including the scientist, works more effectively when he has recognizable goals and a timetable to measure his progress. When this approach is taken, the manager is given the timely information needed to prevent disastrous surprises; while the researcher is given a day-to-day incentive to maintain a uniform pace, avoiding the jam of uncompleted work at the end of a longer planning and control period.

Making a Reward

Rewards must be timely; they must be given as soon as possible following recognition of notable accomplishment; they should never be made indiscriminately; and they must be given to the right person in each situation. It is certainly better not to reward at all than to reward the wrong person. Rewards need not always be financial. Consideration should also be given to other forms, including increased prestige that is attendant upon a title change or something as innocuous as an improved office or laboratory location.

Essentially, an individual's performance relative to the considered norm of the group should be appraised on an ongoing basis, with the significance and value of the individual's accomplishments identified for the determination of rewards. For example, a research team leader's reward might well be expressed in terms of rewards to his research team members *on his recommendation*. There is no reason why an incentive plan cannot be applied for scientific and technical personnel in research and development. The goals for these individuals can be established and measured with appropriate norms, and superior positions can be recognized for comparative purposes.

The Patent in Motivation

Before getting into an incentive plan for research and development personnel, it would be wise to discuss the problem of patents and patent incentives. Patents and proprietary ideas are the principal products of research. The corporate investment in research, as has already been said, should be made to obtain a proprietary position among the company's competitors in today's and tomorrow's markets. The company's motivation program must therefore consider the most effective means of gaining every proprietary position possible through in-house research programs. The procedure of offering the new employee a company patent agreement to sign and paying him a nominal sum (usually one dollar) to make the agreement legally binding is an insult—an insult to both the individual and the company.

Companies must recognize that patentable ideas are the products of fertile minds and that it is impossible to police people's minds and take from them everything that the managers feel rightfully belongs to the company. Each individual with an idea, regardless of the stimulation that fostered it, has a personal stake in its exploitation. If a man does not believe he will receive a reward commensurate with the benefits derived from his idea, he may withhold the idea from the company, seeking other means to exploit it for his personal benefit. The progressive company today will acknowledge that the rights to patentable ideas are the property of the employee originators although derived in partnership with the company. The employee must be made to understand and feel that the company is a partner by virtue of employment and stimulation of the originator and that it should therefore be awarded the first opportunity to exploit the idea for its own benefit *and* for the benefit of the originator. Patents and other royalties should be added to the financial compensation of corporate employees capable of providing the company with improved proprietary interests. Such an approach will stimulate far more worthwhile ideas and result in stronger company proprietary positions than any demand made on an employee and sealed with an insignificant piece of green government script.

The Bonus Incentive

Not all scientists or engineers engaged in meaningful research will be able to provide patentable ideas directly. However, the products of their fertile brains may provide the foundations for many patentable ideas or concepts developed by others and may be the direct stimulus for such development. Any financial incentive plan must make allowances for this factor.

The concept of the annual bonus, usually given at Christmas time on the basis of generalized measurement techniques, is archaic and no longer fits modern concepts of business management. A standard bonus or bonus formula develops into, and is anticipated as, part of the normal employment compensation. Far better for the company and the individual is the concept of the incentive reward, made against measurable and predefined yardsticks. In the incentive approach each individual's reward is more nearly in line with his contributions and in accordance with the success of the whole group as well as the company. Thus each individual has a measurable stake in the contributions and success of his associates. The incentive approach also recognizes that the individual with the greatest responsibility has the greatest potential effect upon the group and should therefore receive a larger reward for his and the group's achievements.

It would be worthwhile for a research group—and for most other company groups—to establish an incentive plan which would provide a single year's goals for the entire group, preferably coinciding with the company's fiscal year. Such goals might include a normally anticipated level of external contract business bookings, of research performance billings, of controlled negative profit, and of return on investment. To these norms would be added the expected superior performance which the group would not be expected to surpass without unusual perseverance and maximum contribution by all group members. The goals would be weighted in importance to the company, with those qualifying for incentive participation passing upon the fairness or equity of the levels.

At the end of the year, any group which had failed to meet the established norms would be excluded from incentive rewards— barring any extenuating circumstances, of course. Meeting the normal or average levels would entitle the group to 10 percent of the money set aside as a burden cost during the year's performance; and the closer the group came to the superior performance level, the more closely it would approach the incentive disbursement of 100 percent of the incentive that had been set aside. As stated earlier, *each individual within the group would share according to his de-*

gree of responsibility and according to his contributions as measured in terms of his established goals. This is the important aspect of the workable incentive plan.

Establishing the Incentive Set-aside

The group's total incentive is determined by totaling the sums of each individual group member's percentage share and that individual's salary. The justification for the individual to receive his incentive payment would be established by his attainment of his specific goals. However, if the group should attain only 75 percent of its goals, only 75 percent of the incentive set-aside would be available for disbursement to the group. Should the individual goals, when summed, exceed the total incentive payment available for disbursement, the individuals would share pro rata and not in full. This is the fact that can be used to motivate individual group members to approach or exceed superior performance so each individual makes his maximum contribution to the group goals.

Selecting the Goals

In research and development, ideas breed ideas, and each individual's contribution to the group is enlarged by his participation in his area of scientific specialization rather than in other areas where he is less qualified. The incentive plan approach to rewards encourages this type of positive interrelationship and discourages the idea of withholding ideas for later personal exploitation. The individual's goals, however, must be removed from the realm of arbitrary decision if the goals are to have significance. To that end, the goals should be prepared by the individual and should be open for review not only by his superiors but also by his peers within the group. In this way the individual will be able to feel that his goals—and his potential rewards—are in line with those of the people with whom he competes in the incentive competition.

The actual nature of an individual's goals can be diverse so as to cover the full requirements of his normal range of efforts. For example, typical goals might include participation in research programs which meet cost and time schedules; participation in contract proposals with at least 50 percent contract award success; preparation of a scientific paper with acceptance by a recognized journal; disclosure, either individually or jointly, of a proprietary advantage or patentable idea applicable to the company's current or future products or services; and successful completion of courses of advanced study. These individual goals, like the group goals, should be weighted in importance to establish the norm and the superior-performance rating of the individual.

Dividing the Incentive Pie

The final aspect of the incentive program comes at year's end, when the members of the group are required to write a critique of their performance under the incentive plan, rating themselves for consideration by their superiors in the distribution of the group-earned incentive set-aside. This should allow the individual to determine introspectively his own worth and should provide the self-motivation for his future improvement. To give the plan meaning, the group should be apprised during the year of its performance relative to the group goals. Thus the group members are made aware of their contributions, and each individual can measure personal successes or failures. This is motivation in its most direct form.

A Salary Plan

In Chapter 6, a concept of ranking individuals within research groups was offered. Exhibit 11 suggested the minimum academic and experience qualifications for each descriptive title. Attainment of each higher-ranking title should become entirely a matter of academic standing and not a matter of dollars. If there were no compensating features to this system, however, it would serve as a motivational depressant. The compensating factor which has been added here is that each individual can make his career in any title from the lowest to the highest. This is possible only if the salary scale provides appropriate overlapping in each grade and if grade advancement possibilities increase with experience. Thus an indi-

Exhibit 12

RESEARCH ORGANIZATION'S SALARY GRADE STRUCTURE

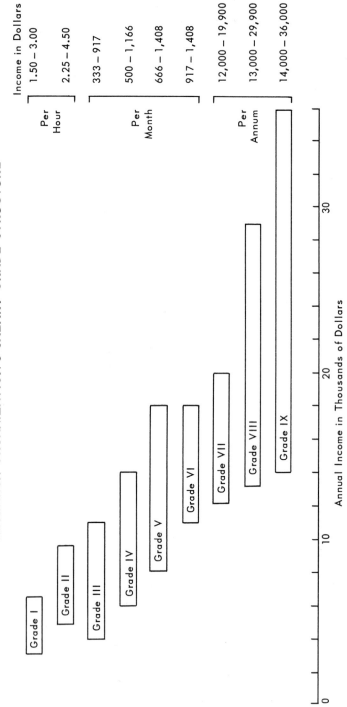

The grade structure for salaries within a research organization is based upon 1968 levels. As noted, this structure provides a natural progression of research employees from hourly through monthly to annual base. (See the text for an explanation of the grade overlaps.)

vidual could enter the organization with the minimum qualifications for a research assistant and then advance by experience alone through three salary grades to the top of the grade V pay scale.

At best, the grade structure for salaries must differ according to company, industry, and geographical location. The structure must be reviewed on a regular basis to eliminate inequities that inevitably develop through changed environmental factors. A form for the grade structure might be that of Exhibit 12. Although grades V and VI have the same top dollar, the top dollar in grade V should be reserved for the research associate or advanced development associate. The grades for the assistant scientist and junior development engineer are V and VI. For these positions, the individual should be promoted from grade V to VI shortly after passing the starting level of the higher grade. This approach is in keeping with the concept of maintaining a career in a title. It is also in keeping with the concept that scientific and technical personnel should be encouraged to pursue careers in their fields of specialization and not transfer to a management or administrative role for the furtherance of their financial well-being.

Employee Loyalty

Finally, in regard to motivation, the company and its management must recognize that the individual who says his first loyalty is to the company is probably lying either to the company or to himself. In the majority of cases the employee's loyalty is given first to his family or himself, with the company rating a poor second. The paternalistic policy of giving an employee stock in the company will not buy his loyalty, as attested to by the labor strikes in predominantly employee-owned companies. Therefore, astute management will make and stand behind a policy statement such as this: "Each employee should recognize that his first obligation is to himself and his family and that his employment is an aid in fulfilling that obligation. Thus the employee's second obligation is essentially to his family through his job." Further, the company should make it absolutely clear that no employee will be forced to violate his moral principles or family obligations as a condition of employment.

This view by management places a responsibility on each employee to seek other employment if he finds the interest of the company to be in conflict with his ethical or moral standards, regardless of where he may be in the company. For example, can a scientist, in clear conscience, work on research and development programs whose objective is the ultimate production of artificial organs (such as the heart, lungs, and kidneys) when the scientist has a moral belief that such organs are counter to the "will of God"—that man should suffer and die when his natural organs fail?

8

Administrative Control

T$_{HE}$ need for control of research and development has been discussed in previous chapters. However, it is one thing to acknowledge that control is desirable or necessary and another thing to provide effective control. This chapter considers control through the media of procedures and program control devices such as network analysis. Management in all areas, not just in research and development, is most effective when controls are well understood and uniformly applied without discrimination or favoritism. Of course, blanket coverage without the application of good judgment to particular situations is not effective management.

Introducing Procedures

Even in a totally involved and fully motivated research and development organization, there is a definite place for procedures. While procedures as such are a basic method of control, they also serve the purpose of providing guidelines for appropriate action in various situations. It remains for the method of introduction to achieve the desired results.

109

Procedures may be presented to the scientific and technical personnel of research and development either as a stout club to be wielded by management to control the actions and reactions of the organization and the individuals in it, or as an action guide in difficult situations as well as a shield for the employees' own protection. The first approach, however thinly disguised it may be, will be bitterly contested, while the second will fail if the content of the procedures is not carefully considered and as carefully worded.

Scientific and technical personnel are astute and generally have an open mind about administrative matters. If the pitfalls which they must face are explained and they are given an opportunity to contribute to the preparation of the procedures, the procedures will become the desired action guide and shield. Almost everyone appreciates a clear statement of how things may be accomplished and within what limits. If the individual has had the opportunity to help in defining and establishing the limits, procedures become self-imposed control.

Shaping the Content of Procedures

In Chapter 7, it was suggested that research and development personnel really expect to receive the opportunity to advance their training and education at company expense; encouragement and assistance in the preparation and presentation of papers before their peers; encouragement to belong to and financial assistance for participation in appropriate professional societies; adequate financial rewards for direct and indirect contributions, including patent royalties and other rewards; financial and status advancement based upon merit as measured by technological contributions; competent supervision; relief from the tedium and intrusion of routine managerial and administrative problems; and an opportunity to engage in challenging work. Procedures must be an extension of these concepts when the concepts have been accepted by management. But more than an extension or even an expression, the formal resulting procedures must be "sold" as to both content and purpose before being officially instituted as controls over research and development.

The procedure which might be perfectly acceptable in the production shop (and would generally be expected by shop personnel as a routine act of managerial control) if enacted for the research and development organization without prior explanation or selling could become the petard which the sophisticated scientist will use to open major chinks in management's armor.

For example, the average production worker on the line expects his time on the job to be fully governed by management. While he may be freed from the stigma of a time clock, he still realizes that his actions must be carefully geared to the production line and that the movement of the line is controlled by management, even after a union agreement sets the maximum rate of movement. The production worker also realizes that at quitting time he can leave his work station and the company premises without taking his work problems home for further consideration and possible after-hours solution. By contrast, the involvement of the average scientist or engineer in his research or development effort knows no set working hours. At quitting time, he cannot just turn off a magical switch in his head and go home. Furthermore, as he moves up the scale of creativity, this inability to "turn it off" also increases. Yet, to satisfy the norms of business, management must establish and maintain some semblance of official business hours for its research and development organizations. To accomplish this purpose poses a very real problem not only of control but also of expression in the written procedures.

Allaying Suspicions of Other Divisions

It is a sad fact, but a true one, that the more unsophisticated a company may be in its production and product engineering programs, the more the research and development components of the company will be viewed with suspicion by the rank and file personnel in all other components. Procedures, to be meaningful, must be published. Even with a controlled distribution system, procedures published for one component of the company will receive unofficial circulation in other components. Thus each procedure must be written with a view toward possible total exposure throughout the company. This means that procedures written specifically for the research and development components must be worded so as not to increase the suspicions of the other divisions that research and development personnel are a special, privileged group—the "darlings of management." However, since the procedures must be written for action, they must convey to the scientist and engineer the real intent of the control. Therein lies the real difficulty—a difficulty which is sometimes viewed as the horns of an unsolvable dilemma.

In an approach to the procedure-writing problem, consider how a procedure to cover the *official periods of business* might be written for a research organization. First note the subtle distinction between the term "official periods of business" and the concept of working hours as used in the production areas. The official periods of business clearly state when the organization will be open to outsiders for the conduct of business. It says in effect that the administrative and managerial personnel of the research organization will be present and available during these periods. It clearly does not say that the research *thinking* will start and end within these hours. If a clause is added to the procedure stating that the scientific and technical personnel are employed for research on the basis of a 40-hours-per-week contribution and that they have the responsibility to establish and work such hours on such days as may be appropriate to them, no one can fault the procedure. Yet clearly the creative personnel are not confined to working only within the official periods of business of the research organization. The full development of the resultant procedure is given in the first of the representative procedures in Appendix B.

Earlier in this chapter it was suggested that management may want to withhold or limit distribution of research and development procedures. It seems likely that any effort toward this end will merely create suspicions within the other divisions, rather than allay them. The procedural examples in Appendix B are of a form that could be widely published without undue repercussions.

Control of Mail, Receiving, and Shipping

In a research and development organization, mail handling, as well as receiving and shipping, becomes a major control problem, a problem somewhat different from that usually experienced in other departments. Part of the problem arises because the average scientist or engineer will write a short note on official company stationery requesting all manner of data, samples, or even detailed information which the recipient of the note will have to generate to fulfill the request. Although the scientist's desire and need for the requested material and data are understandable, such uncontrolled action can readily result in a significant and unexpected cost.

Consider a situation which really did develop. A scientist was considering the possible use of porous media for an experimental research effort. By a literature search, he discovered that a firm more than a thousand miles away produced a line of specialized porous metal media that seemingly offered the qualities of porosity and strength needed. But the literature was too indefinite for him to determine all the qualities. The scientist did not consider that the requirement for the material would justify a trip for a first-hand inspection of the media. Consequently, he sat down and wrote a letter to the firm producing the media. The letter was written on company letterhead stationery. In essence, the letter stated that the scientist was considering the use of porous media for an experiment and requested samples of the firm's products together with specific supporting technical design data.

On the surface, nothing could seem more innocuous than this simple request. However, the samples and requested data arrived promptly, accompanied by an invoice for several hundred dollars to cover the cost of sample and data preparation. In every sense of the word, an official order had been placed by the scientist when he used company stationery, and the company (or the scientist) was legally obligated for payment of the invoice.

Proper mail control would have caught the outgoing letter and amended it by adding a paragraph to this effect: "If this request generates any chargeable costs to the undersigned or the ABC Company, the request shall not be honored until the costs have been conveyed to this company in a formal bid and approved by an official purchase order of ABC Company." In this way, both the company and the scientist would be protected from unauthorized or unexpected charges. Further, if the reason for the control action is explained to the scientist, he should be more than willing to cooperate. In the event that a scientist is still unwilling to cooperate in matters of mail control, it is always possible to make it perfectly clear to him that he must assume personal liability for any costs incurred by his letter writing.

Another problem which faces every research organization housed with production and other elements of a large company is that of receiving. In general, research equipment and materials are foreign to the other operations of the company. Where a formal, company-wide receiving organization has been established, this can create unusual problems in terms of receiving inspection—particularly in a union shop. The receiving personnel will attempt to open and inspect everything received to insure that it conforms to the purchase specification. Their methods of inspection for conventional products may be highly damaging to specialized research equipment.

For example, although forewarned that a special shipment of front-surface mirrors for a research experiment would be arriving and that these mirrors required very delicate handling to prevent damage to the front surfaces, one receiving department accepted the shipment, checked it against the invoice number, took out the specification, and proceeded to open the shipment for inspection without notifying the research department. The specification stated that the mirrors would have a certain degree of concave radius in two perpendicular planes to provide a 20-degree off-axis image at a specific focal length. Each mirror had been specially prepared by the vendor to conform to the required concave shape and then had been silvered on the front face to complete the mirror surface. Together, the three mirrors had cost in excess of $1,500.

When the mirrors arrived, the inspectors laid them on a table in the receiving area and proceeded to use calipers and other gauges to measure their curvature. The front surfaces were liberally fingered in the process, and the thinly silvered surfaces were pocked by the pressure of the various gauges. In effect, the mirrors were destroyed in the receiving room by the ineptness of the inspectors.

Upper management should recognize this possibility and take such administrative action as is necessary to exclude the specialized equipment of research or any other division from the routine inspection of a general receiving department. The second procedure of Appendix B offers one form of a procedure to cover the contingencies which generally arise in handling mail, receiving, and shipping within a research group.

The Official or Unofficial Utterance

Whenever a scientist rises to speak in public or even before a limited audience of his fellow scientists, he presents a dual image to all who hear him. One is the image of his scientific astuteness; the second is the image of his company. In a formal presentation, the two images become inseparable. Thus a need arises for controls over industrial scientists and engineers relative to memberships in various societies, participation in conferences, and public presentations. More than just raising the spectre of exposing company proprietary information, the scientist making any form of presentation before the public or before a limited audience of his peers runs the risk of giving the impression that he speaks the opinions officially held by his company and its management, regardless of the subject matter.

The research and development scientist or engineer's membership in professional societies should be encouraged, and the company should make such memberships easily attainable by assuming the associated expense. However, employee membership in nonprofessional societies is also of company interest.

If the company is engaged in or is seeking government contracts to support its profit plan, then the company and its personnel must have a clean bill of security health. Managers at all levels and in all departments must not now be and must never have been members of any organization which the Justice Department lists as subversive. Similarly, scientists and engineers engaged in research and development under government contract must be above question in terms of national loyalty. The company therefore has a right—even a duty—to ask everyone in the research organization to report all memberships and refuse to hire or dismiss any individual who has jeopardized or would jeopardize the firm's ability to do government contract business because of his membership in any government-disapproved society or organization.

The procedure covering memberships in societies and organizations should also provide guidelines for the scientist or engineer who wishes to speak his mind on any subject when officially or unofficially representing the company at a meeting of any group. A suggested draft for such a procedure is also to be found in Appendix B. This procedure must be worded in such a way that it becomes a guide to the scientist and engineer rather than a blatant form of "Thou shalt not." As with the other example procedures of Appendix B, this one was written with the assistance of the scientists in a research organization after the problems facing the research managers had been explained to the scientists.

From the limited foregoing examples and discussion, the need for individual procedures arising within the company can be seen. The precise number of procedures which may be needed to provide a desired level of control will depend upon many factors and to some degree upon the attitude of the total management organization within the firm. The important thing to bear in mind is that each procedure must be sold on its own merits to the scientists and engineers affected by it.

Program Control

Specific research and development efforts provide yet another control problem. Here, procedures can serve only as an adjunct to the much larger interplay of interpersonal and administrative factors. Many managers of research and development programs fail to recognize that control of a total program effort transcends mere control of people. In this failure, these managers end up with nonproductive research efforts.

Many individuals, including a large percentage now actively engaged in research and development, categorically deny that research or even development can be controlled according to any fundamental management principles. If the scientist or engineer in research and development is to be permitted to erect roadblocks to control, effective control will not be possible. However, virtually all applied research and any product or process development effort *can* be preplanned and controlled by procedures normally termed "network analysis." On the other hand, the effectiveness of any form of direct control over basic research efforts can be questioned. A return to the definitions of research efforts should explain this. Basic research is an effort directed toward the expansion of man's basic knowledge. Thus it becomes knowledge for knowledge's sake. The goal of true basic research is undefined—even undefinable. Without specific goals, it becomes impossible to mark a clear path toward a successful conclusion.

Network Analysis: A Background

Before considering the how of network analysis, it is worthwhile to digress a little and consider the background of this control technique. The full development of network analysis has occurred since 1955. Its most representative system, PERT (program evaluation and review technique), is close kin to the other well-known systems, which include CPM (critical path method), IMPACT (implementation planning and control technique), and PRISM (program reliability information system for management). PERT was developed by the management consulting staff of Booz, Allen & Hamilton Inc. to meet the needs of the U.S. Navy's Special Projects Office in the conduct of the Polaris Project's research, development, and production phases. In this project, the navy set about the deployment of a completely new weapon system which was to include a new missile and a fully compatible at-sea launch subsystem. The missile was a radical departure from previous guided missiles in that it was to have a solid propellant rocket motor and was to be launched from a submerged nuclear submarine.

The Polaris Project was placed on a "short fuze" response to a critical navy and Defense Department requirement. Success became a matter of having every aspect of the effort enter the development stream at the proper time. Essentially, for the first time in any government program, technical breakthroughs were identified *and* scheduled. To accomplish this aim, both research and development efforts were controlled as to total inputs to insure that the breakthroughs were accomplished as required by the schedule. PERT was the form of network analysis which accomplished this control.

Network Analysis: Its Fundamental Purpose

Any network analysis system, including PERT, is designed to establish the critical points in the research, development, or other ongoing processes of a total effort. The first step in network analysis of any effort is to establish and define all the elements of the effort which must be performed for successful completion of the program. In the second step, the elements are sequenced according to their technological and administrative interdependence. Taken together, the two steps provide a system of checks and balances to insure the definition of the total technical aspects of the effort to be planned. Note, however, that to this point nothing has been done toward establishing the time to accomplish each element of the program or the manpower application required by each element.

The third step is the construction of a network using the data and information derived in the previous two steps. The network, if properly laid out, will show that each point or event within it has a logical beginning at a proven development or concept and that the path from that beginning to the event of interest covers all the necessary intermediate events. These paths will include all or any required technical breakthroughs to reach the event of interest. When the network has been drawn in its entirety with no closed loops and no doubling along the various paths from the time of effort initiation to completion of the ultimate program goal, the final step in the network analysis can be taken.

The fundamental value of network analysis, regardless of the type of effort analyzed, is the derivation of a series of rational answers to a series of subjective estimates. Working through the logical progression of events within the network, the analyst must decide how much time is required along each path between events. Of course, this is a subjective effort, and the total analysis will succeed or fail as a result of the evaluation of the effort required between events and the amount of effort that can be effectively applied. These estimates are far more difficult to make in research than in development or production. Managers responsible for the program must select the analyst or analysts with considerable care and a knowledge of their reliability.

Network Analysis of Research

Network analysis is admittedly more difficult to apply to research program planning and control than to development or production efforts. It is also fair to state that theoretical research is more difficult to analyze and control than experimental research. The analyst who attempts to provide the time estimates and scheduling for a research effort must have more than an understanding of research processes—he must have a feeling for them.

In the conventional network analysis methods, the analyst makes three estimates: the most optimistic time required for completion of the effort represented by each program event, the most pessimistic time, and the most logical time. For a research effort, however, the most important element in time estimation may be the maximum number of scientists or engineers who can be applied to the solution of the problems represented by a single program event. In production programs, production can be increased within a fixed time frame, or the same output can be obtained in a shorter time by the application of more personnel and materials.

When a single scientist is the key investigator pursuing a line of reasoning, there is a limit to the number of assistants he can be given to cover the routine factors in the reasoning process. The analyst attempting the time estimates for a research effort must know which scientists or engineers will be assigned to the solution of each event's problems, and he must have some realization of how the assigned individual functions in a problem-solving environment to arrive at meaningful time estimates. In the assignment of personnel, the analyst can utilize the network to check overlapping assignments of various key individuals and can accumulate the estimated time contributions for each individual to achieve a prediction of research costs.

From the foregoing, it is apparent that there must be something of a departure from conventional network analysis if the objectives of research are to be controlled.

Using Network Analysis for Control

The completed network analysis for a research program provides management with all the information needed to adequately control and evaluate progress of the program. It provides the sequence of technical events from program initiation to completion, with a time scale that permits determining when any event in the sequence is throwing the program plan out of control and when the program progress is exceeding or lagging behind the cost estimates. The objective in applying the analysis, however, is more than mere control. In earlier chapters, the concept was advanced that an industrial organization should conduct research only as an investment in an improved or new proprietary position in a competitive market. If this concept is accepted, then the investment must be known at each point in time during its commitment; and the investment should be terminated at the earliest point in time when it is clear that it will prove economically unsound or will not reach its technical objective.

In some companies, and even in areas of government, network analysis techniques and their application to preprogram planning have become a fad. A network is prepared, submitted, and approved for the proposed program. Then the fun begins. At program initiation, the network analysis script is thrown away and there is a return to the old catch-as-catch-can methods for there is always more money to keep the program alive since "we" never kill a research effort. There has to be a better way than this, and the managers who do not seek that better way have abdicated their responsibilities.

Resistance to Control of Research

Managers' abdication of responsibility for control of research is traceable to several reasons, but the principal reason is one of threat. The threat arises out of the challenges implied and imposed by any technological innovation. When the threat (either real or imagined) becomes evident, the resistance to the supporting research will be in direct proportion to the threat.

Upper managers and intermediate managers at the same level as the manager of the research division have an established social status and way of life which have been determined by the current investment in facilities and the current product characteristics, as well as acceptance. Research producing a technological innovation which requires a change in facilities, product characteristics, or even market presentation places a burden on the upper and intermediate managers to optimize the new situation. Their failure to optimize—especially when the failure is obvious—poses a very real threat to their social status and existing way of life. How much easier it is for them to do nothing to encourage the output of the new technological innovation! After all, failure in research is not chargeable to them—or so they rationalize. Their current abilities, knowledge, or recallable skills are not endangered. If need be, supporting resistance to the potential technological innovation can be obtained from other quarters similarly "threatened."

For every potential technological innovation, there can be found some form of active or passive resistance to its introduction coming from the social, economic, or political spheres, if not from within technology itself. For example, the American family car ages primarily because of rusting. Technology has shown that the useful life of a car can be extended at least 50 percent by a chrome plate on galvanized coating of the basic sheet steel of the body and frame. The cost has been estimated to be approximately $35 in new-car sales price. Yet, at the end of five years, the extra cladding would increase the used-car price by at least $150 over that of the unclad metal car. A marketing effort could convince the American public of the value of paying the extra $35. However, this would reduce new-car sales proportionately and make automobile production less economically attractive. Hence, the economic pressure to change styling every three years and reduce the value of five-year-old cars to a level where the average car of that age is worth less than $100. Even safety innovations are resisted by the car makers until political pressure generated in the social sphere forces the change—as witness the results of Ralph Nader's writing of *Unsafe at Any Speed* and his crusade for improved auto safety.

Since network analysis provides a tool to those directly and indirectly affected by research to exercise control over research efforts, while also exposing their duplicity when it exists, it is worthwhile to consider how network analysis can be applied to a research program. The balance of this chapter considers the methods of network analysis in greater depth.

Fundamentals of the Activity Path

In Exhibit 13(a), the activity path moves from event 1 to event 2. This diagrammatic presentation should be read, "The full activity associated with event 1 must be completed before the activity of event 2 can be initiated." Thus event 1 serves to constrain the activity of event 2. To put the concept in a simple perspective, consider the planned construction of a custom-built house on a chosen site. Event 1 might be the surveying of the site to establish the constraints within which the design of the house would have to be drawn. Event 2 would be the preliminary layout of the house on the lot according to the established building codes and land restrictions in effect for the chosen site. It is easily seen that event 1 must precede event 2 in this situation if event 2 is to have any meaning.

A single event in a program may be the beginning point for more than one additional event; or a single event may be the terminal point for the activity paths from more than one event. This is demonstrated by Exhibit 13(b) and (c). In the burst configuration, events 2 and 3 are constrained by event 1, inasmuch as the later events cannot be initiated until all the activity of event 1 has been completed. Event 1 may have two separable activities, as represented by the double rays moving from event 1 to events 2 and 3. It would be entirely possible that one of these separable activities would lead to event 2 as a constraint, with the other activity leading to

Exhibit 13

ELEMENTS OF A NETWORK

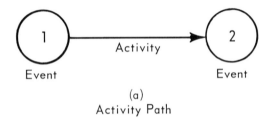

(a)
Activity Path

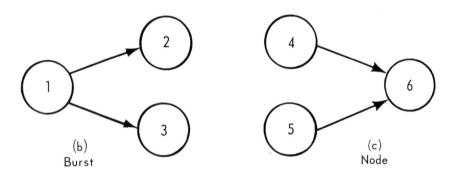

(b)
Burst

(c)
Node

The fundamental elements of a network are the event circles and the respective activity paths which follow. Events may be strung in a continuous series as shown at (a). They may also be arranged in diverging or converging series as shown at (b) and (c).

event 3 as shown. In turn, a separable activity of event 2 might serve as a constraint on event 3. This condition is present in the network of Exhibit 15.

Return a moment to the house construction example, and consider that event 3 might be a legal check of the survey information relative to real estate records, a first action in insuring that a clear title will be obtainable on the completed house. While the legal search is under way, the design of the house to fit the lot can also be undertaken, since a clear title is not a prerequisite for the house design. The effort of event 2 might be separable into the drawing of the plat and the required additional design work. The plat data might also be necessary to the legal search as part of establishing the legal description. If this were the situation, then the network relationship of Exhibit 15 would prevail.

In the node configuration of Exhibit 13(c), both events 4 and 5 must be completed in full before event 6 can be initiated. Whereas, in the burst example, event 1 is critical to and a constraint on events 2 and 3, in the node, events 4 and 5 taken together are critical to and a constraint on event 6.

Rules for Network Layout

The rules for layout of a network are extremely simple and, if followed closely, provide a check on the feasibility of the total effort.

The first rule of network layout states that each line in the network joining two events must be traversed as an activity of the planned program, and no path can be superfluous. This rule does not preclude the possibility that some paths may be such that no actual activity has to occur to move from one event to another. When no activity is required on a path, this means that the second event is constrained from initiation until the prior event's activities have also been initiated.

The second rule states that no event can be initiated until all activity on every path leading back to the event of program initiation has been completed. This rule is merely an extension of the first rule. If the first rule is observed, the second rule is naturally fulfilled.

The third rule states that any activity resulting from an event cannot be started until the event has occurred. This is an outgrowth of the first two rules, yet it is the rule most often violated in network application.

According to the fourth rule, the network must be drawn so that no event occurs more than one time. That is to say, there can be no closed loops within the network. When a reiterative process is necessary in a program, the process is drawn as a sequential series.

The fifth rule requires that only one activity be used to join a pair of events, although a dummy activity may be added to the network if it is assigned a zero activity time. This rule naturally leads to the last rule of network design: that every complete network has only one beginning and one end.

Time Scheduling a Network

The expected time to complete the activity associated with each event is derived by the estimator using the ideal manpower loading, and a value is assigned for the most optimistic time-to-completion estimate *a*, the most likely time-to-completion estimate *m*, and the most pessimistic estimate *b*. The expected time is then calculated from this formula:

$$t_e = \frac{a + 4m + b}{6}$$

An acceptable method of drawing the activity path from one event to the next is shown in Exhibit 14. The estimated time to completion for the activity t_e is placed above the path line as determined from the formula. Figures within the parentheses should be read as follows: the most optimistic estimate for time to completion (2-x-x)(x) is two days; the most likely time to completion (x-4-x)(x) is estimated as four days; the latest allowable or most pessimistic date for completion (x-x-6)(x) is six days; and the maximum practical manpower assignment (x-x-x)(2) is two men simultaneously.

In a research effort, unlike a production program, there is a practical limit to the number of individuals who can be meaningfully assigned to a specific activity. For example, a research activity involving the extension of a single mathematical expression cannot be broken into a series of tasks to be performed simultaneously by a number of different individuals. The addition of the manpower assignment number acknowledges such a limitation and provides a needed dimension normally missing from the conventional network presentation.

Beneath the activity path and within the triangle is the available slack time estimate. Calculation of this number will be discussed later. Below the triangle is an expression v^2, which is a measure of the variance. This number will also be discussed in more detail later.

The Total Network

Exhibit 15 presents a simple research program in the research network analysis form. As with the individual activity paths between events, there is an earliest expected date for completion T_E for the total effort and a latest allowable date for completion T_L. There the similarity essentially ends.

For the total network, the earliest expected date for completion of the program effort is the maximum sum of the values of the individual activity path values of t_e taken along each of the various paths which can be followed from program initiation to completion. In Exhibit 15, there are four possible paths through the network. These paths are via events 1,3,6,8; 1,2,3,6,8; 1,2,5,8; or 1,4,7,8. The

Exhibit 14
FORMAT OF ACTIVITY PATH

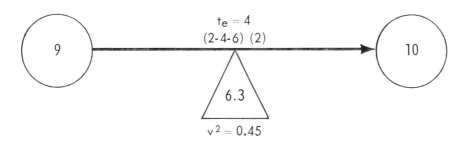

Network analysis for research projects might be presented with the format for each activity path as shown here. The individual notations are explained in the text. The one significantly new notation, not normally found in standard network analysis, is the quantity (x-x-x) (2). This designates the number of scientists who can practically be applied to this specific activity.

Exhibit 15

PROGRAM IN THE RESEARCH NETWORK ANALYSIS FORM

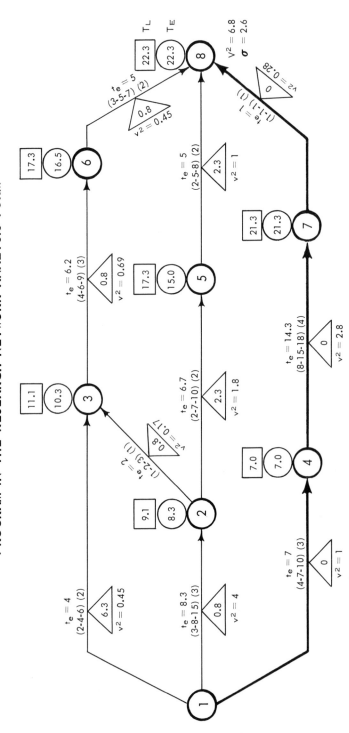

Even the simplest of research efforts can be plotted and controlled through the use of network analysis. Of course, there is a practical limit determined principally by the cost of the analysis effort versus the practical return. Regardless of the size of the effort, however, short in-terval scheduling (SIS) is still practical and a natural adjunct to the network activity. The research effort shown here has been judged a 166 man-day effort with a cost of approximately $5,000. Thus it is a rela-tively modest effort even by research standards.

path which passes through events 1,4,7,8 provides a sum of t_e values along that path equal to 22.3. Each of the other potential paths yields a lesser total. This value of 22.3 then becomes the total network's T_E value and is placed in the circle above event 8.

Each event also has a value of T_E determined in a similar manner. These individual event values of T_E are entered in the circles over the affected event. Note especially that the value of T_E for event 3 is the sum of the t_e's along the path 1,2,3 and not along the direct path 1,3.

As the value of T_E is not the sum of the m values in the parentheses of the activity paths, the determination of the latest allowable date for completion is not the sum of the b values (referring of course to the original formula for t_e). The value of the latest allowable date for completion T_L for the complete network is normally taken to be equal to the value of T_E for the complete network. In this case, that value, 22.3, is entered in the square above event 8.

To establish the value of T_L for each event in the network, it is now necessary to work backward from the last event to the initial event, subtracting the value of t_e along each path. Thus, moving backward from event 8 to 6, T_L at event 6 is $22.3 - 5 = 17.3$; and moving backward from event 8 to 7, T_L at event 7 is $22.3 - 1 = 21.3$. In this manner, the value for T_L for each event is established.

The Critical Path

With the values of T_E and T_L established for each event, it is possible now to establish the slack time available along each event's activity path. Slack is the schedule given in an event's activity accomplishment without a delay to the program as a whole. It is the difference between the values for T_E and T_L for the event; it is expressed by the formula

$$\text{Slack} = T_L - T_E.$$

The determined value for the slack of each event activity is entered in the triangle beneath the path as shown in Exhibit 15.

When all the slack values have been entered on the network, one path will emerge along which the slack for each event is zero. This should be the path which yielded the maximum value of T_E for the total network. This path through the network is termed the "critical" path. Completion of each event on this critical path on schedule will control the completion of the program on schedule. Any effort to solve the critical path problem must be taken with full knowledge of the effect of change upon all other possible paths through the network.

With the critical path identified (and it is usually identified by heavier path lines), it is possible to consider ways and means of reducing its criticalness. Of course, it might be possible to transfer resources to efforts on the critical path from slack segments of the network. This is possible only within the constraints of manpower or facilities application. A second possible action is to deliberately create slack in the critical path by raising the value of T_L at the terminal event to some value greater than T_E for the network. This will have the effect of increasing slack throughout the network, however.

If the latter course of action is followed, consideration should be given to changing values of *a*, *m*, and *b* along various paths and applying fewer individuals to each event activity to achieve better manpower utilization.

Variance

Standard deviation is a coefficient which serves to measure the scatter a group of data may have from the mean of the group. The concept is based upon a "normal distribution" of the data points about the mean. In *Methods of Correlation and Regression Analysis*,[*] Mordecai Ezekiel and Karl Fox aptly defined a normal distribution by stating that it "is such a one as will be obtained from a series of observations of a variable influenced only by a large number of random or chance causes, each one small in proportion to the total." For any random distribution with the normal distribution characteristics, the standard deviation coefficient is determinable from the formula

$$\sigma_x = \sqrt{\frac{\sum x^2}{n}}$$

[*] New York: John Wiley & Sons, Inc., 1941.

where $\sum x^2$ is the sum of the squares of the displacement of each data point in the group from the mean of the group and n is the number of points in the group.

Useful as it is, standard deviation as a mathematical coefficient is sometimes even more useful as a squared value. Standard deviation may be thought of as measuring variability, while the standard deviation squared is the variance.

In network analysis, variance is a useful tool which makes control of the program a little less difficult. While many others use the symbol σ^2 to designate the variance of each event activity path within a network, the symbol v^2 may be easier to use, primarily because few typewriters come equipped with Greek letters. The choice of symbol is of little import provided that there is consistency in its use and calculation. Each event activity path's variance is calculable using the simplified formula

$$v^2 = \left[\frac{b - a}{6} \right]^2$$

where b and a are the values within the parentheses above the activity path. The divisor 6 is an empirical value which provides an adjustment for the form of data distribution which is most likely to occur in a network distribution.

The variance for the complete network is simply the largest sum of variances along any path through the network from origin to termination. It should be noted that the largest sum will generally not be found on the critical path. In Exhibit 15, the largest sum is established along the path 1,2,5,8 as a value of 6.8.

Probability of On-Time Completion

The variance for the total network V^2 provides the basic tool for establishing the probability of completing the network's program according to the value of the expected time for completion T_E. From the total network variance, a value for the standard deviation is obtained by extracting the square root of the value V^2. The resultant value σ is the standard deviation of the network and is expressed in the same time units as those of the network. In the example of Exhibit 15, the standard deviation is 2.6. To lend meaning to this value, consider the following table and Exhibit 16.

Number of Standard Deviations for the Specification of the Range (from Plus to Minus)	Probability that the Actual Time Falls Within the Specified Range (Percent)
$1.0\,\sigma$	68.0
$2.0\,\sigma$	95.0
$3.0\,\sigma$	99.8

Exhibit 16

NORMAL DISTRIBUTION

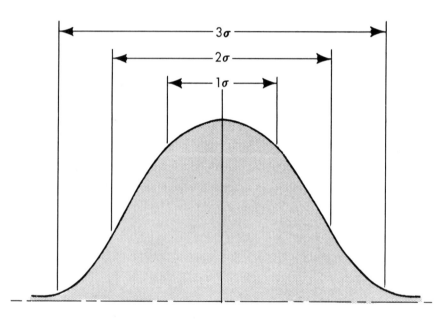

In the theory of probability, if a series of points are randomly obtainable around a specific target, the points will be obtained in accordance with a distribution which is a normal distribution or some close proximation of a normal distribution. The standard deviation of these points is statistically predictable. Thus 68 percent of all the points will be found within a spread of one standard deviation on either side of the target.

From Exhibit 15, there is a 68 percent probability that the program represented by the network will be completed between the 19.7th and the 24.9th days after program initiation. These dates are 1σ on either side of the value for T_E. There is also a reasonable expectation that the program will not be completed before the 17th day (17.1) or later than the 27th day (27.8). These values are determined by a 4σ spread which will include 99.95 percent of all data points.

9

The Planning Function

THE modern concept of a corporation is that of a viable organism with an ongoing character which can be shaped and molded to meet specific, definable objectives. Although a figurative snapshot of the corporation can be made at any moment in time to establish the character and condition of the firm at that moment, what it will be tomorrow and in the future depends entirely upon the reaction of the corporation's managers to today's problems and upon their planning today for tomorrow's eventualities. These managers must extend planning to every segment of the corporation and provide a scenario for future action and reaction. Certainly, research efforts and the research organization cannot be omitted from the planning.

This chapter is concerned with the need for the following action by the corporation:

1. To establish meaningful corporate objectives as a fundamental guide to research *and* development efforts.
2. To see that research and development personnel, as well as operational personnel, are aware of the firm's short- and long-range technological needs and capacities.
3. To make research and development an integral part of the overall business strategy.

4. To insure that research and development priorities and project balance reflect appropriate business judgments.
5. To provide for the maximum transfer of research technology to product operations according to preplanned time schedules.
6. To provide for evaluation milestones within research and development programs so as to minimize investment and maximize return on investment.

Setting Objectives or Goals

Those individuals responsible for overall corporate management —in other words, upper management, but particularly the chief executive officer or president—must be prepared to define *what* research is expected to contribute to the future, not how. Setting total corporate objectives is the vital first step in corporate planning. Research, development, and all other segments of the corporation should then respond to these objectives or goals without equivocation, for these goals are what the managers expect the corporation to achieve in order to fulfill the role it has been given. Taken in this frame of reference, the overall corporate objectives help to define the scope, degree, and timing of the company's technological needs and requirements. If the goals are properly written and defined, they will stimulate research along the most desirable paths, but will not restrict the technological approaches to goal achievement.

Insuring that goals are properly written and defined is the major problem in goal setting. Too often, in our materialistic society, goals or objectives are framed in terms of money or profit. Financial planning is part of the totality of planning and is more properly a supporting part than a leading part. The managers who determine the goals of a corporation must decide what the corporation is to become, with due consideration for its current nature. For example, will the current products or services be supplanted by new products or services, be supplemented with new products or services, or be enlarged to provide greater customer benefits? Viewed in this way, goals cannot be purely financial or financially oriented. However, the value of the goals to the corporation and to the stockholders must be considered in financial terms.

The corporation that sets its prime objective to become an X-billion-dollar corporation by year Y has already lost its first effort toward that goal. Everyone in the corporation with any degree of responsibility will believe he knows the proper path toward that objective. True, such an objective frees the entrepreneurial spirit of achievement-motivated managers, but it also encourages digressions along tangents and into seductive side paths. Any existing team spirit may very well be destroyed, while the upper managers can take no exception to any effort pursued by the research segment. The corporation has set a dollar sign as its goal, and every manager is free to pursue that goal as he judges best. Some individuals and the segments of the corporation under their control may prosper. But who will be able to measure how much more the corporation would have prospered if meaningful goals had been established and *all* segments of the firm had worked together as a team to achieve those goals?

If the corporation is a viable organism, goals must have life also. Goals are subject to review, renewal, and revision to match the changes in society, economics, politics, and even demography. But technology will be the largest affecting factor. Goals can be framed in terms of changing technology but they will be far more meaningful when framed in terms of changing technology as it relates to the other changing factors of society and the like.

Established Company Mission

Quite apart from a company's objectives or goals is its established mission. This mission is the thrust of the company as measurable in terms of products or services now being offered to potential customers. The case of one company is an example of what can happen when the basic thrust of the firm is ignored and goals are established independently of the established company mission.

The firm was a machinery company and a good one when a new president assumed the reins of control. Brilliant to a fault, this man recognized the potential of recreation equipment and launched the firm into the business—with great success. Occurring, as it did, early in his career, his success spurred him to expand the company's research and development commitments to develop another product to match the first. Out of this intense concentration on research came a great many ideas. But some of the great ideas did not mesh with the firm's established mission.

Research produced a number of technologically successful product ideas, which cost millions in new product investment, but provided no return or at most minimal return. These product ideas failed because they ignored the basic thrust of the company—quality machinery lines. To succeed, the president would have had to alter the thrust—the established mission—of the company as well as invest in research and development.

Those managers who control the destiny of any company must recognize that they cannot radically and suddenly change its established mission. The thrust is there, and at best it can be but altered with time and planning. In the case just cited, the first of the new products fit within the company's established mission, while the later efforts were a departure from it. Today, the research and development efforts are essentially in keeping with the thrust of the firm and at a level significantly below that at the end of the cited president's tenure.

Thus it can be seen that goals and objectives must be compatible with the established mission, but they should be flexible. When a conflict arises between the two areas, the resolution by managers should be in favor of the established mission, and the goals should be modified to bring about the long-term change in the thrust of the company.

The Strategic Scenario

Of itself, a goal is useless. To achieve the goal as established, a strategy of action must be developed which considers all the opposing forces and impulses toward the goal. The strategy must provide a blueprint for action which presents broad outlines in terms of "if . . . then. . . ." The strategy can be defined in a scenario form which delineates a series of broad paths with alternative branches. It is expected that the main path will be followed to achieve the desired corporate objective, but *if* an anticipated or unanticipated event occurs at a certain point along the path, *then* a branch is taken according to the preplanning to achieve the objective along another broad path of potential action.

To write the scenario, there must be realistic forecasting in every factor affecting the path to objective achievement. A corporation may accomplish its own in-depth analysis through the applied talents of an internal planning analysis group, or it may rely on purchased services of one of the many service groups—such as Arthur D. Little, Inc., Stanford Research Institute, or Booz, Allen & Hamilton Inc. The course to be followed must be determined, in part at least, by the corporate size. External services are expensive, but they cannot be duplicated by a small internal staff in terms of reliability or objectivity.

The scenario should include the hypothetical possibilities within the several forecasts and define the alternatives that are possible in each predictable change. It is not unusual for a planning group to utilize mathematical models for the development of a scenario for a major expansion program. The models permit the assessment of the impact of the various alternatives open as social, economic, and other factors change. As a minimum, models should be drawn for the market, for the applicability of marketing, for the cash-flow requirements, and for the investment scheduling. If the program requires a research and development input, then it becomes crystal clear that research and development efforts must be managed in terms of cost and schedule or the scenario becomes pointless and the models useless.

In terms of research and development, the scenario must do more than define costing and scheduling. It must also—

1. Determine where the research efforts are to be concentrated to fulfill established objectives.
2. Provide for the research personnel to maintain contact with the scientific community in all directly and indirectly related disciplines.
3. Insure that all technology which could alter any of the planning models is adequately screened to provide a warning of pending change, especially change which could materially alter any of the nontechnical factors.

Tactics Versus Strategy

Given company objectives which are well written and well defined, and given the scenario of action to meet these objectives, the broad strategy is planned. But the strategy is designed to follow the broad paths described earlier. Within these path widths, a certain amount of maneuvering must be possible to bypass small impedimenta and yet retain the action within the limits of the path. Such maneuvering constitutes the tactics to be applied. Whereas the strategy plan set forth in the scenario is the long-term action, the tactics used along the way represent the short-term actions or responses to program externals. Each company's peculiar strengths, weaknesses, and objectives will determine optimum strategy and the tactics required to achieve the objectives through the planned strategy. The effectiveness of tactics is controlled entirely by the ability of managers at all levels to measure, evaluate, and respond to action demands within real time.

Tactics do not permit action as a result of in-depth analysis and weighty deliberation at the very top of the corporation. The upper managers who demand such slavish response to decisions place the corporation in a straitjacket. Tactical response to the demands of strategy must be defined in terms of level of response and the level available to each manager must be made clear to all managers concerned. Within his authorized level of response, each manager should be free to pursue any ethical tactic. It goes without saying at this point that each manager must also be guided by well-written and fully defined objectives.

Measuring and Evaluating Research

Is it possible to measure the progress of research efforts? In many companies, attempts to apply standard control and evaluation techniques to research and development efforts have proved to be very disappointing. In some instances, these attempts have led to gross misunderstandings between research and development personnel and the upper-level managers charged with overall research and development responsibility. Such misunderstandings have caused the erection of barriers to effective research and development programming. Sometimes, these difficulties arise from control and evaluation procedures which are basically inadequate for *any* company activities, much less research and development. More frequently, however, the difficulties come from the application of procedures which are effective in other parts of the company though inappropriate to research and development.

Some of the distinctions that separate the research and development segments of a company from such other segments as production are reflected in the degree of tangibility. In production, cost accounting tools and the physical act of counting output usually serve to measure progress. The managers can readily determine success in meeting production goals by an examination of records.

Research and development managers also need a measurement of progress, but a readily defined physical means of determination is lacking. Many schemes have been tried for keeping track of research and development progress, including Gantt charts, project milestone schedules, sophisticated computer-reporting techniques, and just plain guesswork. But all these processes are dependent upon subjective judgments. Evaluation capabilities move into the picture when the manager attempts to determine for the record whether a milestone has in fact been achieved, or to determine what inputs should be fed into the computer program, or what intangible factors should be entered in progress estimates. Perhaps it is only folklore that such evaluation methods cannot be objective. Certainly, many managers fail to try for various reasons of their own. The network analysis techniques discussed in the previous chapter offer one of the most effective evaluation and control methods available for research and development efforts. Further, the short interval scheduling (SIS) discussed in an earlier chapter is a natural adjunct to the network analysis.

Product Planning

Product planning is most effective when it is based upon technological analysis and forecasting. Technological forecasting, which will be covered separately in the next chapter, is a relatively new art which currently enjoys the dubious status that economic forecasting had approximately 20 years ago, but which is very rapidly developing into a semiscience.

Properly conducted, a technological forecast provides an identification of broad product areas and specific objective potentials for product penetration planning within identified markets. However, technology is not the determining factor in the marketability of a product. There is a matter of social acceptance, technology availability, and human desire. The successful product is the one that has all three of these factors meeting simultaneously.

Over the years there have been many products which were introduced with the availability of the technology, but these products failed because of a lack of social acceptance, a lack of buyer desire, or both. Some of these products have later succeeded, but in other cases the products have faded into obscurity. An interesting example of the introduction of a product too early is that of the numerically controlled machine tool. In the early 1950's the technology was available, and several companies had mastered the technology to produce excellent, efficient equipment. These companies invested heavily in the designs and marketing of numerical control equipment, completely ignoring the social acceptability of automated manufacturing equipment. The cries of anguish raised by the unions forced the potential purchasers to consider their purchases carefully. Most of the available machine tools in industry were good equipment left from the World War II period, and additional supplies of this equipment were available from government surplus storage. The old equipment was fully depreciated and the surplus was available under government bailment contracts, with the potential of eventual acquisition at pennies on the dollar. There was therefore a negative economic factor added to the social one.

The originators of numerical control machine tools rang up a "no sale"; some of them went bankrupt and some quietly merged with other machine tool firms at a loss to their investors. Fortunately, today there is social acceptance of the automation concept and more than adequate economic justification to modernize production. Consequently, there is a new numerically controlled machine tool industry.

Management's Role in Planning

Exhibit 17 presents the total planning and control process as a reiterative, closed-loop system which includes a series of reiterative,

Exhibit 17

CLOSED-LOOP SYSTEM OF TOTAL PLANNING AND CONTROL PROCESS

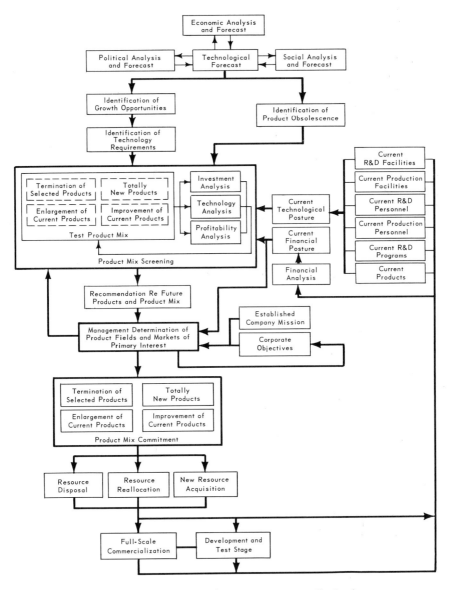

Corporate planning is a reiterative and ongoing process. Each plan must encompass the total status of the company at the moment it is produced, and it must be continually revised and updated with each change in corporate aspect. The planning process begins in the middle of the diagram, with the input of corporate objectives and established company mission at the level of the chief executive.

closed-loop subsystems. The heart of the complete system is the block entitled, "Management Determination of Product Fields and Markets of Primary Interest." This block could as easily have been labeled, "Office of the Chief Executive," for it is this office which has to set the corporate objectives and provide the direction for the firm.

The chief executive does not have to work in a vacuum when making these all-important decisions about the future of the company. While his inputs may be varied and of different levels of reliability, in the final analysis he has to make the decisions which will alter the course of the company—for greater or lesser return on the total corporate investment. As he makes these decisions, he would be wise to keep in mind the reiterative loop which represents the totality of technology.

Technology as a Closed-Loop System

Exhibit 2 (see Chapter 2, page 23) presents the totality of technology, a totality which is a closed-loop system without beginning or termination. All too frequently, the beginnings of advances in the state of the art are assumed to be rooted in basic research, which at best provides increased human understanding of natural phenomena, prediction of change that can be effected, and new or extended theory on which new concepts can be based. In actual practice, human knowledge (which includes knowledge derived from basic research), inquiry, imagination, and observation provide the real stimulus to applied research. As shown in Exhibit 2 and discussed in previous chapters, there is an interaction between the economic, social, geopolitical, and technological spheres of action, with each sphere impacting on the others and responding in turn to their pressures or stimulations.

As the technological state of the art responds to the influences of the other spheres, its requirements for growth draw upon human knowledge, inquiry, imagination, and observation to initiate the background for advancement. Since the effort is directed toward advancement of the state of the art through new commodities and services, the research begins with applied, not basic, research. While the human knowledge may be drawn from the output of basic research, it may also come from prior applied research or new applications from the current state of the art.

Returning to the earlier definitions of basic and applied research, it is possible to understand why the output of applied research is merely new techniques, new knowledge of the physical or technological world, and new materials around which new products can be formed. These advances are the foundation for not only development designed to make use of the discoveries, but also input or stimulation required to produce basic research.

Development takes the output of applied research and produces commodities and services which can be introduced in the market to visibly alter the state of the art in technology. Yet in a very real sense the totality of technological state of the art is the complete status of technology in the loop at any single moment in time. There is nothing static in the loop, and the rate of change within it will be controlled through the actions and reactions (impacts) of the other spheres upon the technology sphere. Human knowledge, inquiry, imagination, and observation are the factors within technology which provide the impacts upon the other spheres.

Consider the nature of the output of the basic research element. Basic research provides increased human understanding of the physical and technological world. It provides the basis for prediction about natural phenomena; and it also provides new or extended theories about natural phenomena or factors within the physical or technological world. Clearly, this type of output cannot provide the basis for development of commodities and services without some intervening process such as applied research.

Future Impact Analysis

Returning again to Exhibit 17, the output of a complete forecast is a series of identifications of potential commodities and services. These identifications are an input to the product mix screening subsystem loop. As is discussed in the next chapter in more depth and has already been touched on briefly, the technological forecast must provide adequate consideration of the political, economic, and social impacts on technology. These can be identified and evaluated only through analysis and forecast in each of the spheres. Hence, in Exhibit 17, the interrelationships of these four spheres are shown to provide a total forecast from which a double path leads downward toward the product mix screening subsystem block.

Along one path, the analyses of the future provide the identification of commodities and services which will become obsolete and a timetable for obsolescence. Along the other path, there is an identification of new commodity and service potentialities as coupled with an identification of the technology requirements imposed by these opportunities. The output of the two paths taken together is simply analysis, and this analysis must be tested and evaluated in terms of potential impacts upon the company's current commodities and services—as well as upon its established future planning.

Product Mix Screening

The subsystem process represented by product mix screening is reiterative and could as easily be called product substitution analysis. In the first step of the subsystem's reiterative analysis, the potential commodities and services of the company are compared with the current commodities and services of the firm and those of the world at large. The singular purpose of this analysis is to establish some measure of how the real world of market will be affected by the potential commodities and services if their full potential is realized and they achieve the public acceptance envisioned by future forecasts. The analysis proceeds by considering the fate of current commodities and services if these are continued by the firm with only normal improvements added to further development of the current market, by considering the effects of a potential commodity or service which offers a direct or indirect substitution for the firm's current commodities and services, or by considering market response if the potential new commodity or service offers no direct or indirect substitution threat.

It must be recognized that any new commodity or service may pose a threat to a firm's current offerings simply because it will draw on the source of money which supports the firm's current commodities and services. For example, a home hair-setting machine for women will have to be purchased from the same source funds (personal disposable income) as an electric razor for men.

In the next step in product mix screening, there must be a consideration and evaluation of the key technologies inherent in both the anticipated improvement of current commodities and services and the research and development required to bring these new commodities and services to market. With the key technologies thus defined, an evaluation must be conducted to identify the technological advances (or breakthroughs) in the state of the art which must be realized before the new commodities and services or improved old ones can be realized as marketable fact. These technological advances are then further analyzed to determine the controlling factors or schedule mileposts in research and development efforts.

The actual analysis involves the corporation's potential reaction to the future commodity and service situation. To accomplish the analysis, it is necessary that the corporation fully understand its current technological posture. It must recognize also that this posture has to be balanced or weighed against future technical requirements.

The current technological posture is determined by current facilities for research, development, and production; by the available personnel in these segments of the firm, as well as their current skills; and by the technical level of complexity within current projects in these areas of research, development, and production. In addition to the current technological posture, the current financial posture of the firm is significant as input to the product mix screening. The final input to the screening process is direction from the office of the chief executive. This will include, but need not be limited to, the stated objectives of the firm.

The managers charged with product planning are continually faced with four basic courses of action. Predicated on an analysis of a commodity or service in terms of its life cycle and its return on investment, both past and future, a proper decision to terminate the commodity or service might be made. On the other hand, a proper decision may be to provide either an improvement or an enlargement of a current commodity or service.

For example, a company may be manufacturing a basic microcircuit amplifier. A product improvement through research and development might reduce the circuit's cost, complexity, or lack of reliability, thus making it more competitive in the market. Enlargement would occur with a decision to advance from the basic amplifier circuit to a complete radio receiver set. In the latter situation, the company would be freed from the competitive pressures of component purchasing by the normal users (that is, the regular manufacturers of radios and instrumentation) of the amplifier circuit, but competition would be renewed at a new level in a different market. Beyond the considerations of the current commodity and service mix and offerings, the planning managers must consider the possibilities of introducing totally new commodities and services.

The product mix screening process can be established as a mathematical model and can be subjected to a computer program. In a large firm with a complex mix of commodities or services having a high order of technical sophistication, this is the most practical approach to the analysis within the reiterative loop.

The loop is initiated by considering a potential mix of commodities and services weighing the four basic courses of action outlined earlier. Utilizing the inputs to the process, an investment analysis, a technology analysis, and a profitability analysis are conducted. The investment analysis considers all the resources (personnel, facilities, and cash flow) required to fulfill the commodity or service objectives of the test product mix in terms of both current availability and necessary acquisition. The technology analysis establishes the requirements for resource disposal, reallocation, and new acquisition to fit the projected needs of the mix. Finally, a profitability prediction analysis is drawn from the proposed mix and is made available for the planners' consideration.

After a series of reiterations around the loop, a pattern of profitability will emerge and the most profitable mix will be evident. If this mix coincides with the goals and objectives of the corporation, it should be recommended to the chief executive. On the other hand, if the mix is not in agreement with the established company mission and objectives, the planners need to move back in the order of profitability to the maximization within the limits.

Implementation of the Mix Recommendation

The planners present the results of the product mix screening as firm recommendations relative to current and proposed commodities and services. In general, these recommendations should be accompanied by the basis for the decision. Within the office of the chief executive, the recommendation should be reviewed and either accepted or rejected. If the recommendation is rejected, the planners must initiate the product mix screening process anew, but hopefully with top management counsel and guidance.

With approval of the planners' recommendation for the mix, the action of the company is established as a commitment. Inherent in the commitment is a schedule for the change from the current mix to the future mix. At this point, the detailed planning of all segments of the corporation should be geared to fulfill the mix commitment according to the preplanned schedule. Certainly, the research and development segments must become an integral part of the effort. The product mix commitment becomes the basic authority for writing the research and development programs. It also forms the justification for the financial investment in the required research and development. Further, all managers having a control responsibility over research and development now have the means for evaluating and controlling such efforts. The real test for any research and development effort then is this: How does the effort contribute to the commitment plan?

As the plan is carried out there is a change in the financial condition of the company, and this is reflected in the ongoing financial analysis. There are also changes in the facilities for research and development as well as production, changes in personnel and personnel skills, and changes in programs at all stages of the life cycle. Thus the total systems loop is closed and planning reevaluation becomes necessary.

10

Technological Forecasting

TECHNOLOGICAL forecasting has been defined by one of its most illustrious proponents as "the probabilistic assessment, on a relatively high confidence level, of future technology transfer." [1]

In 1969, not 10 years after technological forecasting had become recognized as a potential management discipline, it had been characterized as equivalent in development to economic forecasting some 20 years earlier; and it might be prudent to add that the need for technological forecasting today is substantially greater than the need for economic forecasting when it was at the same stage of development.

Few people will deny that the pace of industry today is much faster than it was after World War II and substantially faster than the pace after World War I. Earlier discussions considered the concept of the product life cycle and noted that, although the time span within this cycle for research and development has shown no tendency to become shorter, the productive life of the resultant product is materially reduced. This shortening of the productive life is a direct result of the exponential expansion of technological

[1] Erich Jantsch, *Technological Forecasting in Perspective* (Washington, D.C.: Organization for Economic Cooperation and Development, 1967).

knowledge. Many companies have discovered that new technologies prove more profitable when applied to totally new products rather than to marginal improvement of products already in a competitive market.

If technological innovation is a worthwhile objective, can a company ever expect to be a leader in all technological areas of real or potential interest? While some companies tend toward such a goal, very few offer any evidences of consistent success. Writing in the *Quarterly Journal of Economics*,[2] Edwin Mansfield concluded from a study of industry that the leaders in one innovation are often the followers in another, especially if there are large time lags between two innovations in the same industry.

Technological Forecasting—Art or Science?

Many companies, both large and small, now engage in some form of technological forecasting. Any question as to whether technological forecasting, wherever it is practiced, is art or science must be answered firmly as art and not science. Erich Jantsch has studied the problems and the art of technological forecasting as it is practiced in all the industrial countries of the western world, identifying more than a hundred examples of forecasting techniques already used or currently being tried. In the United States, a variety of techniques or combinations of techniques are used by various government agencies and many industrial firms. Yet not all efforts approach a truly analytical basis. In some companies, technological forecasting is like a game of "twenty questions" with the objective of "divining" a new technology on which a new product or industry can be founded ahead of all potential competitors. If that were all that technological forecasting had to offer, it would not be worth the cost. Carried to its fullest expression, technological forecasting charts the total course of corporate action in terms of a meaningful time schedule providing progress mileposts for evaluation.

While technological forecasting is still an art, it enjoys an advantage over the earlier day of economic forecasting, for technological forecasting's major advocates and developers fully recognize

[2] "The Speed of Response of Firms to New Techniques" (May 1963).

the importance of the related factors in the "future equation." These factors, which were discussed in an earlier chapter, are the sociological, economic, and geopolitical, and they interact with technology and each other to induce interactive changes. Without due consideration of these interactions, technological forecasting becomes meaningless.

Yet there are evidences of technological forecasting's rapid development toward a more scientific plane. The publication of *Technological Forecasting for Industry and Government* [3] is indicative of this movement. In the quarterlies *Futures* [4] and *Technological Forecasting*,[5] technological forecasters may have the first journals in which to report new advances in techniques and explore the needs of industries. Many business and technical journals and publications have carried articles on technological forecasting, and at least one society has been formed to consider the future. (The World Future Society, Washington, D.C. 20036.)

However, no organization or individual has done more to solidify thinking relative to this field than has the Industrial Management Center, Inc. (2108 Trail of the Madrones, Austin, Texas 78746) and its president, James R. Bright. Through both introductory and advanced seminars, the Industrial Management Center has spurred the development of technological forecasting by promoting a frank and open exchange of methodology and nonproprietary forecasting results. The free exchange approaches that of the scientific community.

Interaction in Technological Forecasting

The fact that the successful introduction of a new product bearing a new technology or a technological breakthrough depends on three basic considerations is not always understood. In the first place, the state of the art in the specific technology must be proved by a practical reduction to practice. Second, the product and its application must be acceptable to the potential purchaser in terms of the moral, ethical, and social conscience at the time of marketing. Third,

---

[3] James R. Bright, ed. (Englewood Cliffs, N.J.: Prentice-Hall, Inc., 1968).
[4] Surrey, England, Iliffe Science and Technology Publications Ltd. Published in cooperation with The Institute for the Future, U.S.A.
[5] New York: American Elsevier Publishing Co., Inc.

in terms of consumer desire the product must be able to compete successfully with other products and services making demands on the potential purchaser's available funds. Failure to evaluate any of these three aspects may result in a lack of product success which could have been avoided. Thus properly performed technological forecasting provides a dynamic interpretation of basic future needs as well as the forces of sociological, economic, and political motivation supplementing the purely technological needs and forces. However, technological forecasting is not immune to the affliction suffered by all other forecasting.

Any forecasting must be accomplished within and upon a framework of history—as well as current activity. Yet the rightness or wrongness of a forecast will be determined by the people of the future, not by those of the present or the past. Furthermore, having shown what the future may potentially bring, people can in the interim take whatever action is necessary to alter the future. This fact demonstrates the value of forecasting while pinpointing the inherent danger in accepting forecasts as a finality of fact. This viewpoint relative to technological forecasting may be stated in another way.

When properly performed, a technological forecast is a dynamic interpretation of future events. It is dynamic because it is a mere prediction, made at a single point in time, of events which have no certainty of occurrence. With a change in time, the prediction may have to be altered materially or only insignificantly as a result of the interaction of forces from the sociological, economic, or geo-political spheres.

An Example of Interaction with Technology

As an example of the basics of technological forecasting, consider the case of the cosmetics industry. This industry has had a phenomenal growth and is currently growing at double the rate of the gross national product and disposable income in the United States. At the time of World War II, the growth of the industry seemed limited to (1) greater expenditures by women for facial makeup; (2) acceptance of facial makeup by a greater percentage of women; and (3) the fundamental increase in the female population. "Nice" girls and "respectable" women under 40 did not dye or tint their hair, and body odor was for the most part an unrecognized problem. In the 1960's, a totally new cosmetics and toiletries demand developed—a male-centered demand. Today, men's cosmetics, even though most are merely women's products relabeled, account for roughly 14 percent of all cosmetics sales!

Since World War II, society as a whole has become substantially more permissive and affluent. This sociological and economic change is reflected not only in cosmetics for men but in a greater acceptance of public nudity, even in the relaxation of laws against nudity. Will there be a reversal of this trend? If so, how deeply will it be felt? If there is no significant reversal, in the future there should be a stronger demand for body cosmetics (such as the Love product line which first appeared in 1968). On this point, one forecast predicts that by 1980 the body cosmetics market will equal one-half the value of today's total cosmetics market. Now consider the fact that, except for the aerosol dispenser, both men's cosmetics and body cosmetics technology fully existed before World War II. However, successful products are dependent upon more than available and proven technology even though no product is possible if the technology is not available.

Management's Role in Forecasting

To realize the benefits of a successful forecast, top managers must be convinced of the benefits of long-range forecasting. The responsibility for forecasting belongs to these top managers, and they must give the direction essential to its conduct. The finest staff in the country cannot develop an effective long-range forecast unless the top managers believe in the merits of the effort and accept the responsibility for looking ahead to shape the company's destiny. But who should participate in forecasting? It is essential that key personnel at the intermediate level and executives at the control level participate in the process to some meaningful degree. The ideal participation would also include representatives from top management.

One common forecasting methodology error is to permit the effort to become an informal activity. Generally, the informal activity is separated from communication with the top elements of the company most affected by the results of the analysis. Any forecast separated from corporate realities is an exercise in futility. Insofar as possible, all factors which bear directly on the company's future should be identified and made a part of the forecasting effort. Only in this way will the final forecast reflect the impacts to be anticipated relative to future plans and objectives.

After all, the functions of management and of managers are operation, command, and control. No matter how cleverly written, documents cannot substitute for management. There must be inherent flexibility in a long-range plan; otherwise, management would be unable to take timely action on favorable developments. A rigid program based upon a forecast which does not acknowledge the possibility of prediction error serves only to frustrate and can easily lead to operational disaster. Viewed in this light, forecasting must occur as a staff function near the top of the organization reflecting the thinking and approaches to action which characterize that level of management.

Consensus Forecasting

One of the more popular ways of making a technological forecast is to gather a group of "experts" in a wide range of disciplines and have them make prognostications, playing one event against another until a pattern emerges from the welter of events which seem most likely. Such "fun" occurrences even make the bookstands for the edification of the general public.[6] However, all too frequently the resultant forecast ends on a too-far-out note that has little relevance to the industry manager faced with today's planning problems. Or, more likely, the forecast reflects the opinions and particular insight of the most domineering members of the forecasting group.

The fallacies which can result from the opinions of experts are nowhere better illustrated than in the examples provided to Congress by the Legislative Reference Service of the Library of Congress in April 1967. Here are some of the expert opinions that have been handed down at various times in history:

---

[6] A prize example of this type of book is *Toward the Year 2018* (Cowles Education Corp., 1968).

A committee, organized in 1486 at the command of King Ferdinand and Queen Isabella of Spain and headed by Fray Hernando de Talavera to study Columbus's plans to sail west to find a shorter route to the Indies, concluded in its report of 1490 that a voyage such as Columbus contemplated was impossible because "(1) A voyage to Asia would require three years. (2) The Western Ocean is infinite and perhaps unnavigable. (3) If he reached the Antipodes [the land on the other side of the globe from Europe] he could not get back. (4) There are no antipodes because the greater part of the globe is covered with water, and because Saint Augustine says so. . . . (5) Of the five zones, only three are habitable. (6) So many centuries after Creation, it is unlikely that anyone could find hitherto unknown lands of any value."

In 1837 Sir William Symonds, the surveyor of the British Navy, stated: ". . . even if the propeller had the power of propelling a vessel, it would be found altogether useless in practice, because the power being applied in the stern, it would be absolutely impossible to make the vessel steer."

Although automobiles were already challenging the horse in 1902, *Harper's Weekly* commented: "The actual building of roads devoted to motor cars is not for the near future, in spite of many rumors to that effect."

When Henry Ford wrote his autobiography, he reported that the Edison Company had offered him "the general superintendency of the company but only on the condition that [he] give up [his] gas engine and devote [himself] to something really useful."

Serving in an advisory capacity to the President of the United States, Dr. Vannevar Bush told Harry Truman in the spring of 1945: "The bomb will never go off, and I speak as an expert in explosives."

Delphi Technique in Forecasting

The efforts to circumvent the difficulties and restrictions of the expert opinion or the consensus approach resulted in the development of the Delphi concept of technological forecasting.

The Delphi forecasting technique derives its name from the

famous oracle at Delphi in ancient Greece. According to legend, an individual with a question or a problem would journey to the temple at Delphi and ask the oracle to provide an answer. While the oracle seemed to go into a hypnotic trance, the priests assembled some distance away and used argumentative reasoning to select an appropriate answer. The answer was passed to the oracle, who couched the reply in mumbo-jumbo. Considering that the oracle achieved widespread fame and continued in business for a considerable time, the technique must have been reasonably successful.

The Delphi technique as applied to technological forecasting was developed at the RAND Corporation and is generally credited to Olaf Helmer and T. J. Gordan. In this concept, a panel of technology experts is selected by invitation. The members of the panel are not informed of the names of their fellow panelists, and the entire forecasting procedure is conducted at arm's length. This approach is considered best because it eliminates the committee decision. Members of the panel are initially queried by letter and asked to name technological breakthroughs or advances which appear both urgently needed and realizable within the period of forecast interest. These event statements are then gathered into a questionnaire consisting of the statements and a date block for each. The panel is again approached by letter and asked to decide the year of most probable attainment of the event. On return, the dates presented for each statement are analyzed to establish the median date and the middle 50 percent of the estimates (25 percent on either side of the median). The results of this analysis are put into a second questionnaire and sent to the panelists with a request either to alter their original estimates so as to achieve consensus or near consensus or to state their arguments for choosing a particular date beyond the middle 50 percent. The results of this second questionnaire are gathered and analyzed as before. A third questionnaire is prepared to include the panelists' arguments for a date far removed from the median. The third questionnaire and a similar fourth one are returned to the panelists; with each goes a request to reconsider the event statements and to provide a date estimate more in line with the consensus.

Theoretically, this RAND approach reduces the influence of such psychological factors as persuasion and unwillingness to abandon publicly expressed opinions, as well as the bandwagon effect of a majority opinion.

Objection to the Delphi Technique

As was said earlier, one of the prime objectives of any technological forecasting effort should be the involvement of key management personnel. The Delphi method seems to offer a possibility for companywide involvement, but there are questions, if not reservations, about the efficacy of standard Delphi results. Specifically, these doubts are centered on the following points:

1. While the Delphi method is supposed to eliminate the bandwagon effect, can any method which restricts the scope of answers provide the objectivity necessary to prevent some degree of bandwagon effect? For example, although the approach does replace direct debate with a carefully designed program of sequential questionnaires taken at arm's length, the panelists are told that *never* is an acceptable answer, yet the only answer results reported to them are the dates of the middle 50 percent of answers and the median date. Therefore, there must be a psychological pressure on the panelists to conform, for who wants to be the only one to state categorically that an event will never occur?
2. Since the future state of the art in technology is joined by the interactions of developments and changes in the economic, sociological, and geopolitical spheres, can a purely scientific and technical panel make objective predictions?
3. A date on which a future event may occur is meaningless if there is no measure of the prediction reliability of the event's actually occurring—and no measure of such reliability is possible with the standard Delphi methodology.
4. The standard Delphi results provide no means of relating the results which were forecast to the long-range planning of a company or industry.

A Modified Delphi Technique

What follows is a modified methodology to counter these objections. Panelists should be drawn from the technical and administra-

tive personnel of upper management and from the project and product levels. The number of panelists should be greater than 25 but
smaller than 100. A total of 50 panelists seems a number which is
easily managed during the reiterative process.

In the first questionnaire, each panelist should be asked to list
potential technological changes which will affect his job and his
company. They should also be asked to say what impact these events
will have on the company. The results of this first questionnaire
should be compiled to prepare a second questionnaire. As in the
standard Delphi methodology, there should be no identification of
the panelists, and everything should be handled at arm's length
through the mail.

The second questionnaire should list each of the event statements of the first questionnaire. In some cases, these statements
may have to be edited to conform to the basic Delphi form or to
eliminate ambiguities in the wording. The typical form for statements would be as follows:

> Economically useful desalination of seawater will be possible by
> the year _____.
>
> Development of new synthetic materials suitable for the construc-
> tion of high-rise buildings will have been completed by the
> year _____.
>
> Implanted artificial organs of plastic and electromechanical com-
> ponents will have replaced human organ transplants by the
> year _____.
>
> Central data-storage facilities with wide access for general or
> specialized information retrieval will have been introduced for
> the United States by the year _____.
>
> Of the new cars sold in the United States, 25 percent will have
> other than internal combustion engine power by the year _____.

As noted, each event statement provides a space for the panelist
to enter a date estimate. Instructions accompanying the second
questionnaire should state that *never* is an acceptable answer.

When the second questionnaire is returned by the panelists,
a third questionnaire should be prepared. Each event statement
should be repeated without changing the wording. In addition, a

median date, a range of years in the middle quartile (taken 12.5 percent either side of the median), the date answer extremes, and the percentage of *never* replies expressed relative to all replies should be stated for each event. Median dates and the middle quartile range should be determined only from the positive date answers. This is to say that the *never* answers are excluded from the positive count. Instructions sent with the third questionnaire should request each panelist to reconsider his date estimates and provide an argument for any date before or after the middle quartile range.

With receipt of the third questionnaire from the panelists, things begin to get more complicated. All arguments to support specific dates for each event are added to the fourth questionnaire. Regardless of how lively or salty the arguments may be, in the interests of objectivity the arguments should be presented without editing or rewriting. Exhibit 18 presents a typical event statement with supporting arguments. A fifth questionnaire provides panelists an opportunity to present arguments counter to those of the other panelists. Note that the arguments are given in a descending date order both as an evaluation aid and as a means of preventing any hint of encouraging the choice of a specific date by the order of arrangement.

As the iteration process proceeds, it will be seen that some of the statements will have an increase in the percentage of *never* answers, while the percentage of *never* answers for other event statements will be reduced. It will also be noted that the range of the middle quartile years will narrow materially. In this movement, there will be far less evidence of the bandwagon effect than is characteristic of the standard Delphi methodology.

Confidence Factor

Given these kinds of results, not all the objections voiced about the Delphi methodology will yet have been overcome. A Delphi study is no more valuable than the analysis of the resultant data. Conventional Delphi results provide little opportunity for meaningful analysis beyond that of the probable date of event occurrence. With a conventional method of displaying results, it must be assumed that the events of the forecast will in fact occur. But not

Exhibit 18

EVENT STATEMENT

STATEMENT: A majority of new home construction will include internal power (that is, fuel cells, solar cells, etc.) by the year _____.

ARGUMENTS PREVIOUSLY OFFERED: (Never) Power supplied from nuclear plants will be too economical. (Never) It will not be economically feasible to produce a unit of this type and be in competition with a central powerplant. (Never) Only probable possibility is a safe, reliable, compact, cheap nuclear powerplant. Safe, reliable, and compact it may be, but cheap it won't be. (2010) Community power sources will be more economical and cheaper to the user until a meaningful breakthrough is made. (2006) I agree that the only possibility is a reliable nuclear power unit in the home. This can't occur before the year 2000. Also consider the efficiency and cheapness of centrally generated and distributed power that is being used now. (2000) Assuming that this question refers only to the USA. (2000) If internal power assumes no distribution lines of any kind. (1990) Experiments have been made on the concept of this project for over seven years. Most of the gross concept has been worked out; only the details remain for solution. (1990) I think the nonthinkers who say "never" are ridiculous, for it is just a matter of time and money. Drawing power from long distance with lines running everywhere is *not* in the future with our rapidly growing power needs. (1975) The American Gas Association has conducted successful experiments with natural gas fuel cells and contends that they will be competitive with conventionally generated and distributed electricity by 1970 or 1971. See *Science News* November 1968.

Median: 1998   Inner quartile: 1995-2000   Extremes: 1975 & 2010   % Nevers: 9.1   Your new estimate: [   ]

Your arguments: _____

This is a typical event statement taken from the third iteration of a Delphi conducted in accordance with the modified methodology of the text. Note that the date arguments are presented in descending order from never to the most recent. There has been no editing of any arguments and the panelists are taking full advantage of the cloak of anonymity granted them by this forecasting methodology.

everything that man can conceive of happening in the future will occur. Therefore, there must be room left for doubt as to the probability of occurrence of any conceived event. In the modified method described here, the stress upon the possibility that an event will never occur provides an additional measure for analysis. It provides a means for assessing the confidence of probability of occurrence. Expressed as a confidence factor, this probability of event occurrence is merely the percentage of *never* answers as subtracted from 100 percent. Since no single event can be forecast with complete certainty, a prudent course of action dictates reducing all 100 percent confidence factors by one percentage point.

Establishing Event Priority

Finally, the real test of value of a technological forecast is the usefulness of the derived data for long-range planning. Not all event statements are of equal importance, either within a single company or in toto. However, given a confidence factor and a median date for any event statement, it is possible to place that event in a priority spectrum. Priority values might range downward in importance from I through IV.

In determination of priority, the following criteria have been used for each forecast event in a modified Delphi forecast:

- *Priority I:* Any event statement requiring industrial entry within the next five years for which there is a confidence factor of 95 percent or greater.
- *Priority II:* Any event statement requiring industrial entry within the next five years for which there is a confidence factor of 85 through 94.9 percent; or any event statement requiring industrial entry within the next ten years for which there is a confidence factor of 95 percent or greater.
- *Priority III:* Any event statement requiring industrial entry within the next five years for which there is a confidence factor of 75 through 84.9 percent; or any event statement requiring industrial entry within the next ten years for which there is a confidence factor of 85 through 94.5 percent.
- *Priority IV:* All other event statements.

Clearly, determination of priority is predicated on the required date of industrial entry. This may be the date of the event statement of the forecast, but more likely it will be a significantly earlier date. To provide meaning to the analysis of data, product life cycles must be considered. The ratios of values and the timespan in each phase of the cycle may differ according to the product involved, but the form of the cycle will remain essentially unchanged.

Establishing the Date of Entry

In an example of the interaction of the life cycle and the priority as derived from the modified Delphi methodology, consider a prediction such as this: "Integrated microcircuitry will constitute the major sales volume in the hi-fi home entertainment field by the year 1973." If a firm waits until 1973 to begin preparing to compete in this field, that firm should expect to find itself entering the competition on the declining side of the life cycle. In such a situation, the firm has lost its best opportunity to compete with a product using integrated microcircuitry.

The history of electronic products introduction suggests that the product introduction and market growth phases of the life cycle (see Chapter 2) are probably between five and eight years. Thus a firm in the hi-fi home entertainment field should subtract eight years from the Delphi forecast date of 1973 to establish the year in which it should have begun planning for the introduction of microcircuitry into its product line; in other words, the firm should have made its technical plans not later than 1965. Subtracting five years from the 1973 date would establish a product introduction date of 1968. Prior to 1969, the firm should have completed its initial product designs, made experimental models, conducted testing, made engineering refinements, planned the production phase (including whatever plant conversion is necessary), planned the marketing program, and, most important, planned the financial program.

A significant part of the planning must be directed to the plant and equipment. Before production of an integrated microcircuitry hi-fi home entertainment system can actually begin, new equipment for production has to be purchased. The purchase order must provide for the appropriate delivery lead time to permit manufacture to the buyer's specifications. On arrival at the plant, the equipment has to be installed according to the planned production layout. Then, before production can begin, personnel must be trained in the operation of the equipment. Finally, when production is initiated, allowances must be made for product rejection owing to worker inexperience, as well as for production equipment debugging. Obviously, the more complicated the conversion process, the longer this phase of the life cycle will be.

With such restrictions facing the introduction of full production, a firm expecting to take advantage of the 1973 date derived from the technological forecast should already be moving decisively toward integrated microcircuitry for its line of hi-fi home entertainment equipment. In this particular example, the industrial entry date—the date when "tin is bent" in design and an engineering commitment is made to the event—should have been 1968, or five years prior to the date of the technological forecast giving the peak point on the revenue curve of the life cycle. The industrial entry date for any other Delphi technological forecast event can be logically determined in this manner.

Reliability of Delphi Forecasts

In the cooperative evaluation of a modified Delphi just described 50 key technical and administrative people in management positions in ten diverse-industry companies took part. At the same time Dr. Vincent S. Haneman, associate dean of engineering at Oklahoma State University, conducted an identically modified Delphi study using the same event statements. The OSU participants included 21 faculty members of the architectural, chemical engineering, civil engineering, electrical engineering, industrial engineering, mechanical-aeronautical engineering, and general engineering departments, as well as the office of engineering research and the dean's office.

Comparatively, in only nine of the event statements does the confidence factor as expressed by the industry group fall below that of the university group. In thirty of the event statements, the comparative confidence factors are 5 percentage points apart. Only five confidence factors have a spread of 10 to 15 percentage points;

six have a spread of 15 to 20 percentage points; and the spread for four is greater than 20 percentage points. The lower confidence factors of the university group may be a reflection of what should be anticipated with a totally scientific and technical group. However, this is far too limited a sample to draw such a conclusion.

Variances between the two groups were derived and compared to determine the forecast median dates. Of the 57 event statements, two events had to be discounted on a basis of possible interpretive misunderstanding. In both cases, the arguments presented in each of the two groups clearly indicated that two different interpretations could be placed on the event statements. A reconsideration of the event statements clearly revealed their ambiguity. A standard deviation was derived from the variance of dates for various combinations of the other 55 events.

It is noteworthy that for 55 events, the standard deviation was 3.68 years. For those events predicted for 1990 or earlier (a total of 46) the standard deviation was 3.54 years. Of the 36 events predicted for 1985 or earlier, the standard deviation was 2.64 years. This is to say that 68 percent of the representative, comparative forecast median dates are included within the span of two standard deviations. If the span of years is increased to four standard deviations, then 95 percent of all the representative, comparative dates will be included. This dual group comparative effort seemingly proves that a Delphi panel does not have to be composed exclusively of scientific and technical personnel. It also means that the modified Delphi can be used to involve the key management personnel in a forecasting effort without compromising the forecast data.

Using the Delphi Results as a General Guide

Beyond the use of specific Delphi forecast-generated dates and appropriate life cycles to establish specific product or service planning, these data can be used as a general guide to both planners and managers by conversion of the data into scenarios. The technological forecaster who would write scenarios needs a very large body of data. In general, most technological forecasters willingly exchange nonproprietary forecast data derived from Delphi studies and other consensus efforts.

The technological forecaster should begin his scenario effort by comparative analysis of all similar statements to establish firm predictions for specific technological events. Second, these predictions should be chronologically compared to insure that there is a proper time sequence. For example, if one event statement predicts that 25 percent of all new cars will be equipped with non-internal-combustion engine power by 1975 and a second predicts that the first practical non-internal-combustion engine for automobiles will be ready for production in 1977, there is a chronological inconsistency which must be resolved. If a third event statement exists which says that a low-cost, highly reliable, long-life, and high power-density fuel cell will be commercially available in 1972, the technological forecaster might disregard the prediction relative to the development completion date for a non-internal-combustion engine insofar as it reflects on the sale of cars powered with these engines in 1975. Seemingly, the fuel cell could provide the power system to meet the earlier requirement, and the development anticipated in 1977 might be the logical next step in automotive power.

Scenarios are generally written for a single year and describe the expected state of the art in that year for specific areas of business interest. For example, a scenario for food appears in Appendix D. Others have been written from Delphi data to cover the broad areas of business methods and industrial processes, communications and electronics, education and educational systems, health and medical technology, housing and construction, power generation and distribution, recreation and entertainment, and transportation, with the individual scenarios written for the single years 1975 and 1980. These scenarios have provided planning guides to planners during the preparation of their five- and ten-year technical plans.

Other Forecasting Methods

This chapter on technological forecasting has concentrated on the Delphi method and how its data can be derived and used in the planning process. As stated at the beginning of the chapter, at least 100 different techniques are currently being used in industry and government. There is no right or wrong technique, only a technique which is most applicable in a specific situation. Other techniques which the reader should consider include, but are not limited to, the following: technological monitoring as originated by James R. Bright, Ralph C. Lenz, Jr.'s trend extrapolation technique, envelope curve forecasting of Robert U. Ayres, the PROBE technique of Harper Q. North and Don Pyke, and the relevance techniques of Arthur Lein, William Swager, and Maurice E. Esch.[7]

[7] Technological monitoring is described in a forthcoming book of Professor Bright. This exciting new technique offers the potential of measuring the pace of change toward a specific prediction. The techniques of trend extrapolation, envelope curves, and PROBE are presented in the Prentice-Hall book, *Technological Forecasting for Government and Industry*. Relevance techniques are discussed in the *AMA Management Bulletin 115, Technological Forecasting: Tools, Techniques, Applications*. Additional references are to be found in the Bibliography.

11

The Marketing Problem

W_{HEN} the suggestion is made that a research organization must have sales and marketing ability, many eyebrows are raised not only inside but outside the research organization. Yet the research organization that fails to recognize the need for sales and marketing may survive but has little probability of success. If a research organization is kept going but is not encouraged to sell itself to the product divisions of the company, managers will look on the research organization as a mere façade whose function is to give lip service to the needs of technological growth.

Our concern here is with the R&D marketing problem from three aspects: first, the sale of research efforts within the company; second, internal research and development (IR&D) as a government-industry shared expense; third, the potential contribution of research and development to the total corporate marketing effort.

Internal Sales

Those assigned the task of production or even of product development management seldom understand the problems of research. Yet past research forms the very foundation for their efforts of the present. In a very real sense, this lack of understanding is a failure in communication. Many problems arise in development and production which are solvable through a major effort but which would readily yield to a much smaller effort within the research organization. Such problems occur because appropriate solutions are not to be found in the cookbooks of engineering. Research personnel are trained to break a problem down to its fundamentals and then take a scientific and rational approach toward a workable solution. Hence, they have an ability to reach a solution to many seemingly complex problems using less effort than those without the same training and background.

It is human nature for any individual to resist exposing his inability to solve a problem which might be construed as a natural part of the job. However, if communication and understanding are developed between the research organization and the other components of the company, a oneness of purpose can result.

Marketing by the research organization of its capabilities and of its desire and readiness to be part of the larger corporate picture is essential, for it will never come from the other direction. Here, the term "marketing" is used in a very loose sense. Actually low-key salesmanship is really what is implied. Certainly a formal sales organization within research is not necessary to accomplish this purpose. What is necessary is a demonstration of capability and a sincere interest in the day-to-day problems of the other organizations within the company. This interest must be shown by the managers of the research organization and is increased in effectiveness when the leading scientists of the research organization also come forward to express their interest.

Sales of this nature become the performance of a service to the other organizations—a service designed and offered to reduce their costs and improve their profits. If the research organization is to remain a separate profit center, however, the organization receiving research aid should be charged or debited with the cost of the research effort, and the service costs should be credited to the research organization as a form of income. The real question remains: How can this be effectively accomplished?

When a problem arises in some other segment of the company, generally a key individual is directly concerned with the solution.

The effort toward the required solution should not be completely removed from the concerned individual. To do so would breed distrust—if not positive rejection—of the ultimate solution made in research. Therefore, why not bring the concerned individual into the research organization until the solution is determined? He can participate in the solution effort and thereby not only obtain an understanding of how the research organization functions but also establish comradeship with the scientists and other members of the research organization. When a firm basis for mutual trust and understanding exists between the personnel of a research division and the rest of the company, there will be fewer transition problems as product or service concepts pass from research to development to production or application. (For a more complete discussion of the co-op effort, see Chapter 7.)

Research Contract Support

A research organization might consider enriching itself by soliciting outside research contracts from customers in government or industry. In such a situation, the research organization must expect to conduct proposal efforts to obtain the external contract business.

In its solicitation of outside contracts, the research organization must show a theoretical understanding of the problems involved in the proposed effort, and it must present relevant data developed internally by the scientific staff to show capability. Data taken from the work of others may be identified as such by the customer, and its identification on that basis can be detrimental.

If the research organization does seek external contracts, it must either perform a percentage of its total technological effort in house in direct anticipation of further program solicitation or expand facilities and personnel continually, building upon knowledge already developed in prior contractual efforts.

Unlimited expansion of a research organization, however, is irreconcilable with proper management of research and development to meet corporate goals—unless, of course, the corporate goal is to become a research-for-profit company with little or no production capability. The research organization must serve the corporation in the capacity of an adjunct organization rather than as a directive force. At some point, a balance between the total research efforts (both internal and external) must be achieved relative to the total corporate effort. Further or more rapid expansion of the research organization and efforts is economically impractical and unsound management practice.

Should one of the objectives of a research organization be to obtain external contracts, these contracts should be solicited to initiate and establish (insofar as possible) proprietary positions in commodity and service programs of the customers. Research managers must recognize that in this situation the organization's scientific and technical personnel whose services are offered to the customer as investigators or team support members must be scientifically noncontroversial. Still, the individual scientific and technical talent must be acknowledged or acknowledgeable on the basis of education and prior experience (expressed in terms of projects, publications, and presentations) as fully competent to perform the proposed effort.

One significant purpose for seeking external contracts is sometimes overlooked: penetration of new technology. External research contracts provide a means for penetrating new technological concepts which otherwise would not be open to the research organization and the company of which it is a part. For example, the government enters many new technologies to meet the requirements of future military threats, space exploration, and the social community. The military and some space exploration efforts are normally cloaked in secrecy. Knowledge of, as well as participation in, these efforts is limited to companies contracting with the government to perform the specific services needed. These efforts, when they are of a research nature, can be the opening wedge into major programs of future importance to the company's profit picture.

Internal Research and Development

For those companies which normally do a significant share of their total business with the government, IR&D is an important source of future business. Independent research and development can be conducted by these companies with special government sanction and support. It is not, however, government sponsored by any contract, grant, or other arrangement. It is scientific and technical activity sponsored by the company on its own initiative to meet the company's best estimate of the government's future technological needs. It should be viewed as a management tool for improving the company's future capacity to perform in the marketplace where advanced technology controls sales.

IR&D provides a company with the means for achieving a competitive position in new areas of technology related to the company's normal line of business. It also provides the fundamental knowledge to apply technological innovation to both current and future products of the firm. Given this knowledge, the company is in a better position to assume the risks associated with new technologies and remain competitive.

Prior to World War I, the government and its military establishment relied upon a government in-house arsenal system to conduct the research and development required to support weapons advances and to provide the production of weapons. While the mobilization of industry to provide the sinews of war for World War I proved the ineffectiveness of the military arsenal concept, the United States returned to this concept in the 1920's forsaking the potential of industry. World War II was rapidly approaching before the government again turned to industry to develop new weapons and produce them. Certainly, the aviation industry's development and the developing need for more sophisticated aircraft proved the ultimate value of private industry in meeting military needs. Yet, even into World War II, the military arsenal system as represented by the Naval Aircraft Factory in Philadelphia was attempting to produce aircraft to meet the needs of the navy. Generally speaking, the results of this effort are not fondly remembered by those who flew in the resulting product.

(In shipbuilding and many other facets of naval needs, the U.S. Navy has never abandoned its arsenal concept. Today there are evidences in the latest reorganization of the navy that there will be a strong return to this outmoded approach to weapon development and production. Similarly, the army's continued emphasis on the establishment of larger and more sophisticated research and development centers within arsenals demonstrates a positive thrust toward the arsenal concept. Although the air force lacks the history of the other two services, it is also demonstrating a strong move toward in-house research, development, and even production in what amounts to an arsenal syndrome. Added to these clues to future thinking must be the utterances of key personnel in the Nixon administration. In talks before the National Security Industrial Association and similar forums, these people have warned industry that the military will be drawing more and more of its research and development into the arsenals and spending less and less with industry. Anyone wishing to explore the outlook for the future should look to the history of the past, as presented most effectively in Nevil Shute's *Slide Rule: The Autobiography of an Engineer*. Although best known for his fiction [such as *On the Beach*], Mr. Shute was an excellent aeronautical engineer, whose personal experiences with the arsenal mentality in England prior to World War II make fascinating reading.)

If the potential of industry is to be realized in the support of military and social needs, the government must frame its policies relative to industry so as to derive maximum benefit. Only by encouraging and fostering IR&D in support of these needs can the government expect the support of industry. Further, through IR&D the government is encouraging industry to be keenly competitive. It is competition (missing in the arsenal approach) which encourages technological innovation and breakthrough. The government's original IR&D policy was formulated with an understanding of the need for competition, as well as a need for encouragement of industry.

Industry derives its stimulation for specific IR&D projects from presentations of the military relative to future needs and requirements, which generally are based upon the military's projections of technological advancements. No formal requirement actually exists, and the industrial listeners have to project the needs of the future into concrete terms and then relate these terms to the current and potential abilities of their companies to meet those needs. The commitment of funds to IR&D requires careful planning plus an assumption of substantial risk. After all, a company is applying its limited available resources to the satisfaction of a need long before the customer has fully defined the requirement.

What does the government receive? The return is twofold. First there are the broad technological advances which provide new capabilities. These can and do shape new requirements and provide the military edge required for bargaining to maintain the tenuous peace we now enjoy. IR&D also upgrades the ability of industry to supply the more sophisticated needs of government. Thus in a very real sense IR&D is a cost of doing business with the government, and it should be viewed as a cost of sales.

Costing Internal Research and Development

As a cost of sales, internal research and development is an overhead cost. As such, it is not chargeable to any specific commodity or service of the firm or any specific customer's account. Therefore, it has become common practice to allocate a share of the cost of IR&D to all commodities and services, with the government accepting the cost as a normal fact of doing business with industry. Not uncommonly, IR&D costs include basic or fundamental research, applied research, advanced development, *and* bidding and proposal effort costs.

IR&D is conceived to be independent of government control. Theoretically, industry will use IR&D efforts to remain responsive to the needs of government, and failure to remain responsive can only mean the loss of government business. Thus, while IR&D may include support of commercial ventures which have no direct response to government needs, the belief is that the company which allocates the principal level of its IR&D efforts to support its commercial ventures will ultimately lose its government customer through an inability to meet government needs.

Actually, theory and fact part company when the government begins to evaluate a specific company's IR&D effort. In its procurement of commodities and services, the government has the authority, if not the right, to audit a company's books and to establish what is proper in terms of overhead and other costs. Thus government auditors have assumed the role of evaluators of IR&D. This has resulted in a highly formalized procedure for approving a company's IR&D allowable costs in advance of their commitment.

Most frequently, the system is based upon a triservice agreement which is negotiated each year. A company begins the negotiation process by preparing a summary of the efforts proposed for the following year. The summary includes details of past related efforts, some degree of justification on the basis of what is expected from the effort, manpower and facilities estimates, and costs. This summary, which is usually in the form of a bound report, is presented to the government committee assigned to evaluate the proposed effort and approve it for the three services. The committee considers the proposed cost of the effort in the light of the level of the firm's current business with the government and in terms of the previous year's agreement as to level of spending. In a company which is rapidly expanding its government business, there is little likelihood that the allowed percentage increase in IR&D commitment will approach the percentage increase in sales. Thus the IR&D approval method has a retardant effect upon the development of companies performing work for the government.

Through a triservice agreement, the government committee sets a maximum level of IR&D expenditures, in essence approving the proposed specific IR&D efforts set forth in the firm's proposal to the committee. This maximum level should not be interpreted to mean that the firm cannot spend more money on IR&D than is approved by the committee. It means the company which does spend more on IR&D than the approved level will discover that the government demands exclusion of the additional cost from both direct and indirect charges, and only profit remains to cover this additional cost. But, as was discussed in Chapter 3, there is little real profit to be realized in government contracting. (In the final analysis, it is usually less than 4 percent of the value of the work performed.) A company must therefore carefully weigh the consequences of overspending on internal research and development to support its government contracting.

Any company which resorts to IR&D as a support for its government efforts is not home free with the finalization of an IR&D triservice agreement. The government expects the firm to share in the cost of the IR&D efforts. Consequently, the government committee will establish some formula whereby the firm can charge only a fixed percentage of its IR&D costs to overhead or other direct and indirect charges made to the government. At the present time, this allowance has been of the order of only 90 percent up to the maximum level of allowable IR&D. The firm is expected to absorb the remaining 10 percent from its profits.

Future of Internal Research and Development

The entire concept of IR&D is under attack from many quarters. Today, even the organization of government and industry cooperation in military and other areas is under fire, with the term "military and industrial complex" being used in both a derogatory and a "scare" fashion. There are people both in and out of government who claim that the IR&D program should not be continued unless the government obtains all the proprietary rights (both patents and data) derived as a result of work performed under IR&D agreements. Further, these people say, any company seeking IR&D relief should be required to compete for the allocation, with the government making every effort to insure that there is no duplication of effort among firms doing business with the government. (It is the latter reasoning which is most often advanced to support the concept of government arsenals.)

Without question, IR&D is not immune to these attacks. There are obvious signs that the character of IR&D support by the government will be altered, with more rigid controls and with less latitude remaining for the firms involved. Elimination of IR&D could mark a total retreat to the arsenal system.

Research's Part in the Larger Marketing Plan

Research per se and the research organization have little part to play and little responsibility in the marketing of commodities and services. However, when system programs are in the offing, an entirely different set of conditions prevails. Consider the sale of a major system of the military or paramilitary type as offered to the government. There are four stages in the marketing effort, with each stage a complete entity and a logical successor to the preceding one.

In the first stage, customers (in this case, agencies of government) are selected by a marketing analysis, which considers not only the currently demonstrated capabilities of the company but also its inherent potentials. These customers are contacted formally and informally by sales and R&D representatives, coordinating their visits and exchanging trip and analysis reports to minimize confusion and to properly assess the climate for business. The principal objective of these contacts should be to determine the technical needs and operational requirements of the customer prior to its issuance of a formal request for quotation (RFQ) or request for proposal (RFP). Whenever possible, the exchange of information between the potential government customer and the company representatives should form the basis for unsolicited systems proposals to that customer.

Early in the first stage, the customer attempts to codify and define its needs and potentials. The research segment of the firm should be ever ready to assist the customer in these efforts by seeking and accepting limited objective contracts of a scientific and technical analysis nature.

The Unsolicited Proposal

An unsolicited systems proposal action should result from a request by sales or development, made through sales, to the company managers responsible for proposal action authorization. The unsolicited proposal should be prepared with all the care of a more formal proposal. Yet, since there is no certainty that financial support will be given the proposal by the selected customer, the preparation effort should be limited to a minimum expenditure of funds. But what constitutes a minimum? First, the obvious technical barriers must be identified and sufficient technical data must be developed for presentation to indicate clearly that a solution is possible. If the company proposes research or development of an invention, conceived independently of any government contract or effort but not yet actually reduced to practice, the company must be wary of giving up its rights in the invention with the award of a contract.

To be appealing, an unsolicited proposal must offer a new or novel concept. The proposal must therefore indicate the approach which will be taken to solve all the obvious technical problems and a significant number of the less obvious ones. The Office of Naval Research (ONR) publication, "Contract Research Program (ONR-1)," provides a guide for the preparation of research proposals. This guide has been paraphrased as follows:

1. Prepare a one-page summary statement of the proposed work.
2. Include a definition of the application or field of specific interest, with some indication of performance increases or improvements which might result.
3. Prepare a summary of the related state of the art in the technical area.
4. Incorporate a reasonably complete technical description of the proposed work, including a specific work statement and a statement of the relationship of the proposed work to other work being performed in the same field.
5. Present the names and qualifications of the principal investigator and his associates in sufficient detail to permit meaningful appraisal.
6. Include the estimated duration of the effort and a budget which shows an estimated cost of capital equipment and expendable supplies.
7. Present the facilities required and a knowledge of their availability.
8. Finally, relate the proposed effort to other work being performed by the firm for the government or for other industrial firms.

The Formal Proposal

When it is obvious that an unsolicited proposal would be inappropriate because of a pending RFQ or RFP of the customer, sales and development representatives should anticipate the coming required action, prepare the company proposal authorization request to management, and submit it through the sales department, as at step 1 of Exhibit 19. There are times when sales and development representatives cannot "shotgun" potential customers or when it is undesirable for them to do so. At those times, RFQ's and RFP's will be received without prior knowledge or anticipation. When this happens and the content meets company objectives, the sales department is faced with a real dilemma.

Many government agencies broadly solicit proposals in an honest

Exhibit 19

STAGE I: OBTAINING PROPOSAL APPROVAL

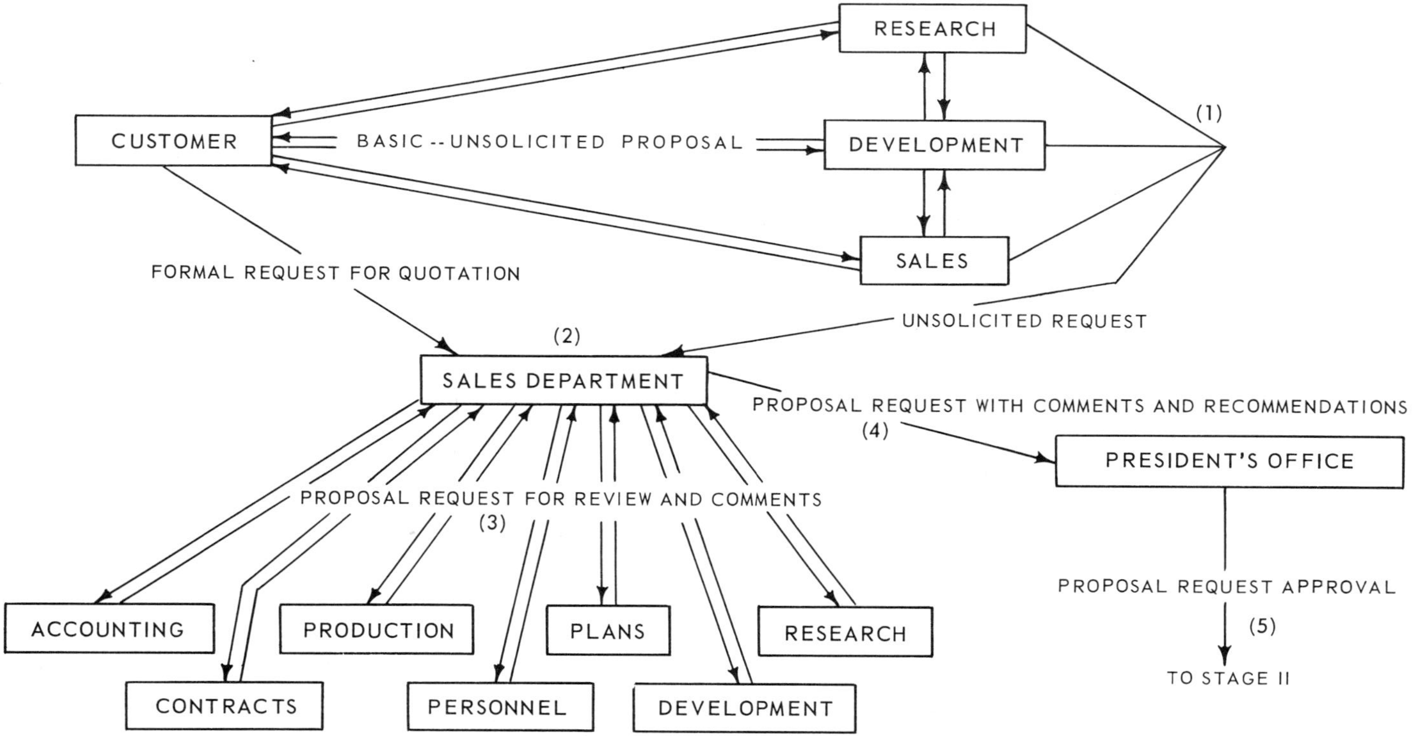

effort to receive the best reply and proposal possible. Other agencies have preconceived notions of what the proposal should present and which company should be awarded the contract. In the latter case, the solicitation is a sham to comply with the legal requirements to obtain a multiplicity of bids. The companies which respond to such requests when they are clearly not favored do so foolishly unless the response can be justified on some practical basis.

Every unexpected request for quotation and proposal should be investigated by the sales department to establish its potential. A "no bid" response may be all that the government expects or wants. If so, it is the response that should be given. Or the government agency may be expecting, on the basis of past good relationships, a token response to justify an award to the selected contractor. However, if the sales department determines that a complete proposal is in order, the regular steps toward the preparation of a proposal should be followed.

To initiate a formal proposal effort, the sales department should prepare a company request for proposal authorization (step 2 in Exhibit 19). Whether the proposal is solicited or unsolicited, the sales department has the responsibility of formally or informally coordinating the company request for proposal authorization with appropriate organizations within the company, and these organizations have a responsibility for review (step 3 in Exhibit 19). These organizations and the sales department share equal responsibility to provide appropriate comments upon the company request for proposal authorization.

All parties to a major systems proposal effort should realize that this is a major expense item and involves substantial risk. Seldom will a company be able to mount a systems proposal effort for less than $75,000, and many such efforts will approach or exceed $1 million before a contract decision is rendered by the customer. (The latter situation exists in virtually every major aircraft system contract, and the fate of industry leaders hangs on the selection of the ultimate contractor.) However, the reward for a contract may be 100 to 1,000 times the initial proposal cost. If the company is going to gamble for such high stakes, even with IR&D agreements, it must be assured that it is playing with a full deck, not merely satisfying whims.

The Proposal Authorization

The sales department should transmit the company request for proposal authorization, the comments of the various review organizations, and its own comments and recommendations to the president's office. The decision to bid a systems proposal is much too important to be made at any lower level. The recommendations of the sales department to the president should reflect marketing decisions or plans previously adopted as company policy, and should present fairly and faithfully the comments of other company organizations (step 4 of Exhibit 19). The president's office, after reviewing the comments of the various departments and the recommendations of the sales department, must render a decision to proceed with a proposal effort or disapprove the company proposal authorization request. If the request is approved, the president's office should transmit this approval to the sales department to initiate stage II of the total systems sales effort (step 5 of Exhibit 19). The approval, if it does not contain limitations, implicitly approves the proposed bidding budget which is submitted with the request.

Any one department of the company is able to initiate a proposal authorization request, including the research organization. This request should be directed through the sales department, and the sales department is obligated, even when it has a contrary recommendation, to submit the request to the president's office with all the supporting information provided with any other request. Thus, a check and balance of the sales department's actions is maintained, and its potential authoritarian character in matters of new business is minimized.

Forming the Proposal Committee

Stage II (Exhibit 20) begins with the sales department's receiving the approved company proposal authorization. Upon its receipt, the sales department should call together a proposal committee, which is chaired by a key sales department representative (step 1 in Exhibit 20). The committee's sole reason for existence is to make a coordinated review of the systems proposal, which must reflect the

Exhibit 20

STAGE II: PREPARING THE PROPOSAL

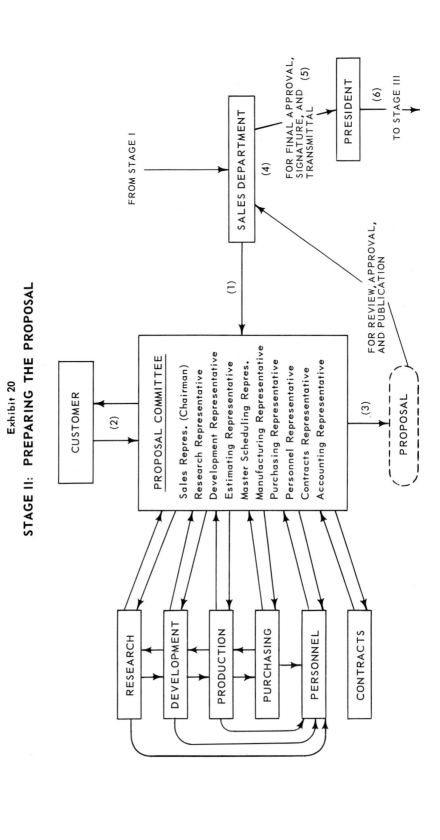

company's capabilities to satisfy the potential customer's needs and requirements. Representation on this proposal committee must be extended to all key and affected departments of the company.

During the preparation of the proposal, any contact with the customer relative to this particular proposal should be made through and by the proposal committee (step 2 in Exhibit 20), and all information pertinent to the proposal preparation coming from the customer should come to the committee directly. The sole function of the committee should be to schedule, plan, prepare, and assemble the proposal (step 3 in Exhibit 20). Each affected department should make its direct contribution to the proposal through the committee.

The final proposal is presented by the proposal committee to the sales department for review, approval, and publication. Review by the sales department should consist of a comparison of the proposal with a checklist designed to insure that the proposal provides all the contractual protection required of any proposal. Review should also extend to insuring that the proposal provides all the essential answers to all the points raised by the customer relative to its expressed needs and requirements. When published, the sales department should prepare a letter of transmittal for the proposal (step 4 in Exhibit 20). This letter is presented with the published proposal to the president for his ultimate approval, signature, and transmittal to the customer (step 5 in Exhibit 20). The actual transmittal of the proposal to the customer initiates stage III (see Exhibit 21).

Closing the Contract

With delivery of the proposal package to the customer from the president, the sales department has the responsibility of coordinating with the research and development organizations to prepare a sales plan which will favorably influence the customer's decision and evaluation of the proposal. This sales plan (step 1 in Exhibit 21), which includes a budgetary estimate, is offered to the president for his approval. Approval (step 2 in Exhibit 21) by the president, if without limitations, establishes the budget authorization to implement the sales plan.

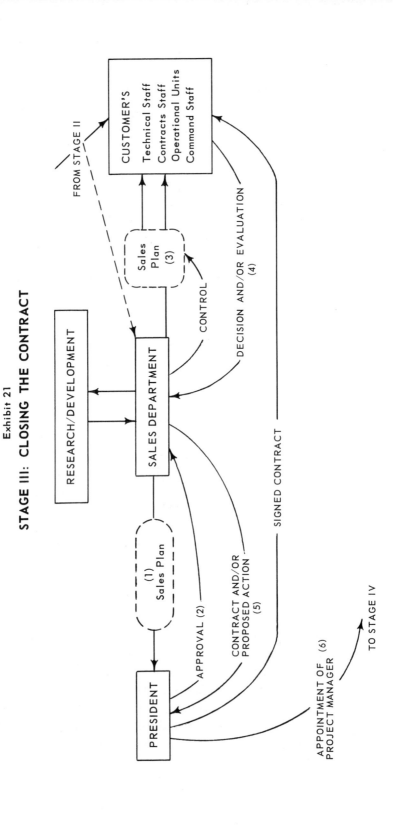

Exhibit 21
STAGE III: CLOSING THE CONTRACT

The sales plan must involve contacts by both sales and technical representatives on a cooperative-coordinated basis with the customer's key decision-making personnel (step 3 in Exhibit 21). While the customer is in the process of evaluating a proposal and reaching a contract award decision, action through the sales plan should be designed to influence the customer's decision by affecting the viewpoint of "command staff," operational units, and technical and administrative personnel within the customer's organization. A decision will be rendered by the customer, and this decision will be either a contract, a total rejection, or an evaluation which indicates merit for a part of the proposed program (step 4 in Exhibit 21).

It is the function of the sales department to review and evaluate the decision rendered by the customer and to draw from the evaluation recommendations for appropriate action. In the case of a contract tender, the contract must be reviewed by the sales department, drawing upon knowledge available in other departments to recommend to the president that the contract be signed, rejected, or signed subject to modification (step 5 in Exhibit 21). Any recommendation to the president for nonsignature or signature on the basis of modification, or an unfavorable decision by the customer, should be passed to the president with the sales department's recommendations of proposed future action in this area of interest and relative to this particular customer. When a satisfactory contract offer results, the president should have the responsibility for signing the contract and returning the executed contract to the customer (step 6 in Exhibit 21) for implementation. At the same time, the president should transmit to the research and development organizations authorization to initiate a project to accomplish the required work under the contract in accordance with the precontract planning. This action initiates stage IV (see Exhibit 22).

Satisfying the Customer

Research and development managers, upon receipt of the project approval, have the responsibility of establishing a project committee (step 1 in Exhibit 22). This committee is chaired by the project

Exhibit 22

THE MATURE PROJECT

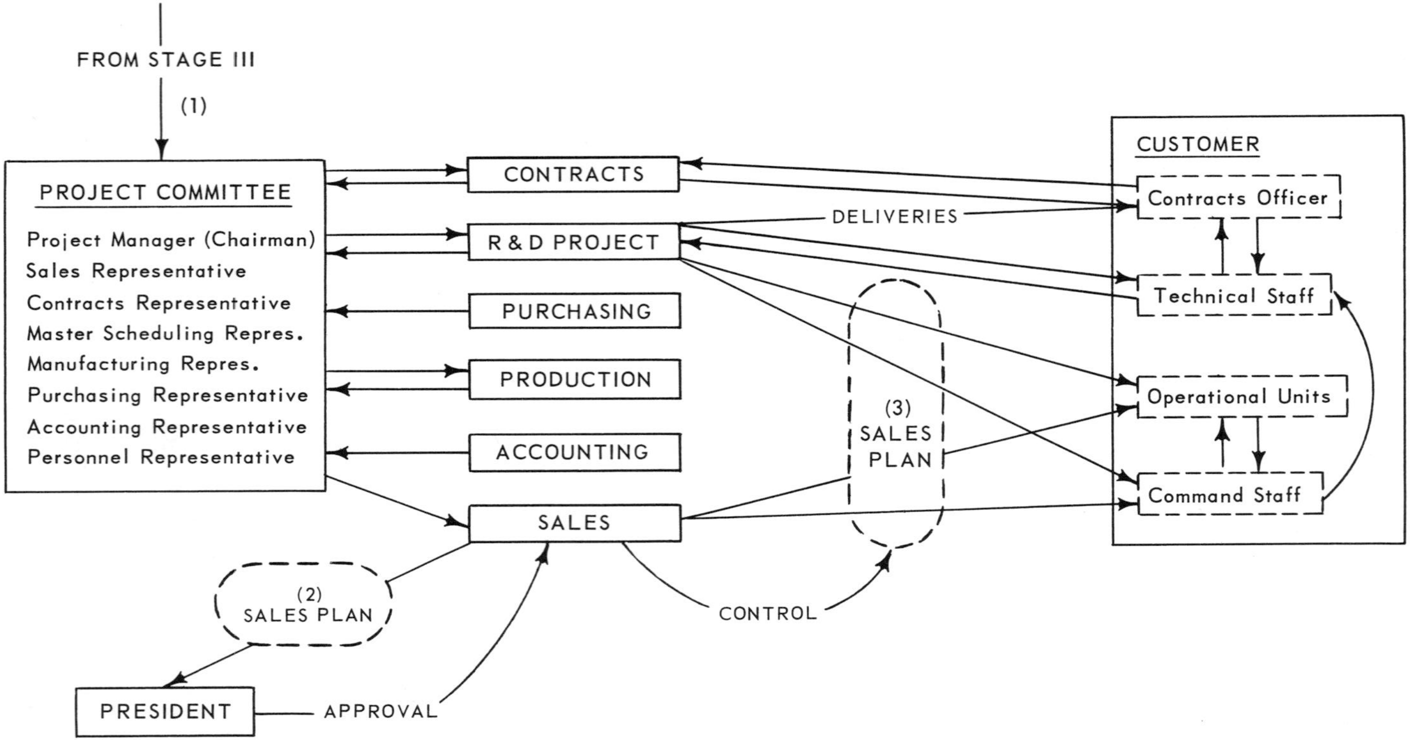

manager as assigned. He must be supported by the contributions of all company departments essential to the proper function of the project, and his committee should consist of representatives of these departments. The contracts department, whose information is provided in and through the project committee, is in a position to monitor the program to insure fulfillment of contractual obligations and is able through the committee to provide appropriate direction to all departments associated with the program.

The purchasing department should work in close, direct coordination with the research, development, project, and manufacturing organizations through the project committee to insure the purchase of all essential items in the program according to preplanning and to provide status information which affects the scheduling of the program. The accounting department has the responsibility of assembling all related cost data. This information should be passed through the project committee to the organizations which need this knowledge so that they will be able to execute their responsibilities properly.

The sales department should draw information from the project committee to permit the formulation of a continuing sales plan (step 2 in Exhibit 22). This plan should have as its objective convincing the customer's operational units and command staff that the item is desirable, is required, fulfills the needs of the customer, and has proper operational functions. The sales plan, when approved by the president, should be administered by the sales department with cooperative-coordinated participation by sales and technical representatives (step 3 in Exhibit 22).

Contacts with the customer's contract officer, as they relate to all things pertaining to contract requirements, must be limited to the company's contracts department. All contacts with the customer's technical staff (that is, those responsible for the technical administration of the program) which do not affect contract terms or conditions should be limited to the project manager or the project committee. This arrangement insures a minimum of contract confusion and prevents transmittal of misinformation with its subsequent misunderstandings. It is the joint responsibility of contracts, research, development, and sales to explore the possibilities for enlarging the scope of the project with increased customer funds and their attendant increase in potential profits.

Research Staff for Marketing

Where a research organization is actively seeking contracts outside the company, a marketing staff is essential. It is entirely appropriate to have a marketing manager, but it is not appropriate to give that title to someone who is really a salesman and not a manager. The real sales of research efforts occur through the understanding of scientific and technical personnel in the research organization and their counterparts in the customer's technical staff. Most scientific and technical personnel distrust anyone with a title of salesman. Even the title of marketing manager will produce some distrust. One possibility for circumventing this problem is to call a salesman a research coordinator. Appendix A offers professional job descriptions for a marketing manager in a research organization and for the position of research coordinator.

The marketing staff for research is presented with administrative problems which differ significantly from other marketing staffs. It is not possible for them to lay a finely manufactured component or part on the customer's desk to provide evidence of the research organization's capabilities. The very best the salesman can offer is a sampling of technical reports. This restriction on doing business clearly pinpoints the necessity for the research organization to make each report a significant presentation of capabilities.

Maintaining the administrative records and controlling the contracting aspects of an effort both before contract award and afterward present some unique problems within the research organization. A procedure originally designed to overcome some of these problems appears in Appendix B. This procedure is not suitable for all situations, but it can serve as a foundation for establishing a workable procedure for a research organization's marketing staff.

Appendix A

Professional Job Descriptions

Position descriptions for a research organization should be composed with full recognition of the professionalism required to make such an organization successful. Also, the position descriptions should be in keeping with the levels of education required for each position. That is, they should provide and delineate the limit of freedom and responsibility that are commensurate with equivalent academic positions.

The position descriptions which follow have been drawn with these considerations foremost. These descriptions were prepared to meet a specific set of circumstances in the management of a research organization. While each is relatively general in nature, to be appropriate in other circumstances they should be reviewed and altered to fit. No single, cut-and-dried position description will cover all personnel in all industrial situations. By the same token, there is significant difficulty, if not danger, in trying to apply any broad personnel concepts to research and development personnel.

For the sake of brevity and space, this set of position descriptions is not complete. Reference should be made to the chapters dealing with the organization and motivation of the research organization to establish the relationship which exists between and among the various personnel.

The order of the position descriptions presented here is as follows:

185

Research general manager.
Research manager.
Senior scientist.
Assistant scientist.
Research assistant.
Sales-marketing manager.
Research coordinator (that is, salesman).

Using these position descriptions as a base, it is possible to draw the missing descriptions for

Services manager.
Administrative manager.
Scientist.
Associate scientist.
Research associate.

Each of these positions is merely an extension of or an adjunct to the position descriptions actually presented.

As was stated in the text, the position descriptions which follow should be reserved exclusively for the research organization. This is especially true for the scientific and technical positions. Whenever these titles are permitted to diffuse into the other divisions or even into the staff of corporate headquarters, their prestige is severely diminished and their value is eroded.

Job Title: Research General Manager
Division: Research
Department: All

Basic Functions

Manages the activities of the research division to achieve the profit objectives of the corporation.

Insures that all research proposals are adequately reviewed for scientific and technical feasibility.

Provides scientific and technical assurance that ideas and concepts accepted for development are within the company's scientific and technical capability or technical growth.

Creates an effective image to the industry and public by participating in scientific and technical as well as management seminars, writing articles for publication, and attending recognized courses in fields of scientific and technical as well as managerial interest.

Manages theoretical and experimental research and advanced development completely through breadboard or advanced development stage as proof of new designs and concepts accepted as projects.

Manages all the analytical studies of a research or advanced development nature as accepted by the division.

Personal Responsibilities

Planning and Policy Responsibilities

1. Complies with policy as set forth in the "Corporate Policy Manual" and recommends changes as necessary or appropriate.

2. Prepares periodic budgets as required to include people, services, facilities, materials, and dollars.

3. Formulates plans for the orderly growth of the division as the corporation increases its volume of business.

Procedural Responsibilities

1. Insures compliance with corporate and appropriate division procedures as outlined in the corporate and divisional procedures manuals.

2. Establishes and maintains divisional procedures.

Other Personally Performed Responsibilities

1. Initiates and/or writes scientific and technical research or study proposals.

2. Sets up and/or approves time schedules for work, progress reports, and drafts for contract solicitation proposals.

3. Reviews time and dollar schedules and personnel assignments established for research proposals with the administrative manager to insure that schedules are met.

4. Integrates schedules on divisional projects involving interdepartmental activities.

5. Establishes program assignments along with time and dollar schedules and budgets for proper conduct of projects.

6. Directs divisional scientific and technical activities from initial conception through breadboarding to publication of appropriate final reports.

7. Authenticates the necessary paperwork prior to submission for fabrication or procurement orders for research instrumentation, equipment, and facilities.

8. Insures proper scientific and technical feasibility review for all project schedules and for bid proposals.

9. Furnishes scientific and technical assistance, as requested, to production divisions in difficult scientific and technical problem areas encountered in development, product engineering, or production.

10. Indoctrinates research personnel in their role as the source of new conceptual ideas and development programs, emphasizing the significance of "cash flow" by keeping ideas and concepts from stagnating in research.

11. Provides an understanding as to the part research plays in assisting the corporation in producing a profit.

12. Assists the corporation by
   a. Supporting scientific and technical articles for publication in appropriate journals.
   b. Maintaining an awareness of patentable concepts or ideas and taking the initiative to patent these items.
   c. Furnishing the marketing manager with new research or study ideas as they are developed.
   d. Meeting customer requirements on presentation of scientific and technical research or study proposals.
   e. Supporting efforts to present an appropriate technical image to customers of the corporation during capability surveys.
   f. Reviewing requests by customers with a view toward formally presenting research or study concepts as unsolicited bids at a later date, slanting such unsolicited proposals toward corporate demonstrated capabilities.
   g. Preparing progress reports to customers on research or study projects.

13. Insures the maintenance of a very high degree of scientific and technical knowledge in all areas of interest.

14. Provides a complete and current scientific and technical research library that will serve the needs of research and study efforts. Prevents technical books, surveys, studies, and reports from getting sidetracked into individual files of personnel in the division.

15. Maintains constant vigilance to develop and expand the capability of the division through planned growth of the personnel within the division.

Delegated Responsibilities

Administrative manager.
Services manager.
Marketing manager.
Research manager.

Inside Relationships

1. Maintains interdivisional and intradivisional relationships to insure the effective coordination of the profit objectives of the corporation.

2. Maintains relationship with the corporate attorneys concerning patent and legal problems.

3. Maintains relationship with appropriate personnel in other divisions to have a knowledge of overall business activities.

Outside Relationships

1. Maintains relationships with current and potential customers to solicit new business and assist in the solicitation of scientific and technical problems.

2. Maintains relationships with the scientific and technical community to keep abreast of the changing state of the art and to insure a proper image relative to capabilities.

Job Title: Research Manager
Reports to: Research General Manager
Division: Research
Department: Scientific

Basic Functions

Manages the scientific and technical activities relating to research to achieve the cost control and other appropriate objectives of the research division.

Manages the research efforts through review and guidance to insure adequate support of the research objectives of the division.

Provides administrative and other appropriate assistance to individual researchers and research teams in the performance of their assigned efforts.

Manages the administrative aspects of the research efforts to insure fulfillment of program objectives and time schedules within contractual or other commitments. Plans research efforts and schedules to comply with contract and other commitments.

Creates an effective image to current and potential customers, as well as the public at large, by participating in appropriate seminars and conferences, attending recognized courses relating to his responsibilities, and writing articles for publication or for public presentation.

Manages completely the initiation and assignment of research programs to insure meeting the objectives established for such programs.

Personal Responsibilities

Planning and Policy Responsibilities

1. Complies with policy as set forth in the "Corporate Policy Manual" and recommends changes, as necessary, to the research general manager.

2. Interprets company and divisional policy and procedure to all subordinates reporting directly to him.

3. Obtains clarification relative to any policy matter which is unclear or unresolvable.

4. Prepares periodic budgets as required, including support services, personnel, facilities, materials, and dollars reflecting the scientific and technical planning required to support all programs within the division.

5. Formulates plans for the orderly growth of the research effort as the division increases volume of business.

6. Formulates plans to insure that research progress and completion are in accordance with contractual and other commitments.

Procedural Responsibilities

1. Insures compliance with corporate and divisional procedures as outlined in the corporate and divisional procedures manuals.

2. Establishes and maintains division procedures relating to research functions.

Other Personally Performed Responsibilities

1. Initiates and directs the writing of scientific and technical research reports and proposals.

2. Sets up time schedules, progress reports, and drafts for research proposals.

3. Reviews time and dollar schedules on research proposals and assignments with the services manager to insure that schedules are met.

4. Establishes program assignments along with time and dollar schedules and budgets for research projects.

5. Prepares and authenticates the necessary paperwork prior to submission to the services manager and/or research general manager for scheduling of research.

6. Assures the research general manager that proper research feasibility review is given to all program schedules.

7. Furnishes scientific and technical assistance as required by the research general manager to establish objectives and controls of the division.

8. Indoctrinates research personnel in their role as the research function of the division, emphasizing the significance of cost-consciousness and adherence to contractual or other commitments.

9. Provides an understanding as to the part a research function plays in assisting the division in producing a profit.

10. Assists the marketing department by
   a. Maintaining an awareness of patentable concepts or devices; taking the initiative to insure patent protection.
   b. Preparing and/or submitting scientific and technical articles for publication in appropriate journals or presentation before appropriate society meetings.
   c. Furnishing competent scientific and technical personnel to support marketing's presentations to customers.
   d. Meeting customer requirements for the presentation of scientific and technical proposals in research areas.
   e. Preparing progress reports for customers on research programs.

11. Insures the maintenance of a high degree of scientific and technical state-of-the-art capability throughout the research division.

12. Maintains constant vigilance to develop and expand the capability of the research function through the planned growth of personnel in the department.

Delegated Reponsibilities

Individual principal investigators.
Research team leaders.
Clerical.

Inside Relationships

1. Maintains relationships with other departments within the division to insure effective coordination of the profit objective of the division.

2. Maintains relationships with the corporate patent attorney concerning corporate patent and legal problems.

3. Maintains relationships with personnel in the other divisions so as to have a knowledge of the corporation's business activities.

Outside Relationships

1. Maintains relations with direct customers to insure that they are satisfied that the division is functioning in accordance with the proper management control of research.

2. Maintains relations with the scientific and technical community to keep abreast of the changing state of the art and to insure a proper image relative to corporate capabilities.

Job Title: Senior Scientist
Reports to: Research Manager or Research General Manager with approval of the Research Manager
Division: Research
Department: Scientific

Basic Functions

Serves as principal or lead researcher or investigator in areas of his scientific and technical specialization.

Provides scientific and technical direction as a research team leader for assigned research programs.

Provides scientific and technical recommendations to enhance research programs under his cognizance.

Provides scientific and technical recommendations to other principal or lead researchers or research team leaders in his area of specialization to insure the fulfillment of program objectives of the division.

Assists the research manager in the evaluation and analysis of programs, both internal and external to the corporation.

Creates an effective image to current and potential customers, peers, and the public at large by direct and indirect participation in appropriate seminars and conferences, attendance at recognized technical courses relating to his areas of responsibility, and the writing, presenting, and publishing of scientific and technical reports in appropriate journals and the like.

Personal Responsibilities

Planning and Policy Responsibilities

1. Complies with policy as set forth in the "Corporate Policy Manual" and recommends changes, if necessary, to the research manager.

2. Complies with policy as set forth in the division procedures and recommends changes, if necessary, to the research manager.

3. Interprets corporate and divisional policy and procedure to all subordinates reporting directly to him.

4. Obtains clarification relative to any policy matter which is unclear or unresolvable.

5. Prepares periodic estimates as required to reflect scientific and technical planning required to support all programs within the division.

6. As requested, formulates plans for the orderly growth of the division's scientific and technical effort as there is an increase in the volume of research activity.

Procedural Responsibilities

1. Insures compliance with corporate and divisional procedures by direct subordinates.

2. Recommends, through the research manager, divisional procedures relating to scientific and technical matters.

Other Personally Performed Responsibilities

1. Conducts scientific and technical planning on all assigned programs to insure that work progress and completion is in accordance with contractual requirements or other commitments.

2. Submits all timely data and information required for the proper administrative control of programs under his direct control.

3. Exercises professional review of all personnel directly reporting to him for periods in excess of ninety (90) days and passes upon the reviews prepared by subordinates relative to personnel under them.

4. Establishes program assignments along with time schedules and expenditure authorizations for assigned scientific and technical programs. Coordinates scientific and technical efforts with the services manager to insure the timely availability of experimental instrumentation and equipment for assigned programs.

5. Indoctrinates subordinate scientific and technical personnel in their knowledge as a research function, emphasizing the significance of effective research with attention to cost factors and schedules established by contractual or other commitments.

6. Provides an understanding as to the part research plays in assisting the corporation in complying with future planning and product growth.

7. Insures that research efforts under his control are conducted within the frame of approved program planning as established by appropriate documentation or within the frame of normal requirements for the operation of a research organization.

8. Maintains constant vigilance to develop and expand the capability of the research function through the planned growth of the personnel assigned to his programs.

9. Exercises unrestricted scientific and technical judgment and action within the framework of approved programs.

10. Relates the scientific and technical content of assigned programs to the everyday requirements and future planning of the corporation.

Delegated Responsibilities

Researchers.

Inside Relationships

1. Maintains relationships with other scientific and technical personnel within the division to insure effective coordination and timely conclusion of scientific and technical programs.

2. Maintains relationships with other departments within the division to insure effective coordination of the profit objective of the division.

3. Maintains relations with the services manager to insure effective coordination in requirements for laboratory facilities, equipment, and support services, as well as patent protection for advanced and original thinking.

4. Maintains relations with technical personnel in other divisions and departments so as to have knowledge of corporate business activities and objectives.

Outside Relationships

1. Maintains, in conjunction with marketing, relations with customers and potential customers, aiding in the solicitation of new research and assisting marketing in presenting a more complete image of the corporation and division.

2. Maintains relations with personnel in the scientific and technical community so as to remain abreast of the advancing state of the art.

Job Title: Assistant Scientist
Reports to: Research Team Leader or Research Manager as assigned
Division: Research
Department: Scientific

Basic Functions

Serves as a principal or lead researcher or investigator in areas of his scientific or technical specialization.

Supports scientific and technical programs as a member of a research team.

Provides scientific and technical consultation in his specialization to enhance research efforts with which he is associated.

Provides scientific and technical consultation in his areas of specialization as requested by researchers outside his own team and as approved by his research team leader or research manager (in the case of an individual researcher).

Personal Responsibilities

Planning and Policy Responsibilities

1. Complies with policy as set forth in corporate and division policy manuals and recommends changes, if necessary, through his intermediate to the research manager.

2. Obtains clarification relative to any policy matter which is unclear or unresolvable.

3. Prepares periodic estimates as required to reflect scientific and technical planning essential to support his efforts.

Procedural Responsibilities

1. Recommends to the research manager, through any intermediate superiors, division procedures relating to scientific and technical matters.

2. Insures compliance with corporate and division procedures as outlined in appropriate manuals.

Other Personally Performed Responsibilities

1. Conducts personal scientific and technical planning on all assigned efforts to insure work progress and completion in accordance with contractual requirements or other commitments.

2. Submits all timely data and information required for the proper administrative control of personal efforts.

3. Coordinates scientific and technical efforts with the research team leader to insure the timely availability of experimental instrumentation, equipment, and support for assigned scientific and technical efforts.

4. Emphasizes, in personal research efforts, cost factors and schedules established by contractual requirements or other commitments.

5. Insures that personal research efforts are conducted within the frame of approved program planning as established by appropriate documentation.

6. Maintains constant vigilance to aid development and expansion of the capabilities of the research function through planned growth.

7. Subject to review, exercises sound scientific and technical judgment and action within the framework of assigned research efforts.

8. Obtains scientific and technical consultation in areas of nonspecialization as required to support personal efforts.

9. Relates the scientific and technical content of assigned efforts to the everyday requirements and future planning of the corporation.

Delegated Responsibilities

Research associates.
Research assistants.

Inside Relationships

1. Maintains relationships with other scientific and technical personnel within the division to insure coordination and timely conclusion of personal scientific and technical efforts.

2. Maintains such relationships as are necessary to insure effective coordination of the profit objective of the division.

3. Maintains relations with the services manager to insure patent protection for personally advanced ideas and original thinking.

Outside Relationships

1. Maintains, as approved by superiors, in conjunction with marketing, relationships with customers and potential customers, aiding in the solicitation of new research efforts and assisting marketing in presenting a more complete image of the corporation and division.

2. Maintains relations with personnel in the scientific and technical community so as to remain abreast of the advancing state of the art.

Job Title: Research Assistant
Reports to: Research Team Leader or Services Manager as assigned
Division: Research
Department: Scientific or Services as assigned

Basic Functions

Serves as an experimenter, data analyst, or technical aide in areas of his qualifications.

Supports scientific and technical programs as a direct member of a research team or as a member of the services department.

Carries out special assignments in support of scientific and technical efforts, as assigned.

Supports design, fabrication, assembly, operation, repair, and calibration of laboratory instrumentation, equipment, and facilities through application of his specialized skills and knowledge.

Personal Responsibilities

Planning and Policy Responsibilities
1. Complies with policy as set forth in corporate and division policy manuals.
2. Obtains clarification relative to any policy matter which is unclear or unresolvable.

Procedural Responsibilities
Insures personal compliance with corporate and division procedures as outlined in appropriate manuals.

Other Personally Performed Responsibilities
1. Conducts all assigned efforts to insure work progress and completion in accordance with contractual requirements or other commitments.
2. Coordinates personal efforts with the appropriate supervisor to insure timely availability of equipment and materials required to perform his personal functions.
3. Emphasizes, in personal efforts, cost factors and schedules established by contractual requirements or other commitments.
4. Insures that personal efforts are conducted within the frame of approved program planning as established by appropriate documentation.
5. Obtains scientific and/or technical direction to insure proper support of the principal effort.
6. Exercises sound judgment and action, with supervision, within the framework of assigned efforts.

Delegated Responsibilities
None.

Inside Relationships
1. Maintains relationships with scientific and technical personnel within the department to insure effective coordination and timely conclusion of personal efforts.
2. Maintains such relationships as are necessary to insure scientific and/or technical advancement within his area of capabilities.

3. Maintains appropriate relations to insure patent protection of personally advanced ideas and original thinking.

Outside Relationships

Maintains relations with his peers and with others in the scientific and technical community so as to remain abreast of the advancing state of the art affecting his capabilities.

Job Title: Sales-Marketing Manager
Reports to: Research General Manager
Division: Research
Department: Marketing

Basic Functions

Manages the sales activities and related marketing analysis to achieve the level of effort and growth objectives of the division.

Conducts sales and preliminary contract negotiations with agencies and groups in accordance with the division's plans and established objectives.

Provides marketing and sales intelligence to permit the establishment of marketing plans and objectives.

Organizes, directs, and contributes to division proposal efforts by coordinating scientific and technical inputs, insuring proper graphics and format preparation, editing and writing, and insuring that printing, collation, and binding meet division standards.

Provides sales budget control coordination with the administrative manager and prepares appropriate estimates of sales to insure the adequacy of division forecasts.

Creates an effective image to the customers and the public at large beyond that required to achieve sales objectives.

Personal Responsibilities

Planning and Policy Responsibilities

1. Complies with policy as set forth in corporate and division policy manuals and recommends changes, as necessary, to the research general manager.

2. Obtains clarification relative to any policy matter which is unfamiliar or personally unresolvable.

3. Interprets company and division policy and procedure to all assigned personnel.

4. Formulates plans for the orderly growth of sales to insure work and/or program progress and completion compatible with the overall growth objectives of the division.

5. Prepares periodic estimates to reflect sales planning and costs to support the division programs and efforts.

Procedural Responsibilities

1. Within the marketing department, insures compliance with procedures as outlined in corporate and division procedures manuals.

2. Recommends to the research general manager division procedures to be established to govern sales and marketing activities and functions.

3. Establishes division procedures relating to sales and marketing.

Other Personally Performed Responsibilities

1. Conducts overall sales planning on all programs to insure that sales promotion and contract finalization are accomplished in the best interests of the division.

2. Submits all timely data and information required for the proper administrative control of sales and precontract efforts.

3. Coordinates sales efforts to insure the timely presentation of proposals and the coordination of such proposals without conflict between contracting agencies.

4. Emphasizes the significance of effective sales and marketing efforts, with attention to cost factors and timely contract execution.

5. Assures that sales-marketing efforts are conducted within the frame of appropriate planning as established by approved documentation or within the frame of normal requirements of the operations of a research organization.

6. Maintains constant vigilance to develop and expand the capability of sales and marketing in the division's program of planned growth.

7. Exercises sound sales-marketing judgment and action within the framework of the capabilities and planned growth of the division.

8. Develops and maintains all appropriate records relating to the sales and marketing functions described in this job description.

9. Initiates and directs procedures for the control and implementation of sales and marketing functions.

10. Indoctrinates department personnel in their role as the sales function of the division, emphasizing the significance of planned growth and controlled sales-marketing costs.

11. Conducts precontract and in-process contract negotiations with customers' contract personnel.

Delegated Responsibilities

Research coordinators.
Clerical.

Inside Relationships

1. Maintains relations with scientific and technical personnel within the division to insure effective coordination and timely presentation of scientific and technical data required to support sales efforts.

2. Maintains relationships with other personnel within the division to insure effective coordination of the profit objectives of the division.

3. Maintains relations, as appropriate, with sales and marketing functions of other divisions to insure proper development of the total corporate sales and marketing effort.

4. Maintains relations, as appropriate, with the administrative manager to insure proper development and maintenance of records and costing.

Outside Relationships

1. Maintains relations with customers and potential customers essential to solicit new business and to present a more complete image of the division as a research organization.

2. Maintains relations with personnel in the sales and marketing community to remain abreast of changing sales and marketing techniques and to insure current marketing intelligence.

Job Title: Research Coordinator
Reports to: Marketing Manager
Division: Research
Department: Marketing

Basic Functions

Conducts sales and preliminary contract negotiations with assigned agencies and groups in accordance with the division's plans and established objectives.

Provides marketing and sales intelligence on which marketing plans and objectives can be established.

Organizes, directs, and contributes to division proposal efforts by coordinating scientific and technical inputs, insuring proper graphics and format preparation, editing and writing, and insuring that printing, collation, and binding meet division standards.

Personal Responsibilities

Planning and Policy Responsibilities

1. Complies with policy as set forth in corporate and division policy manuals and recommends changes, as necessary, to the marketing manager.

2. Obtains clarification relative to any policy matter which is unfamiliar or personally unresolvable.

3. Prepares periodic estimates as required to reflect sales planning to support division programs and efforts.

4. As requested, formulates plans for the orderly growth of the division's sales and marketing efforts as the division increases in activity.

Procedural Responsibilities

1. Insures compliance with corporate and division procedures as outlined in the appropriate manuals.

2. Recommends to the marketing manager procedures relating to sales.

Other Personally Performed Responsibilities

1. Conducts sales planning on all assigned programs to insure that sales promotion and finalization are accomplished in the best interests of the division and corporation.

2. Submits all timely data and information required for the proper administrative control of sales programs under his responsibility.

3. Coordinates sales efforts to insure the timely presentation of proposals without conflict between customers.

4. Emphasizes the significance of effective sales with attention to cost factors and timely contract execution.

5. Insures that sales efforts under his direct control are conducted within the frame of appropriate planning as established by documentation or within the frame of normal requirements of the operations of a research organization.

6. Maintains constant vigilance to aid in development and expansion of the capability for sales and marketing in a program of planned growth.

7. Subject to review, exercises sound sales judgment and action within the framework of assigned, approved programs.

Delegated Responsibilities

None.

Inside Relationships

1. Maintains relations with scientific and technical personnel within the division to insure effective coordination and timely presentation of scientific and technical data required to support sales efforts.

2. Maintains relationships with other personnel within the division to insure effective coordination of the profit objectives of the division.

3. Maintains relations, as appropriate, with the administrative manager to insure proper development and maintenance of records and costs.

Outside Relationships

1. Maintains relationships with customers, government agencies, and potential customers essential to solicit new research efforts and to present a more complete image of the corporation and division.

2. Maintains relations with personnel in the sales and marketing community so as to remain abreast of changing sales and marketing techniques.

Appendix B

Typical Procedures

Management through administration and control within a company is normally effected through published procedures. Such procedures may be written as companywide and published as part of a corporate procedures manual. Or companywide procedures may be supplemented by additional divisional procedures covering specialized problems of a specific component of the company.

In general, a research component of a company should have a separate division procedure manual with procedures specifically written to cope with the problems which arise with and through the management of highly creative people.

A well-written procedure clearly delineates the limits of individual action available in specific situations. However, it should also serve as a guide to the research personnel attempting to follow the proper course of action in specific situations. The procedures which follow were drafted to cover the administration and control of a specific research organization. These procedures are not amenable to unqualified adoption by every research organization, but they are indicative of the type and scope of procedures which must be adopted.

As each procedure is reviewed, consider the fact that each procedure was written in conjunction with the scientific and technical personnel who were affected by its terms. Before each procedure was published, the need for the procedure was explored in regular staff meetings and the wording was experimentally tested in these same meetings. When finally published, the procedures reflected the thinking of those most affected and were readily accepted by them.

| SUBJECT: | DISTRIBUTION: |
| Official Periods of Business | All Division Personnel |

1. Purpose. This procedure defines the hours of operation of the division and the administrative controls which will exist relative to the hours of operation. There will be no exemptions to this procedure.

2. Workweek.

   2.1. Period of Week.

      2.1.1. The workweek officially begins at 00:01 A.M. on Saturday morning.

      2.1.2. The workweek officially ends at 12:00 P.M. on Friday night.

   2.2. Overtime.

      2.2.1. Definition. Overtime will be computed on the basis of hours and/or tenths of hours worked in excess of forty (40) hours within the official workweek.

      2.2.2. Control nonexempt overtime. Nonexempt personnel will not work overtime except as previously approved by the employee's immediate supervisor and the administrative manager.

   2.3. Time Records.

      2.3.1. In lieu of time clocks, each employee will work a full forty (40) hours in each official workweek, except as excused by official holidays, approved vacations, and illnesses.

      2.3.2. Each employee will keep his own time records. Nonexempt employees will complete their own time cards, indicating both hours worked and projects assigned. Time cards of exempt employees will be completed by the administrative manager.

      2.3.3. All time cards will be submitted to the administrative manager in the morning of the last working day in each official workweek.

3. Workday.

   3.1. Period of Day.

      3.1.1. The workday officially begins at 8:15 A.M. local time on each designated workday.

      3.1.2. The workday officially ends at 5:00 P.M. local time on each designated workday.

      3.1.3. Between official opening and official closing, the division offices will be continuously open to visitors and to the reception of telephone calls.

SUPERSEDES:

3.2. Individual Responsibilities.

3.2.1. In lieu of time clocks, each individual is expected to regulate his work schedule to perform his assigned projects, tasks, and obligations to the division and the corporation.

3.2.2. Formal coffee breaks and other relaxation periods will not be established. Each individual will regulate his or her own work habits.

3.2.3. Formal lunch or meal periods will not be established. A period of forty-five (45) minutes will be set aside by each employee for a midday break for lunch and/or other purposes. Each individual will regulate his or her own work habits to take a midday break in keeping with the requirements of division operating procedures.

3.2.4. Each nonexempt employee will report an anticipated tardiness to his or her immediate supervisor prior to 8:30 A.M. on the day affected. Each such tardiness must be excused by the affected supervisor.

3.2.5. Each employee will report to his or her immediate supervisor an anticipated absence from work regardless of cause. Such report will be made prior to 8:30 A.M. on the day affected. All absences will be covered by a report of the immediate supervisor to the administrative manager on the date of absence prior to 11:00 A.M.

4. Vacations.

4.1. Branch.

4.1.1. Holidays. The division will observe six regular holidays (New Year's Day, Memorial Day, 4th of July, Labor Day, Thanksgiving, and Christmas Day) and one floating holiday to be chosen by the general manager.

4.1.2. Vacations. The division will not observe any vacation periods. It will be open year-round on a full operational basis.

4.2. Individual.

4.2.1. Holidays. All employees will be given all holidays of the division as official days of absence from work.

4.2.2. Vacations.

4.2.2.1. Compensated. Vacation time will be fully accrued prior to a compensated vacation.

4.2.2.2. Noncompensated. Noncompensated vacations will be discouraged. Such vacations must have the prior approval of the supervisory staff up to and including the administrative manager.

4.2.2.3. Split. Split vacations will be discouraged. A full year's vacation (normally ten working days) will be taken as an integral whole. Any other arrangement must have the prior approval of the supervisory staff up to and including the administrative manager.

RESEARCH DIVISION PROCEDURE	PROCEDURE NO.: 1-2
	PAGE 1 OF 5 PAGES
	APPROVED: _(signature)_ DATED: August 4, 19__

SUBJECT:	DISTRIBUTION:
Mail, Receiving and Shipping	All Division Personnel

1. **Purpose.** This procedure defines the transmittal and receipt of all material (correspondence, memoranda, reports, equipment, and the like) which enters or leaves the division. The procedures for handling and control are established, as are the responsibilities of division personnel. The various forms which materials may assume are defined also. All division personnel will comply with the procedures set forth herein, unless specifically exempted in writing by the general manager.

2. **Correspondence.**

   2.1. **Outgoing.**

      2.1.1. **Definition.** Any form of letter mail which leaves this division over the signature of any bona fide employee of this division and which is written, typed, reproduced, or printed on the letterhead or facsimile letterhead of this division must be considered as official correspondence of this division, reflecting its opinions, procedures, and directives.

      2.1.2. **Signature control.**

         2.1.2.1. Any correspondence which submits or transmits a firm or a "planning purposes only" proposal, either with or without a cost quotation, will be approved by the general manager and will be signed either by the general manager or the president's office.

         2.1.2.2. Any correspondence which pertains to the terms and conditions of a contract within the division, or which transmits any report, article, or item required for delivery under the terms of such a contract, will be approved and signed by the general manager.

         2.1.2.3. Any correspondence which provides a statement or interpretation of either division or corporate policy, directives, or procedures will be approved and signed by the general manager.

         2.1.2.4. All other correspondence will be approved and/or signed by the administrative manager.

      2.1.3. **Administrative control.**

         2.1.3.1. All correspondence which is written, typed, reproduced, or printed on the letterhead or facsimile letterhead of this division will be assigned a proper log number by the typist and recorded as to initiator, designee, date, and subject. The administrative manager will see that a copy of all correspondence is placed in the permanent files of the division.

         2.1.3.2. The permanent file copy will bear the initials of the originator within the division, any intermediate individuals responsible for approval, and the individual who

SUPERSEDES: 1-2 of September 7, 19__.

signs. These initials will appear in the upper left-hand margin of the file copy. No item of correspondence will be transmitted until the proper initials and the final signature have been affixed to the correspondence. Obtaining the initials and the final signature is the responsibility of the originator.

2.1.3.3. The originator of any correspondence and the one who signs (if he is not the originator) will be provided with with a reading file copy.

2.1.4. Transmittal.

2.1.4.1. All correspondence will be sent by the most expeditious method (normally, air mail).

2.1.4.2. Correspondence will not be hand-carried to the addressee by the originator, the individual who signs, or other division employee or representative without the knowledge and consent of the general manager or the administrative manager.

2.1.5. Personal correspondence and mail.

2.1.5.1. Any correspondence which does not serve the operating purpose of this division or of the corporation shall not be written, typed, reproduced, or printed on the letterhead or facsimile letterhead of this division or corporation.

2.1.5.2. Nothing of a personal nature shall be mailed in the envelopes bearing the logo, name, or address of this division or corporation.

2.1.5.3. Nothing of a personal nature shall be sent at the expense of this division or of the corporation without the prior, written approval for each item by the administrative manager.

2.2 Incoming.

2.2.1. Definition. Any letter or package mail (excluding periodicals and newspapers) which arrives addressed to the division or any individual within the division at the division's regular address.

2.2.2. Control.

2.2.2.1. Even though correspondence may be addressed to a particular individual within the division, any correspondence which arrives in the division bearing the letterhead and/or logo of any external company, government agency, institution, or other corporate entity, unless marked "Personal," shall be considered to be official business directed to the division. All such correspondence will be subject to opening and first reading by the administrative manager.

2.2.2.2. All other correspondence will be considered to be personal and will be delivered directly (unopened) to the designated addressee. If there is no designated addressee, such mail will be delivered to the administrative manager for action consideration. Anyone within the division receiving mail directly and finding any item of such mail to be of a nature affecting the operation of this division shall be responsible for bringing that item to the immediate attention of the administrative manager. The administrative manager shall immediately deliver to the appropriate employee any correspondence which is obviously personal in nature or content and does not affect the operation of this division.

2.2.2.3. Official correspondence received shall be appropriately logged as to date of receipt, date of correspondence, source, addressee, subject, suspense date (where applicable), and disposition. The administrative manager, who will control the logging procedure, shall assign all official correspondence to the appropriate department or employee for action. Where a suspense date is involved, the administrative manager will attach a suspense notice and shall be responsible for action follow-up control.

2.2.2.4. A copy of all incoming correspondence pertaining to or affecting the operation of this division will be retained in the permanent files of the division.

2.2.3. Personal correspondence and mail.

2.2.3.1. All employees will discourage others from sending personal correspondence to them at the corporate address.

2.2.3.2. No objection is imposed to the direct receipt by any employee of periodicals, newspapers, and other reference material relating to the employee's duties and position.

2.2.3.3. Any employee may elect to have correspondence reflecting the official business of any professional society directed to him at the division address, whether as a member or an official of the society.

3. Memoranda:

3.1. Definition. Any written notes, informal letters, or memoranda form communications which are written "for the record" or to transmit information or instructions of either a specific or a general nature.

3.2. Use.

3.2.1. Memoranda are not to be used outside the corporate entity unless specifically approved by the administrative manager.

3.2.2. All personnel are encouraged to use memoranda freely, particularly to transmit instructions and orders and to report the contents of telephone and personal conferences affecting the operation of this division. The memorandum will also be used to report specialized problems arising within the technical and administrative areas of the division.

3.3. Approval to Sign.

3.3.1. Any memoranda which transmit division opinions, policies, procedures, and directives either to corporate headquarters or to other corporate entities will approved or signed by the general manager.

3.3.2. All other memoranda will not require approval and will be signed by initials of the originator.

3.4. Control. Only memoranda which are directed to corporate headquarters or to other corporate entities will be controlled by assignment of a division memorandum number and will be filed in the permanent files of the division.

3.5. Preparation. In all but exceptional cases, each memorandum will be submitted as an original and a courtesy copy. The originator will retain one copy of each in his personal reading file.

4. Reports:

4.1. Definition. Any bound or unbound document designed to convey information, technical data, terms, and the like in a formal manner.

4.2. Reports. Except where specifically exempted by the general manager, all contract, proposal, and technical reports will be bound in the format of the division, and each subject report will be assigned an appropriate number for the record.

4.3. External Reports. All reports originating from outside the division and mailed, shipped, or hand-delivered to the division are to be considered the property of the division, to be made a part of the division library wherever appropriate.

4.4. Control.

4.4.1. Except where specifically exempted by the general manager or the administrative manager, any report transmitted outside the division will be transmitted either by an appropriate transmittal letter or by memorandum.

4.4.2. No employee will release any report originated by or for the division to any person, company, government agency, institution, or other corporate entity without prior approval of the general manager or the administrative manager.

4.4.3. All reports involving military security will be handled in strict accordance with the security section of these procedures.

4.4.4. The administrative manager will be responsible for the controlled disposition of all reports.

5. Receiving.

   5.1. Definition. Any item procured by or for the division under a purchase order of the corporation, or any item supplied as support for any contract held by the division, or any item supplied by any vendor for evaluation by the division is the subject of receiving.

   5.2. Control.

      5.2.1. Any receiving item will be delivered to the services manager in an unopened condition.

      5.2.2. The services manager shall be responsible for proper recording, inspection, preparation, acceptance on the basis of procurement specifications, and delivery to the appropriate department of the division.

6. Shipping.

   6.1. Definition. Any item (other than a report) produced by the division, any item supplied under any contract of the division, or any item supplied by any vendor for evaluation by the division, which is shipped from the division by any means.

   6.2. Control.

      6.2.1. Any shipping item will be shipped by the services manager.

      6.2.2. The services manager shall be responsible for all shipping documentation, packing, and consignment.

RESEARCH DIVISION PROCEDURE	PROCEDURE NO.: 1-3
	PAGE 1 OF 5 PAGES
	APPROVED: _(signature)_ DATED: February 11, 19__

SUBJECT: Memberships, Conferences, and Presentations	DISTRIBUTION: All Division Personnel

1. Purpose. This procedure defines the policy of the division and corporation relative to employee membership in societies, groups, and organizations; attendance at conferences and meetings as an employee or representative of the division or corporation; and any sales, administrative, or scientific-technical presentation (either formal or informal) to anyone outside the corporation.

2. Membership.

   2.1 Definition. The division recognizes that individual employee membership in professional societies is of direct and indirect benefit to the division and the corporation. Professional societies in this context are those groups or associations, legally chartered and constituted, which exist for the purpose of increasing, disseminating, or evaluating managerial, administrative, technical, or scientific knowledge for its members and the total community of professions. Such societies are not engaged in labor organization, bargaining, or related activities, nor are they engaged in political or religious promotional activities.

   2.2 Membership in Professional Societies. Only the general manager or administrative manager with the general manager's knowledge and approval can commit the division to membership in any society or organization as a corporate member. Any employee who considers that division membership in any society or organization will materially benefit the division in conducting its business is urged to make a recommendation for division membership, setting forth the reasons for the recommendation.

   2.3. Individual Membership in Professional Societies.

      2.3.1. Noncompany reimbursed.

         2.3.1.1. Limitations. The division imposes no restrictions on employee membership in any society, group, or organization, so long as the society, group, or organization is not inimical to the national security of the United States within the meaning of the list of organizations prepared and released by the attorney general's office of the United States. All personnel are urged to seek membership in and actively participate in activities of professional societies relating to their occupational specialties.

         2.3.1.2. Reporting memberships. Each employee is required to report all former, current, and new memberships in any society, group, or organization to the administrative manager. Only memberships in purely religious or national political societies, groups, or organi-

SUPERSEDES:

zations not inimical to the security of the United States are exempt from this requirement. Failure to report any such membership is cause for disciplinary action.

2.3.2. Company reimbursed.

2.3.2.1. Limitations. The division will consider reimbursement of membership dues and related expenses for employee membership in professional societies, groups, or organizations when such membership benefits the professional standing of the employee within his chosen field of endeavor and/or when such membership is advantageous to the corporate image.

2.3.2.2. Eligibility. Any professional employee of the division is eligible for reimbursement of professional membership dues and related expenses when all other requirements are met.

2.3.2.3. Control. Any professional employee requesting division reimbursement for membership in any professional society or societies will submit a memorandum request to the administrative manager with the following information:

2.3.2.3.1. Name, address, and nature of society, group, or organization in which membership is held and for which division reimbursement is desired.

2.3.2.3.2. Degree of membership held in the society, group, or organization, with any offices previously or currently held.

2.3.2.3.3. Statement of all direct and indirect costs, excluding periodicals costs (see procedure on books and periodicals).

2.3.2.3.4. Comparative statement of all professional memberships held, showing which are company reimbursed and which are personally paid.

2.3.2.4. Convenience memberships. The division reserves the right to enroll in membership any professional employee in any professional society at company expense, if membership of the employee in that professional society will benefit the division in its operations and the employee has no objections to such membership.

3. Conferences.

3.1 Definition. A conference is any formal or informal gathering called by the division or its employees for the purpose of discussing, defining, or transmitting opinions, procedures, directives, technical and/or scientific findings, activities, or information of the division to nondivision employees. A conference is also defined as any formal gathering, which is attended by division employees, called by any nondivision group or professional society for the purpose of increasing, disseminating, or evaluating knowledge. Any comments made by division employees at any conference are subject to interpretation by nondivision employees as expressions of official division policy, directives, or opinions.

3.2. Attendance at Conferences.

    3.2.1. Division formal conference.

        3.2.1.1. Definition. Any conference called by the division, to which nondivision personnel are invited, for the purpose of disseminating or evaluating any information relating to or pertaining to the division or its programs is a division formal conference.

        3.2.1.2. Control. Only the general manager will officially call and issue invitations to a formal conference. However, any employee can request and/or recommend such a conference, as well as recommend others as invitees. The general manager may designate any employee as conference chairman and/or coordinator, with all powers normally associated with such responsibilities.

        3.2.1.3. Employee attendance. Division employee attendance at division formal conferences will be approved and designated by the administrative manager on the basis of the recommendation of the research manager or other key division personnel.

    3.2.2. External formal conference.

        3.2.2.1. Definition. An external formal conference is a meeting called for any purpose by any nondivision group or organization for which individual or general invitations are issued for either attendance or direct participation by the division or its employees. Nondirect participation in such conferences will consist of attendance without expression of division opinions, recommendations, directives, or statements re scientific and technical work or efforts of the division, before the assemblage, either from the stage or from the floor. Direct participation will consist of any participation which includes delivering a formal paper or report, or which includes informal presentation of results of any division efforts before the assemblage from either the stage or the floor.

        3.2.2.2. Control.

            3.2.2.2.1. Nondirect participation. The division will not exercise control over employee attendance at any conference called by any recognized professional society or group which is held outside of normal working hours provided there is nondirect participation by the employee. Employees wishing to attend conferences of recognized professional societies or groups which are related to the activities of the division and the employee, and which are held during working hours, will be accommodated insofar as is practical. Unless otherwise approved, such attendance must be on a nondirect participation basis.

3.2.2.2.2. Direct participation. Direct participation in any conference by any division employee is subject to prior, written approval by the research manager, administrative manager, or general manager. The approval will authorize the degree of direct participation as well as the subject matter presented. Any violation of this rule will be cause for disciplinary action.

3.2.3. External informal conference.

3.2.3.1. Definition. Any meeting between division and nondivision employees at which there is discussion, defining, or transmitting of opinions, procedures, directives, technical and/or scientific findings, or information pertaining to the division and/or corporation is an informal conference.

3.2.3.2. Control. Division personnel are expected, at all times, to conduct themselves in the best interests of the division and/or corporation. Following any external informal conference, division employees attending will prepare a memorandum reporting what took place. The memorandum will be directed to appropriate key division personnel and the appropriate record files. No other control will be exercised.

4. Presentations:

4.1. Purpose. The division recognizes that individual scientific or technical presentations in the form of oral or written reports or papers are essential to the development of professional personnel. Such presentations are also essential to the development of the professional image of the division. Accordingly, the division encourages such presentations within certain controls. This section of the procedure defines the types of acceptable presentations and the appropriate controls which will be exercised.

4.2. Definition. A presentation is an oral or written report or paper given to an assembly or submitted for publication for the purpose of disseminating information relative to the division's programs and efforts or the author's professional specialties. All such information presented is subject to interpretation by nondivision personnel as official statements or opinions of the division.

4.3. Control.

4.3.1. Direct invitation to make a presentation. Insofar as is practical, any direct invitation to make a presentation normally will be extended in writing to the individual through the division. However, any division employee receiving a direct invitation to make a presentation, regardless of form, will make the full details of the invitation and the full details of the meeting or publication known to the research manager, administrative manager, or general manager, as appropriate. Acceptance of any presentation invitation will be made officially by the division and not informally by the employee. This is not to say that the employee will not sign the letter of acceptance. However, each such letter must, in essence, contain the following statement: "The research division___is pleased to be represented by this paper at the ___and the contents reflect the accepted opinions of this company, having been approved by management." All pre-presentation information supplied to the organization extending the invitation, including abstracts, summaries, and biographical information, will be officially transmitted by the division and not by the employee. All submitted material will have prior approval of the corporation's public information staff member, as well as division management.

4.3.2. Indirect invitation to make a presentation. Any division employee desiring to make a presentation in the form of an oral or written report or paper (including those in letter form) to any organization or publication will request and receive, in writing, permission of the research manager, administrative manager, or general manager, as appropriate, before conveying his request outside the division. The request for permission will provide details of the intended presentation and of the organizational meeting or publication.

4.3.3. Presentation contents. The form and substance of any presentation will be approved prior to presentation or submittal by the general manager and the corporation's public information staff member. The approval will be made on the basis of complete graphics and informational content. No control will be exercised over literary form, grammar, or oral diction of the presenter. See paragraph 3.2.2.2.2. of this procedure. Each presentation will attempt to portray the division and corporation in the most favorable light possible and must give appropriate credits to co-workers and other corporate groups as well as outsiders who have contributed to or have controlled the program under a contract. All rules and regulations governing military security must be rigidly adhered to, as must any special contract provisions relating to the program.

1. Purpose. This procedure establishes the records and defines the controls to be exercised in marketing within the division, with special emphasis upon unsolicited proposals and responses to RFQ's, RFP's, and the like.

2. Solicited Proposals.

   2.1. Definition. A solicited proposal is any formal, written request from a government agency or a private company directed to the corporation or the research division specifically. Such requests will contain a complete definition of work, terms and conditions of the proposed contract, and such other pertinent information as due date for submittal.

   2.2. Control.

   2.2.1. Receipt. Each RFQ, RFP, or other formal request for proposal will be logged immediately upon receipt by the secretary to the marketing manager. The log will indicate date of receipt, due date, requesting agency or company, and originator's subject. After logging, the marketing manager will see that the request for proposal is transmitted to the appropriate department and individual for review, consideration, and action recommendation.

   2.2.2. Decision to bid. The marketing manager will, not later than two working days after initial receipt of request, prepare a recommendation, predicated upon review by the appropriate division personnel, to the general manager for a bid or no-bid action.

   2.2.3. Decision to bid or no-bid. The general manager, based upon the information supplied relative to the request for proposal, will provide the marketing manager with a decision to bid or no-bid. Except as may be specifically approved by the general manager, work on a proposal will not be initiated prior to this decision. In the event of a no-bid decision, the marketing manager must submit to the requestee a letter stating the division's no-bid decision and requesting consideration for future bids. This letter of no-bid statement must be transmitted to the requestee in advance of the proposal due date. In the event of a bid decision, the marketing manager will assume responsibility for proposal coordination and for proposal final preparation. As appropriate, the research manager, his research personnel, the administrative manager, his appropriate personnel, and other such key personnel inside and outside the division shall make direct contributions to the proposal.

   2.2.4. Proposal transmittal. The marketing manager shall have the responsibility for assembling the complete proposal and for insuring that its contents satisfy all the requirements of the request received by the division. The assembled proposal will be transmitted by a cover letter, which letter will be initialed by the research manager, the administrative manager, and the marketing manager. The letter will be prepared for transmittal signature of the general manager. In the absence of the general manager, the transmittal letter will be prepared for the signature of the president's office of the corporation. All company proposals are considered to be company proprietary, company classified information, and shall not be kept by any individual within the division without the specific, written permission of the general manager.

2.2.5. Overall control. The overall control of solicited proposals will be accomplished by the case file system. (See paragraph 4 of this procedure.)

3. Unsolicited Proposals.

3.1. Definition. An unsolicited proposal will be generated on the basis of an internal idea which fits a need of an external group, whether within the company or without. An unsolicited proposal may also be generated as a result of conversations between division personnel and others. The unsolicited proposal may be either formal or informal. The formal proposal is prepared as though and as complete as though it had been generated in response to a formal request; that is, it contains a basic proposal report, full program planning, costing, support information, certifications, and, as appropriate, contractual "boiler plate." The informal proposal is submitted with or without costing and planning information for the purpose of inducing interest in a concept or of providing the basis for "planning only" action.

3.2. Control.

3.2.1. Initiation of unsolicited proposal. Any employee of the division can suggest preparation and submittal of an unsolicited proposal. The suggestion is to be made in the form of a written recommendation which details the reasons for the recommendation, all reasonable background information, data re the potential customer, and a statement of the probability of success, as well as financial return. Each such recommendation will be submitted to the marketing manager directly by the employee. The secretary to the marketing manager will log such recommendations as though they were formal requests.

3.2.2. Action on unsolicited proposals. Within two working days of the submission of a recommendation for an unsolicited proposal, the marketing manager will submit to the general manager a suggestion to proceed with or set aside the recommendation. The marketing manager's presentation to the general manager shall include an evaluation of the original recommendation predicated upon his own knowledge plus such other knowledge as he may gain from within the division. If, within two working days, the marketing manager feels that he is unable to provide a proper recommendation either to proceed or not to proceed with the unsolicited proposal, he will make known to the general manager what course of action, in what time frame, he proposes to follow in determining his recommendation.

3.2.3. Implementation of unsolicited proposal. Only the general manager shall authorize proceeding with an unsolicited proposal. He will establish and approve a budget covering all facets of the proposal effort and its subsequent sales effort. The marketing manager will be assigned the responsibility for the preparation and assembly of the proposal in accordance with the authorization of the general manager's office.

4. Case File.

4.1. Definition. A case file is a complete record maintained by marketing of everything leading up to, as well as the presentation and marketing of, a proposal either solicited or unsolicited. Its contents include all technical support information, pricing information, sales data, and related correspondence. It forms the record from which a contract negotiation can be conducted.

4.2. Control.

4.2.1. General responsibility. Everyone associated with a proposal effort has a direct responsibility to see that all the material related to the preparation of the proposal is made available to the marketing department for inclusion in the case file. Such material will include records of telephone calls, correspondence, notes, rough drafts, sketches, supporting information. Nothing relating to the proposal effort should be considered too trivial for submittal to the marketing manager for the case file.

4.2.2. Marketing. Each case file is considered to be company classified, and safeguarding its contents becomes the responsibility of the marketing manager. Except as approved by the general manager, the individual case files will be kept by the marketing manager at all times. As necessary for bid extensions, other proposal efforts, and contract files, the marketing manager may release portions of the contents of any case file, maintaining a record of what is released and to whom. Marketing will maintain case files in two categories: active and closed. Active case files will represent proposal efforts upon which a decision has not been finally rendered. Closed case files will consist of all proposal efforts on which a final decision has been reached. If a contract results from a proposal effort, the marketing manager will permanently release significant portions of the case file to the contract file as precontractual records.

4.3. Construction of case file. The case file will consist of a folder, preferably semihardback, into which is bound by Acco Press Fasteners all loose material. When the folder is opened as a book, it will have two distinct orders.

4.3.1. Left order. On the left side of the folder will be bound or fastened in descending order the following:

4.3.1.1. The request for proposal with its appropriate amendments or the memorandum generating an unsolicited proposal (see paragraph 3.2.1.).

4.3.1.2. The complete proposal as actually submitted (bound proposal reports may be loosely placed in the folder between the left and right order, but must be included).

4.3.1.3. Cost and pricing analysis utilized in determining the price submitted.

4.3.1.4. Technical supporting information, notes, and the like.

4.3.2. Right order. Chronologically, all memoranda for records and related material and correspondence relating to the proposal effort will be bound into the folder. The material of the right order will be logged and serialized for quick and easy reference.

Appendix C

Sample Patent

T<small>HE</small> patent which follows is a typical example of the form of presentation and publication for all patents awarded by the U.S. Patent Office. The stylized drawings provide sufficient technical information to permit any reader to conduct a feasibility assessment but not competitive production without extensive engineering design translation.

As taken verbatim from the original patent application, the patent description opens with a statement of objective and proceeds to establish the basis for the design need and the approach. After a detailed description of the design, with particular emphasis on the unique features and characteristics, the patent enters the claims section. Claims at the beginning of the list are the most generalized, embracing the widest possible concepts. Subsequent claims descend toward more specific and limiting factors, referring consistently back to earlier, more general claims. Thus a total body of claims is established with a tie from one to the others.

Note that the only semblance of an official signature on the patent is that of the patent attorney(s) as added to the drawings. Of course, the inventor had to sign the original application. The application was accompanied by the drawings as reproduced with the patent and it contained all the information finally incorporated in the patent. Notification of the patent award as made to the inventor and his assigns is an official certificate with the seal of the U.S. Patent Office affixed beneath the appropriate signatures of U.S. Patent Office officials. This latter is the document which must be presented in a court of law in any case which challenges the patent.

The chapter on patents discusses the question of patent assignment. Where such an assignment has been made prior to award of the patent, and notification of assignment has been given to the patent office, the assignment by the inventor is made a matter of record on the patent, as seen in the opening of the descriptive material of the example.

Since very few patents are so unique that there is no other related prior art, the patent office provides references relative to these patents for the reader to consider. Any effort to circumvent the claims of the patent must also circumvent these additional patents and their respective claims. Failure to accomplish this will result in a patent infringement and will not be patentable as new art. Anyone is of course free to use the art of any patent that has expired. However, it is always wise to check with the U.S. Patent Office relative to the expiration of a patent. Under some situations, a patent can be renewed or extended beyond the normal period.

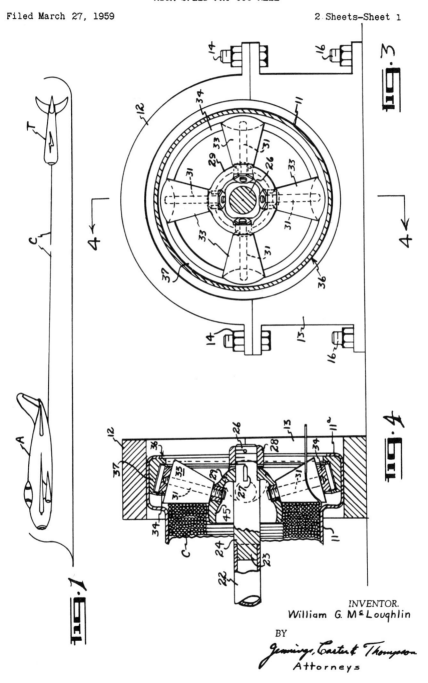

INVENTOR.

William G. McLoughlin

BY

Jennings, Carter & Thompson

Attorneys

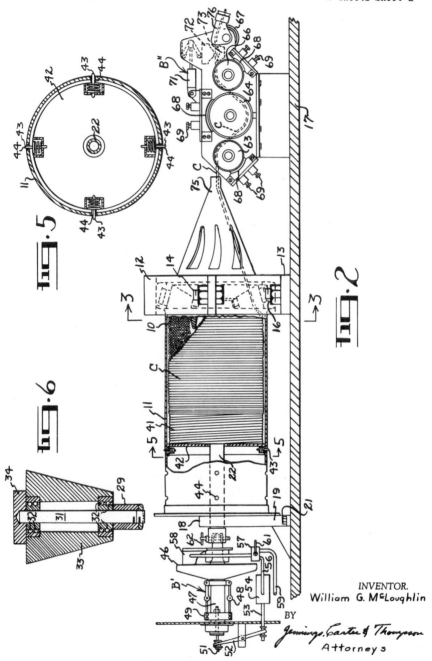

INVENTOR.
William G. McLoughlin
BY
Jennings, Carter & Thompson
Attorneys

1

2,950,876

HIGH SPEED PAY OUT REEL

William G. McLoughlin, Birmingham, Ala., assignor to
Hayes Aircraft Corporation, a corporation of Alabama

Filed Mar. 27, 1959, Ser. No. 802,380

12 Claims. (Cl. 242—128)

This invention relates to apparatus for paying out cable at high speeds, and particularly to the paying out of cable from aircraft at speeds near to and above sonic speed.

A specific use to which my apparatus is particularly adaptable is in towing targets for gunnery and guided missile target practice at high speeds and in which the target is a great distance behind the towing aircraft. Distances of eight to fourteen thousand feet are quite common. Due to the forces involved the size of the towing cable may vary from piano wire size to as much as wire of ⅝ inch in diameter depending upon such factors as speed, drag of target, line length, etc.

It is highly desirable that the tow cable be safely and smoothly payed out in minimum time. With certain short range, high speed aircraft and due primarly to their short range, even as much as a minute required to pay out the tow cable can be an important part of the total flight time for accomplishment of the mission at hand. Therefore, in order to prolong the useful flight time as much as possible it is desirable not only to pay out the cable as quickly as possible but also to jettison it upon completion of the mission, saving the time required to rewind the cable.

Heretofore in the art to which my invention relates, it has been proposed to pay out tow cable by mounting a cable drum for rotation with its axis athwart the fore and aft axis of the aircraft. This results in a system in which, particularly at the start of the pay out, there is a very large rotating mass of material, involving considerable kinetic energy. The problems of originally balancing a drum of cable of this kind and of keeping it in balance in such system during the pay out are quite complicated. Bearing problems in such systems are acute. Very large and heavy braking systems must be associated with such rotating drums in order to stop the pay out at the proper time. These and other problems make such prior cable pay out systems difficult and dangerous to use.

In view of the foregoing, the prime object of my invention is to provide high speed cable pay out apparatus which eliminates or materially reduces the disadvantages set out above.

A more specific object is to provide apparatus of the character designated in which the cable package itself is non-rotatably mounted and in which the cable pays out by being "peeled off" the end of the package with the package embodying a plurality of flat coils arranged in side-by-side relation to be paid out successively.

Another and more specific object is to provide cable pay off means comprising a shaft mounted adjacent the longitudinal axis of the cable package, a generally radially extending spindle on the end of the shaft at the pay off end of the cable, and a frusto-conical roller mounted for rotation on the spindle and disposed with its surface in rolling contact with the end of the cable package, whereby the shaft may be coupled to a brake, thus afford-

2

ing control over the cable being payed out as the roller rotates bodily around the end of the cable.

Another object is to provide apparatus embodying the foregoing features in which the cable package is retained against the rotating pay off roller with the surface of the roller extending for the entire radius of the package, holding the end coil of the package in position as the cable is payed out.

While I have shown a specific use for my pay out reel in the paying out of cable for towing targets, it is understood that my apparatus may be used for other high speed uses. One such use is in the paying out of communication wire from aircraft in military operations.

Briefly, my invention comprises a cylindrical receiver for a coil of cable. The cable package preferably embodies a plurality of flat cable coils arranged in side-by-side relation and formed in the shape of a cylinder whereby the package is slipped into the cylindrical receiver, there being an axially extending opening in the cable package. Passing through the central opening in the package and journaled at the rear end of the package in a suitable bearing is a shaft. Immediately adjacent the forward end of the receiver and mounted non-rotatably on the shaft are spindles, preferably four in number, extending generally radially of the shaft and cable package. Rotatably mounted on the spindles are frusto-conical rollers. The spindles are so directed from the shaft that the surfaces of the rollers adjacent the end of the cable package lie parallel to the end surface of the package. A spring located at the rear end of the receiver urges the entire cable package forwardly against the rollers. The forward end of the shaft carries a speed control means in the form of a centrifugally actuated brake, thereby to limit the pay out speed of the cable. Also, this brake may be applied by manual controls, thus to stop the pay out of the cable when desired. A second brake which frictionally engages the cable itself may be located at the rear of the pay out roller, serving further to limit the speed of pay out. In order that the cable may pay out evenly and also to permit the end of the cable package to bear against the rollers, the cable is wound into the package by a type of winding wherein the individual flat coils are arranged in side-by-side relation and pay out successively from between the outer and inner circumferences of the rear end of the package.

Apparatus illustrating features of my invention is shown in the accompanying drawings, forming a part of this application, in which:

Fig. 1 is a wholly diagrammatic view of an aircraft towing a target;

Fig. 2 is a side elevational view of my improved apparatus together with the forward and rear brakes, the view being partly broken away and in section;

Fig. 3 is an enlarged detail sectional view taken generally along line 3—3 of Fig. 2;

Fig. 4 is a detail sectional view taken generally along line 4—4 of Fig. 3;

Fig. 5 is a detail sectional view taken generally along line 5—5 of Fig. 2; and,

Fig. 6 is a sectional view showing the bearing arrangement for one of the pay out rollers.

In Fig. 1, I show an aircraft A which may be towing a target T through the cable C. The cable C may be anywhere from eight to forty thousand feet long and may be from piano wire sizes to wire of ⅝ inch in diameter.

As best shown in Fig. 2 the cable C is wound in the form of a cylindrical package having an opening 10 therethrough. Further, the package is wound into a plurality of generally parallel flat coils or layers arranged in side-by-side relation with each flat coil comprising

3

a plurality of cable turns, and pays out between the inner and outer circumferences thereof.

My improved apparatus comprises a cylindrical holder or receiver 11 for the package of cable C. The receiver may be supported at the rear end of the package as shown in Fig. 4 by inserting the end 11ᵃ of the same in the end of a split annular support member having upper and lower halves 12 and 13. The semi-circular halves of the support member are held together by nuts and bolts indicated at 14. The lower half may be secured by bolts 16 to a suitable supporting part of the aircraft which is indicated generally as a floor member 17.

At the rear of the receiver is a bearing 18 which is mounted on a standard 19, the latter being bolted to the floor by studs 21. Mounted in the bearing 18 is a tube 22 which extends rearwardly toward the support members 12 and 13. The tube carries at its rear end a length of shaft 23 which is welded thereto as indicated at 24. The shaft 23 is threaded as indicated at 26 and also may be provided with a keyway 27.

Fitting non-rotatably on the shaft 23 and secured thereto by a key in the keyway 27 and a nut 28 is a spider 29. The spider 29 is adapted to support four outwardly extending spindles 31. Mounted on suitable bearings 32 secured about each spindle 31 are anti-friction means comprising frusto-conical rollers 33. It will be noted that the angle of the spindles is such that the surfaces of the rollers adjacent the end of the cable package C are radial to the end of the package.

The outer ends of the spindles fit into suitable openings in the inner race 34 of a heavy duty roller bearing indicated generally by the numeral 36. The outer race 37 of the bearing 36 fits into the annular end 11ᵃ of the receiver 11 and is held assembled by the support members 12 and 13 as shown. Thus, the spider 29 and the rollers 33 are supported for the rollers both to rotate about the spindle 31 in rolling contact with the surface of the end coil for substantially the entire radius thereof and for the rollers to rotate bodily, in planetary fashion, about the end of the cable package C.

At the forward end of the package in the receiver is a compression spring 41. The spring 41 is backed up by a plate 42 which is held against left-hand or forward movement as viewed in Fig. 2 by means of a plurality of pins 43 which enter openings 44 in the receiver 11. The pins 43 are spring biased outwardly so that they may be pushed in and the plate 42 removed. The receiver is provided with a plurality of spaced rows of holes 44 as shown in Fig. 2 thus to accommodate longer or shorter coils of cable C. With the cable package in the receiver as shown and with the spring 41 in place and the pins 43 in the holes as illustrated, the entire cable package C is pushed to the right as viewed in Fig. 2, and held against the rollers 33. A cable retention sleeve 45 is integrally formed on spider 29 to retain the cable in rolling contact on the surface of roller 33 and thereby keep the cable from slipping off the end of roller 33.

At the forward end of the receiver is a brake indicated generally by the letter B'. The brake B' may be of the centrifugal type in which a drum 46 is mounted on a shaft 47. Fly balls 48 are operatively connected through a collar 49 to a shaft 51. The shaft 51 operates a lever 52 which is connected as shown to piston rod 53 of a master cylinder 54. The master cylinder 54 supplies fluid under pressure, when the piston rod is actuated, through a line 56 to a valve 57 and to a brake cylinder 58, thus to slow the rotation of drum 46. A line 59 from a source of fluid under pressure, not shown, leads also to the valve 57. By means of a control handle 61 the master cylinder 54 may be cut out of operation and fluid under pressure supplied to the cylinder 58 directly from line 59.

The shaft 47 is connected by a quick connector pin 62 to the forward end of the tube 22.

Rearwardly of the receiver and pay out rollers, I pro-

4.

vide a line brake indicated generally by the letter B''. In view of the fact that brakes of this general type are known in the art a detail description is not believed necessary. Suffice it to say that the cable C passes over a pulley 63, under a pulley 64 and over another pulley 66. The cable finally passes out over a guide roller 67. Each of the pulleys 63, 64 and 66 have associated therewith a brake shoe 68. Suitable mechanism in the form of bolt adjusted springs 69 are provided to urge the brake shoes against the pulleys. Furthermore, a hydraulic cylinder 71 may be provided which is adapted to force a shoe 72 downwardly onto cable C, engaging it against a stationary shoe 73, thus to slow down the cable.

From the foregoing, the method of constructing and using my improved apparatus may now be more fully explained and understood. First, it will be understood that the holder is mounted parallel to the fore and aft axis of the aircraft and suitably secured therein. When it is desired to load the receiver, pin 62 may be withdrawn and the receiver lifted up by removing the bolts 21 and 14. The cable may be coated with plastic resins, such as acrylic resins, or the like applied thereto to cause the coils to adhere thus to prevent displacement during handling. With the cable package inserted in place in holder 11 the spring 41 and plate 42 are assembled, thus to push the entire package rearwardly with its rear end lying against the surface of the rollers 33. The holder is now reinstalled in the aircraft and the pin 62 put in place thus connecting the tube 22 to the drum 46 of the forward brake B'. The cable is threaded over one of the rollers 33 and out the hawse tube 75, through the brake B'' and a second hawse tube 76, and thence out of the aircraft to the target. With the aircraft in flight the target is let out to towing position by releasing the hydraulically controlled brake 72—73. The cable pays out in accordance with the setting of the brakes B' and B''. When it is desired to stop the pay out, the brake 72—73 is applied and valve 61 is opened, thereby gradually applying both the forward and rear brakes. It will be appreciated that the tube 22 is a torque tube, and since the tube is being driven by the rollers 33, the brake B' is driven through a resilient connection. This aids in preventing backlash on the cable when both brakes are applied.

It will be understood that the cable pays out from the end of the coil, remaining always in contact with the one of the rollers 33 over which it has been threaded. Since the surfaces of the rollers adjacent the end of the package are radial, the flights of the winding of the coil pay out evenly and smoothly and rotate the rollers bodily about the end of the package with the individual rollers themselves rotating on their spindles 31. The spring 41 continues to bias the package rearwardly, maintaining good and firm contact with the rollers. If desired, the rollers may be mounted for sliding movement along the shaft with the cable package remaining stationary within receiver 11.

It will be understood that my invention is particularly characterized by the provision of a stationary cable package and a rotating pay out member together with a rotating pay out member driven by the rotating pay out member. My invention thus eliminates the large amount of kinetic energy present in cable packages which themselves rotate and I have thereby eliminated the many disadvantages of such systems. It will further be appreciated that the speed at which the cable can be payed out with my invention is extremely great due to the relatively small mass of the rotating members used to effect the pay out. My invention therefore increases the useful mission time of high speed aircraft used for tow purposes. It will be further understood that when the mission is completed the brakes B' and B'' may simply be released, letting go of the remaining cable, thus to jettison it from the aircraft. Likewise, it will be apparent that remote control cable cutters of

5

known types can be installed to cut the cable if that is desired.

While I have shown my invention in but one form, it will be obvious to persons skilled in the art that it is not so limited but is susceptible of various changes and modi- 5 fications without departing from the spirit thereof and I desire, therefore, that only such limitations be placed thereupon as are specifically set forth in the appended claims.

What I claim is: 10

1. In apparatus for paying out cable, a holder disposed to support a cable package wound in a plurality of flat coils in side-by-side relation with each coil comprising a plurality of cable turns for paying out the cable from one end thereof, a roller contacting the end coil of the pack- 15 age and over which the cable passes from the package in paying out, means supporting the roller for rotation about an axis generally parallel to the direction of payout of the cable, means to maintain the roller in contact with the end coil of the package as the cable pays out, and means 20 to brake the rotation of the roller about said axis.

2. In cable pay out apparatus, a receiver for a cable package wound in a plurality of flat coils in side-by-side relation with each coil comprising a plurality of cable turns for paying out from an end of the package, a roller 25 located at the pay out end of the package and over which the cable passes, means supporting the roller with the surface thereof adjacent the package parallel to the end surface of the package and in rolling contact with the end coil, means mounting the roller for bodily rotary 30 movement about an axis generally parallel to the direction of pay out of the cable, means to maintain the roller in contact with one end of the cable package as the cable pays out, and brake means operatively connected to the roller for controlling the rate of pay out of the cable. 35

3. In cable pay out apparatus, a cylindrical receiver for receiving a wound hollow cable package embodying a plurality of generally parallel flat coils in side-by-side relation with each coil comprising a plurality of cable turns, a shaft passing through the cable package and 40 mounted for rotation in suitable bearings, a rotary pay out roller on the shaft disposed to bear against the rear pay out end coil of the package and mounted for plane-tary-like movement about the end of the package with the shaft as the center of rotation, means to maintain 45 the end of the cable package in contact with the roller as the cable pays out, and speed control means connected to the shaft.

4. In cable pay out apparatus, a holder, a cable pack-age in the holder adapted to pay out from the rear end of 50 the holder, said package embodying a plurality of gen-erally parallel flat coils arranged in side-by-side relation with each coil comprising a plurality of cable turns whereby the coils are payed out successively from the outer and inner circumferences of the rear end of the 55 package, anti-friction means adjacent the pay out end of the package and contacting the cable as it is payed out, means supporting the anti-friction means with the surface thereof in contact with the end coil of the package along substantially the entire radius of the package, means 60 mounting said anti-friction means for bodily concentric movement about the end coil of the package, said anti-friction means being driven by the unwinding of the coils as the cable pays out, means to maintain the anti-friction means in contact with the pay out end of the package as 65 the cable is payed out, and means operatively connected to the anti-friction means and controlling the rate of pay out of the cable.

5. In cable pay out apparatus, a holder, a cable pack-age in the holder adapted to pay out from the rear end of 70 the holder, said package embodying a plurality of flat coils arranged in side-by-side relation whereby the coils are payed out successively from between the outer and inner circumferences of the rear end of the package, a frusto-conical roller adjacent the pay out end of the 75

6

cable over which the cable passes as it is payed out, means supporting the roller with the surface thereof contacting the rear end coil along substantially the entire radius of the end coil, the small diameter end of the roller being disposed adjacent the inner circumference of the end coil and the large diameter end thereof disposed adjacent the outer circumference of the end coil whereby the end of the cable being payed out is directed toward the shaft by the inclined shape of the roller, means mounting said roller for bodily concentric movement about the end coil of the package, means to maintain the roller in contact with the pay out end of the coil as the cable is payed out, and means operatively connected to the roller and con-trolling the rate of pay out of the cable.

6. In cable pay out apparatus, a holder, a cable pack-age in the holder adapted to pay out from the rear end of the holder, said package embodying a plurality of gen-erally parallel flat coils arranged in side-by-side relation with each coil comprising a plurality of cable turns whereby the coils are payed out successively from between the outer and inner circumferences of the rear end of the package, a shaft passing through the package and the holder and mounted for rotation relatively thereto, anti-friction means mounted on the shaft adjacent the pay out end of the cable and contacting the cable as it is payed out, means mounting the anti-friction means on the shaft for rotation bodily with the shaft in concentric relation about the entire end surface of the end coil, said shaft being driven through said anti-friction means by the unwinding of the coils as the cable pays out, means to maintain the anti-friction means in contact with the end surface of the end coil as the cable is payed out, and means operatively connected to the anti-friction means and controlling the rate of pay out of the cable.

7. In cable pay out apparatus, a holder, a cable pack-age in the holder adapted to pay out from the rear end of the holder, said package embodying a plurality of flat coils arranged in side-by-side relation whereby the coils are payed out successively from between the outer and inner circumferences of the rear end of the package, a shaft passing through the package and the holder and mounted for rotation relatively thereto, a frusto-conical rotary pay out roller mounted on the shaft adjacent the pay out end of the cable over which the cable passes as it is payed out, means mounting the roller on the shaft for rotation bodily with the shaft about the entire end surface of the end coil and in rolling contact with the end coil as the cable is payed out, the surface of the roller adjacent the end coil being parallel to the end surface of the rear end coil with the small diameter end of the roller being disposed adjacent the inner circum-ference of the end coil and the large diameter end dis-posed adjacent the outer circumference of the end coil whereby the cable being payed out is directed toward the shaft by the inclined surface of the roller, means to main-tain the roller in rolling contact with the end surface of the end coil as the cable is payed out, and means op-eratively connected to the roller and controlling the rate of pay out of the cable.

8. In cable pay out apparatus, a shaft mounted for rotation in suitable bearings, a plurality of generally parallel flat coils arranged in side-by-side relation and forming a cable package with each coil comprising a plurality of cable turns and disposed around said shaft in spaced relation therefrom for paying out successively from an end of the shaft, means to support said package about said shaft whereby said shaft rotates relative to the package, a rotary pay out roller mounted on the shaft adjacent the pay out end of the cable over which the cable passes as it is payed out, means mounting the roller on the shaft for rotation bodily with the shaft and for rolling contact with the end coil of the package as the cable is payed out, the surface of the roller adjacent the end coil being parallel to said end coil whereby cable rotates the shaft about its axis as the cable is payed

7

out by moving the roller thereon about the end of the package, means to maintain the roller in contact with the end of the package as the cable is payed out, and means operatively connected to the roller and controlling the rate of pay out of the cable.

9. In apparatus for/paying out cable, a cylindrical receiver, a cable package embodying a plurality of flat cable coils supported within said receiver and arranged in side-by-side relation so that the coils pay out successively from the rear end of the receiver, a shaft passing through the package and the receiver and mounted for rotation relative to the receiver, a pair of oppositely arranged rotary pay out rollers mounted on the shaft adjacent the pay out end of the cable with the cable passing over one of the rollers as it is payed out, means mounting the rollers on the shaft for rotation bodily with the shaft about the end surface of the package and for rolling contact with the end coil as the cable is payed out, the surface of the rollers adjacent the end coil disposed parallel to and contacting the end surface of the end coil, means to maintain the cable package in contact with the rollers as the cable pays out, brake means positioned rearwardly of the rear end of the receiver and operatively connected to the payed out end of the cable to control the rate of paying out of the cable, and brake means operatively connected to the shaft to control the speed of rotation of said shaft and thereby the rate of paying out of the cable.

8

10. Apparatus defined in claim 9 further characterized in that said means to maintain the cable package in contact with the rollers comprises an end plate removably positioned over the shaft adjacent the forward end of the cable package, and a coiled spring positioned between the end plate and the package to urge the package rearwardly as the cable is payed out.

11. Apparatus defined in claim 9 further characterized in that said rollers are frusto-conically shaped with the small diameter ends of the rollers being disposed adjacent the inner circumference of the end coil and the large diameter ends disposed adjacent the outer circumference of the end coil whereby the cable being payed out is directed toward the shaft by the inclined surfaces of the rollers.

12. Apparatus defined in claim 9 further characterized in that said brake means operatively connected to the shaft comprises a fluid operated centrifugal type brake disposed forwardly of and releasably connected to said shaft, and control means to actuate said brake.

References Cited in the file of this patent

UNITED STATES PATENTS

1,329,240	Hays	Jan. 27,	1920
2,842,323	Rayburn	July 8,	1958
2,898,605	Pearson	Aug. 11,	1959

Appendix D

Technological Forecasting Scenario

I<small>N</small> the chapter on technological forecasting, the concept of the fore-casting scenario is mentioned. The scenario offers the means of translating Delphi prediction and other forecasting data into a presentation which is readily understood by the average planner. A scenario is an interpretive document, and it has to be written with a substantial amount of "if . . . , then . . ." decision making.

It is not uncommon to merely prepare the scenario for a specific year or for a series of specific years. However, scenarios have more value and more meaning as well when they also have an introduction which provides a base for the predictions included in the scenario proper. The following scenario was prepared on this basis.

FOOD

According to the U.S. Department of Agriculture,* food production is increasing approximately 3 percent per year in the agriculturally developed nations; approximately 0.33 percent per year in the less developed countries; and approximately 2.9 percent per year worldwide. With

---

* From data supplied by Dr. Q. West, Economic Research Service, U.S. Department of Agriculture. Data excludes Communist Asia.

a world population growth rate exceeding 3 percent per year, this food increase does not match the increase in world population. In some areas, such as Latin America, which were formerly food exporters, production has fallen so far behind the population increase that these areas have become essentially food importers. But what is really disheartening is that, unless the population problem can be solved, the prospects for meeting future worldwide food requirements are dim.

In years past, the United States has been a surplus food nation; but these surpluses, on which so much of the rest of the world has depended in the past, are now rapidly dwindling. In 1969, the United States exported $6.8 billion worth of agricultural products—up 51 percent from ten years earlier. This trade level, plus increased internal demands for food, has reduced this country's agricultural surplus commodities 60 percent—from $8 billion to $3.2 billion in value—as measured in current dollars. The magnitude of this ten-year drop is better understood when it is realized that the wheat surplus was reduced 72 percent—from 1.2 billion bushels to 0.34 billion bushels—and that the corn surplus was reduced 50 percent—from 1.5 billion to 0.74 billion bushels.

The reduction in U.S. agriculture surpluses is caused by many factors. While this country's increased export trade is a significant factor, a more significant one is political. The government, through the Department of Agriculture, has limited the acreage and production of most agricultural products as a price support ploy. This has resulted in many abuses which will affect agriculture in the future. For example, to increase the yield of crops within the allowed acreage, growers have resorted to the intensive application of pesticides and plant nutrients. In many cases, these additives have entered streams and water sources in sufficient quantity to provide a most insidious form of pollution. Already, evidences of reaction to this are being felt in laws pertaining to water pollution. Overreaction could lead to tight restrictions on all agricultural use of pesticides and nutrients.

Within the United States there are approximately 450 million acres of arable land suited to agriculture. This supply of land cannot be increased significantly on an economic basis. If today's restrictions on growing and agricultural methods are continued without change or improvement, this acreage is adequate to meet this country's needs for expanding and more affluent population and to provide an exportable surplus only until 1980 (utilizing the U.S. Census Bureau's most likely population statistics). Change, then, is reasonably assured.

It is worth noting that the factor of increased affluence is not as critical as it might seem. Studies made by the U.S. Department of Agriculture have shown that a 10 percent increase in the national real income results in only a 3 to 4 percent increase in the actual demand for farm products. However, a 10 percent increase in real income produces a 10 percent increase in the demand for food service, where food service is defined as retail food pre-processing, as well as restaurant services. Expressed in more meaningful terms this means that, with an increase in national real income, discretionary spending is attracted less to additional food and more to other satisfactions, so that food per se receives a smaller percentage of total consumer expenditures.

Forecast Scenario—1975

The demand for protein in 1975 will have expanded significantly over the demand that existed in 1968, and thus it will give more emphasis to the production of livestock and poultry, feed grains, and oil meal crops. In fact, nearly half our food will not be grown or raised, but will come closer to being a manufactured product. Through ongoing computer analysis of all factors, planting, cultivating (including the times for and amounts of water and chemicals to be added), and harvesting will be more efficiently controlled on the large-scale, fully business-managed farm. Such farms will have materially increased yields by achieving more efficiency than their 1968 counterparts.

For example, 1968's maximum corn yield, which approximated 150 bushels per acre, will have been increased by more than 80 percent by improved methods of crop management. A part of the increased yield will have resulted from an acceleration of growth (which in some crops may be as high as 20 percent less time to maturity), while another part will be attributable to management methods which permit increases in the yields per season through multiple plantings of the same or different crops.

In 1975, accelerated agricultural production will not be limited to grain and vegetable crops. A significant percentage of cattle and hogs will be raised on accelerated growth schedules in environmentally controlled "animal hotels." The first evidences of the economies of full-scale production, processing, and handling obtained through a high concentration of crop and animal growing and processing in specialized areas of the country will also be evident. This specialization will ultimately result in lower costs and prices to permit processed foods to compete more effectively in the world food market, as well as go a long way toward reestablishing the U.S. agricultural balance.

In 1968, 70 percent of all foods sold in a food market had some degree of processing before retail sale. In 1975, more than 80 percent of all foods will be pre-retail processed, and most of these will be in a convenience form or approaching convenience in character. A substantially higher percentage of meat, poultry, dairy, and fish products will be consumed in pre-processed forms. In fact, fresh red meats cut to order in the retail store will be moving toward the high-priced, low-volume food items group. Some meat and poultry products will be sold as brown-and-serve items in portion-controlled cuts to match various individuals' eating habits. A significant portion of meat and poultry products sold will have been prepared by the processor as frozen cuts in portion-controlled sizes. Including the processed meats, one-fourth of all supermarket food sales will be prepackaged meals with portion-controlled servings especially adapted to quick preparation in microwave ovens, or quick boiling in the container pouch, or warming in the conventional oven. Typical of the rapid growth of the convenience food market will be sales of casserole dinners, which will have topped $130 million in annual sales. Similarly, cake mixes and frostings will provide a substantially larger market. A major spur to the convenience products will be the microwave oven. It will constitute the major means of food preparation in restaurants (where almost all meals will be portion-controlled and prepackaged) and will be prevalent in middle-class and higher-income homes constructed after 1970. Another spur will have been the emergence of essences to control flavor and aroma of all foods. As a result of the development of a wide variety of essences, there will be lemonless lemonade, coffeeless coffee, and unaged neutral spirits that taste like liquor.

Processors of food will be able to further heat-sensitize the microorganisms in food, thus permitting the use of less energy for food sterilization. Continuous-process sterilization of milk will have been introduced to produce a product which can be shipped without refrigeration. A significant percentage of animals will have injections of tenderizing enzymes just before commercial slaughter, and poultry meats will be processed in large volumes by fully automated methods.

A revolution in containers and shipping methods will have occurred. Individual portion size, flexible pouches of aluminum, internally laminated with chemically inert plastics film, will provide a substitute for cans. Vacuum-formed polyvinyl chloride thermoplastic containers for consumable liquids will have replaced the more expensive polyethylene and glass. Many heat-and-serve foods will be packed in their own disposable cooking containers, while "no-sink" (coating) salad dressings will be sold in spray cans. Typical combinations such as peanut butter and jelly will also be offered in pressurized containers for squirting a fast sandwich filler. Liquid cake batter will be offered in a disposable baking pan carton. Edible covers for some foods will be in general use.

The forerunner of synthetic foods will be very much in evidence. Meat-substitute products such as vegetable-based frankfurters and hamburgers will be widely accepted and less expensive than meat. More than 5,000 tons of petroleum-derived protein foodstuffs will be fed to cattle and poultry, while the introduction of petroleum-based foods for human consumption will already have occurred. Similarly, both natural and artificial protein concentrates in liquid, solid, and flour form will constitute a major international sales product from the United States.

Improved transportion at lower costs will permit the importation of greater quantities and varieties of tropical fruits. Compaction food processing and other advanced techniques will lower the bulk and weight of foods to a point permitting economical use of air cargo for shipment overseas. Lightweight containerized refrigerated loads will be moved in or on nonrefrigerated vehicles. Mounted on casters, these containers will be in sizes for ease of warehouse stacking or movement by fork-lift trucks.

Forecast Scenario—1980

Food processing methods in 1980 will include freeze-drying, continuous vacuum drying, infrared/microwave drying, aseptic canning, freeze concentration and compaction, osmotic dehydration, and sonic wave tenderization. Laser-beam meat cutting will provide the processor with high-speed cutting plus searing of the surfaces to retain juice and flavor within individual cuts. Virtually all natural food products will be available as freeze-dried or will receive other processing to permit virtually indefinite shelf life at room temperature. Freeze-dried food processing will be approaching one billion pounds annually, up from a mere 80 million pounds in 1968.

The sea will be a major source of food. It will be yielding more than 130 million metric tons of food as compared with 1968's 35 million metric tons. A significant portion of this increase will come from mariculture (fish and sea farming under controlled conditions).

Just as butter and coffee cream were replaced earlier by substitute nondairy products, fresh whole milk will have given way to dried whole milk powder and soybean milk, an imitation milk produced by a catalytic chemical process using vegetable oil, water, and other ingredients including flavor essences. Dried egg powders also will have replaced whole fresh eggs.

Farming will have been placed on a production basis throughout the United States. Machine planting, cultivation, and harvesting of all crops will be prevalent—even strawberries, asparagus, and other purely hand crops of the 1960's. Contributing to the world's agricultural improvement of previously unarable land will be a major irrigation desalination plant using nuclear energy. Close to half of all food animals will be bred in "animal hotels" on accelerated maturity cycles.

Synthesis of food will have been carried to the point where 5,000 pounds of high protein, vitamin enriched powder will be produced from the fermentation of only 1,000 pounds of bacteria, certain yeasts, water, crude oil stock, nitrogen, and phosphate. Through the addition of essences, the resultant product will be made to look and taste like meat or fish at a fraction of the cost of the real item. Such petrochemical-derived food will be moving toward a significant percentage of the total world food market.

As these technological changes occur over a period of ten years, food producers will have moved into nonfood lines on a large scale. Similarly, nonfood companies will have also moved into food production on a large scale. From 25 to 35 percent of total food processing (including meat) will be controlled by nonfood companies, and the major food processors will receive from 25 to 35 percent of their total revenues from nonfoods.

Bibliography

Adler, Phillip, Jr., and Thomas W. Jackson. "Motivating Research Technicians." *Research Management* XI (May 1968): 183–191.

Ansoff, H. I. *Corporate Strategy: An Analytical Approach to Business Policy for Growth and Expansion.* New York: McGraw-Hill Book Co., 1965.

Ayres, Robert U. *A Technological Forecasting.* Report HI-484 DP (rev.). Harmon-on-Hudson, New York: The Hudson Institute, January 1966.

Bichowsky, F. R. *Industrial Research.* Brooklyn, N.Y.: Chemical Publishing Co., 1942.

Blood, Jerome W., ed. *The Management of Scientific Talent.* New York: American Management Association, 1963.

Bradley, W. E. "The Job of the Research Manager." *Research Management* XI (May 1968): 167–175.

Bright, James R., ed. *Research, Development and Technological Innovation.* Homewood, Ill.: Richard D. Irwin, 1964.

———— *Technological Forecasting for Industry and Government.* Englewood Cliffs, N.J.: Prentice-Hall, 1968.

Cockcroft, Sir John. *The Organization of Research Establishments.* Cambridge: Cambridge University Press, 1965.

Dean, Burton V. *Evaluating, Selecting, and Controlling R&D Projects.* Bulletin 89. New York: American Management Association, 1968.

236 *Fundamentals of Research Management*

Drucker, Peter F. *The Practice of Management,* New York: Harper & Row, 1954.

—— "Managing for Business Effectiveness." *Harvard Business Review* (May–June 1963).

Evans, Gordon H. *The Product Manager's Job.* Research Study 69. New York: American Management Association, 1968.

Ewing, David W., ed. *Long-Range Planning for Management.* New York: Harper & Row, 1958.

Fayol, Henri. *General and Industrial Management.* London: Sir Isaac Pitman & Sons, Ltd., 1949.

Gellerman, Saul W. *Motivation and Productivity.* New York: American Management Association, 1963.

Hagstrom, Warren O. *The Scientific Community.* New York: Basic Books, 1965.

Hainer, Raymond, Sherman Kingsbury, and David B. Gleicher. *Uncertainty in Research Management and New Product Development.* New York: Reinhold Publishing Corp., 1967.

Harris, Milton. "The Education–Industry Interface." *Research Management* XI (May 1968): 159–166.

Hertz, David Bendel, *The Theory and Practice of Industrial Research.* New York: McGraw-Hill Book Co., 1950.

Howard, George W. *Common Sense in Research and Development Management.* New York: Vantage Press, 1955.

Hugh-Jones, E. M., ed. *Human Relations and Modern Management.* Amsterdam: North-Holland Publishing Co., 1958.

Hughes, E. C. "Preserving Individualism on the R&D Team." *Harvard Business Review* (Jan.–Feb. 1968): 72–82.

Jantsch, Erich. *Technological Forecasting in Perspective.* Washington, D.C.: Organization for Economic Cooperation and Development, 1967.

Jones, Edward E., and Harold B. Gerard. *Foundations of Social Psychology.* New York: John Wiley & Sons, 1967.

Karger, Delmar W., and Robert G. Murdick. *Managing Engineering and Research.* New York: Industrial Press, 1963.

Kelley, Eugene J., and William Lazer. *Managerial Marketing: Perspective and Viewpoints.* Homewood, Ill.: Richard D. Irwin, 1967.

Koontz, Harold, and Cyril O'Donnell. *Principles of Management: An Analysis of Managerial Functions.* New York: McGraw-Hill Book Co., 1964.

Lawrie, John W. "Motivation and Organization." *Personnel Journal* 46 (Jan. 1967): 42–49.

Lazo, Hector, and Arnold Corbin. *Management in Marketing.* New York: McGraw-Hill Book Co., 1961.

Lemke, B. C., and James Don Edwards, eds. *Administrative Control and Executive Action.* Columbus, Ohio: Charles E. Merrill Books, 1961.

Lenz, Ralph Charles, Jr. *Technological Forecasting,* 2nd ed., Report ASD-TDR-62-414, Wright-Patterson Air Force Base, Ohio: Aeronautical Systems Division, AFSC, U.S. Air Force, June 1962.

Lien, Arthur P., Paul Anton, and Joseph W. Duncan. *Technological Forecasting: Tools, Techniques, Applications.* New York: American Management Association, 1968.

Mansfield, Edwin. "The Speed of Response of Firms to New Technologies." *The Quarterly 'ournal of Economics* 77 (May 1963).

March, James G., and Herbert A. Simon. *Organizations,* New York: John Wiley & Sons, 1958.

Marcson, Simon. *The Scientist in American Industry.* New York: Harper & Bros., 1960.

Maslow, A. H. "A Theory of Human Motivation." *Psychological Review* 50 (July 1943): 370–396.

Massie, Joseph L. *Essentials of Management.* Englewood Cliffs, N.J.: Prentice-Hall, 1965.

McGregor, Douglas. *The Human Side of Enterprise.* New York: McGraw-Hill Book Co., 1960.

McNeill, Winfield I. *Effective Cost Control Systems,* Englewood Cliffs, N.J.: Prentice-Hall, 1965.

Mees, C. E. Kenneth, and John A. Leermakers. *The Organization of Industrial Research.* New York: McGraw-Hill Book Co., 1950.

Merton, Robert K. *Social Theory and Social Structure: Toward the Codification of Theory and Research.* Glencoe, Ill.: Free Press, 1949.

Moore, Franklin G. *Manufacturing Management.* Homewood, Ill.: Richard D. Irwin, 1965.

Moranian, Thomas. *The Research and Development Engineer as Manager.* New York: Holt, Rinehart and Winston, 1963.

Mordka, Irwin. "A Comparison of Research and Development Laboratory's Organization Structures," *IEEE Transactions on Engineering Management,* EM-14 (Dec. 1967): 170–176.

Myers, M. Scott. "Who Are Your Motivated Workers?" *Harvard Business Review* 42 (Jan.–Feb. 1964): 73–88.

Noltingk, B. E. *The Human Element in Research Management.* Amsterdam: Elsevier Publishing Co., 1959.

Orth, Charles D. 3rd, Joseph C. Bailey, and Francis W. Wolek, eds. *Administering Research and Development: the Behavior of Scientists and Engineers in Organizations.* Homewood, Ill.: Richard D. Irwin, 1964.

Pelz, Donald C., and Frank M. Andrews. *Scientists in Organizations: Productive Climates for Research and Development.* New York: John Wiley & Sons, 1966.

Quinn, James. "Transferring Research Results to Operations." In R&D Management Series, *Harvard Business Review*. Jan.–Feb. 1963.

Roberts, Edward B. *The Dynamics of Research and Development.* New York: Harper & Row, 1964.

Roman, D. D. *Research and Development Management: The Economics and Administration of Technology.* New York: Appleton-Century-Crofts, 1968.

Schon, Donald A. *Technology and Change: The New Heraclitus.* New York: Delacorte Press, 1967.

Seiler, Robert E. *Improving the Effectiveness of Research and Development.* New York: McGraw-Hill Book Co., 1965.

Singer, T. E. R. *Information and Communication Practice in Industry.* New York: Reinhold Publishing Corp., 1958.

Stanley, Alexander O., and K. K. White. *Organizing the R&D Function.* Management Bulletin 72. New York: American Management Association, 1965.

Starr, Martin Kenneth. *Production Management—Systems and Synthesis.* Englewood Cliffs, N.J.: Prentice-Hall, 1964.

Steiner, Gary A., ed. *The Creative Organization.* Chicago: University of Chicago Press, 1965.

Walters, J. E. *Research Management: Principles and Practice.* Washington, D.C.: Spartan Books, 1965.

Research and Development Contracting. Washington, D.C.: Federal Publications, 1963.

Management of New Products. New York: Booz, Allen & Hamilton Inc., 1968.

Index

About the Author

William G. McLoughlin is the director of technological planning at Ling-Temco-Vought, Inc. in Dallas, Texas. He received his Bachelor of Aeronautical Engineering degree from The Catholic University of America and his Master of Business Administration degree from the Braniff Graduate School of Management at the University of Dallas.

Mr. McLoughlin is also an adjunct professor at the Braniff School of Management and has previously been an instructor of physics at George Washington University. He has also held the positions of general manager of the physical sciences laboratories at Varo, Inc., manager of advanced planning for Marshall Laboratories, and chief of research at both Del Mar Engineering Laboratories and Hayes International Corporation.

A member of the American Physical Society and the American Institute of Aeronautics and Astronautics, Mr. McLoughlin serves as chairman of the Electronics Division of the American Ordnance Association and as director of Hydroponics in Texas, Inc. He is the author of *The Case for Research Accountability* (AMA, 1967) and co-author of *Introduction to the Principles of Infrared Physics* (Birmingham, Ala.: Hayes International Corporation, 1956).

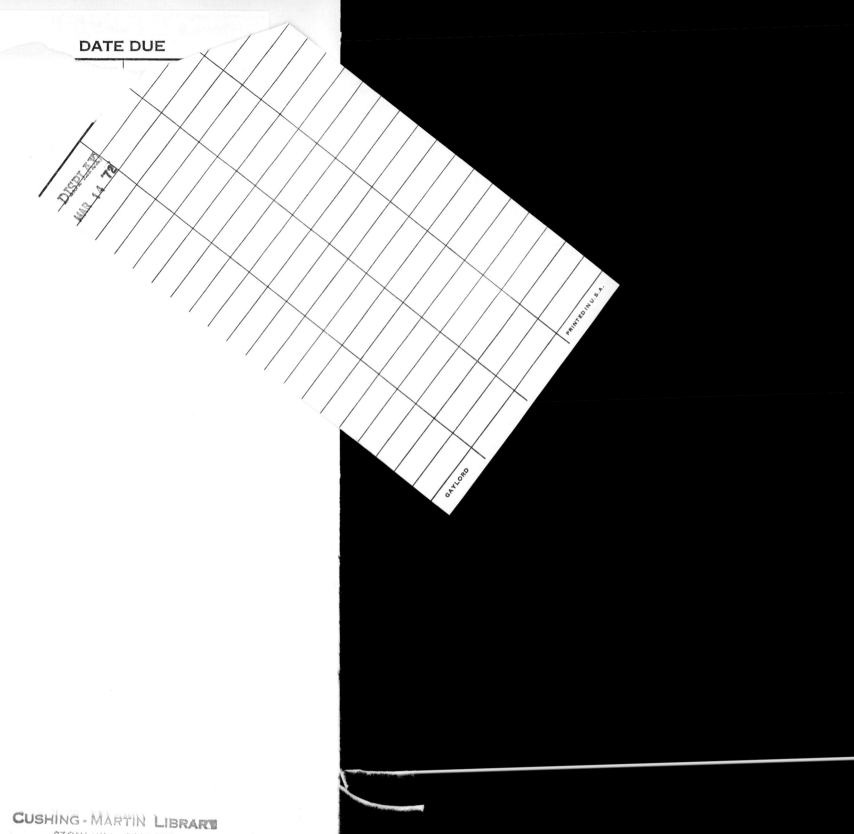

GAYLORD

PRINTED IN U.S.A.